Shine Forth

- The Soul's Magical Destiny -

William A. Meader

Source Publications — Mariposa, California

Copyright © 2004 by William A. Meader. All rights reserved. No part of this book may be reproduced in any form or by any means, electronic or mechanical, including photocopying, recording, or by any information storage and retrieval system, without permission in writing from the publisher, except by a reviewer, who may quote brief passages in a review.

Published by:
Source Publications
P.O. Box 1160, Mariposa, California 95338
source@yosemite.net
http://www.sourcepublications.com
http://www.meader.org

Cover design by:
Sabine Maria Barij
Steinen, Switzerland

Printed and bound in the United States of America

Library of Congress Cataloging-in-Publication Data

Meader, William A., 1955-
   Shine forth : the soul's magical destiny / William A. Meader.
     p. cm.
   Includes bibliographical references and index.
   ISBN 978-0-9635766-5-1
   1. Magic. 2. Occultism. I. Title.
BF1611 .M412 2004
131--dc21
                                       2003012231

Forgetting the things which lie behind,

I will strive towards my higher spiritual possibilities.

I dedicate myself anew to the service of the Coming One

and will do all I can to prepare men's minds and hearts

for that event. I have no other life intention.

Alice A. Bailey

Table of Contents

Preface *1*

Acknowledgements *3*

Introduction *5*

Part I

The Foundation

Initial Ponderings *13*
The Primary Principle 13
Resolution of Paradox 15
The Universal Fiat 17
The Original Condition 19
Emergent Duality 21
    Attributes of the Cosmic Father 23
    Attributes of the Cosmic Mother 25
The Masculine Pronoun 29
Monadic Sojourn 32
    Entrance into the Mineral Kingdom 35
    Entrance into the Plant Kingdom 41
    Entrance into the Animal Kingdom 48
    Entrance into the Human Kingdom 51
The Nature of the Soul 57
    Soul as Universal Matrix 59
    Soul as the Principle of Love 64
    Soul as Sentiency and Consciousness 66
    Soul as the Organizing Principle 69
    Soul as Individualized Identity 71
    Soul as the Quality of Divinity (Seven Rays) 73
The Formation of the Causal Body 83

Part II

The Art and Science

of Magic

The Point of Light Emerges	91
The Direction of Soul Communication	93
The Downward Gazing Soul	95
The Alignment of the Personality	98
The Role of Meditation	99
The Cave	103
The Standing Place of the Magician	103
The Anchor Point of Soul-Inspired Thought	105
The Origin Point of Creative Projection	107
Meditation for Finding the Cave	108
The Emerging Point of Light	111
The Nature and Composition of Thought	112
The Synergy of Thought	118
The Diminishment Factor	120
Sound as the Creator of Effects	122
Dangers of Thoughtform Construction	123
The Danger of Obsession	124
The Danger of the Vacuum	125
The Danger of Unbridled Thought	127
The Danger of Astral Neglect	128
The Contemplative Antidote	130
The Etheric Triangle of Magic	131
The Reversal of Etheric Polarity	133
Spiritual Initiation	137
The Common Features of Initiation	141
The Principle of Hierarchy	145
The Probationary Path	148
First Initiation	151
Second Initiation	157
Third Initiation	160

Table of Contents

    Fourth Initiation 165
    Fifth Initiation 168
The Third Eye 173
    Right Relations with the Devas 182

Condensation Next Ensues *185*
The Attributes of Emotion 185
The Problem of Desire 187
    Sons of Necessity 189
    The Root of Ahamkara 191
    Desire and Karma 193
    Overcoming Desire 195
The Problem of Inversion 198
    The Inversion of Love 203
    The Inversion of Intuition 204
    The Inversion of Group Consciousness 207
    Unanimity and its Inversion 210
    Hierarchy and its Inversion 210
The Emerging Mist 214
Meeting the Left-Hand Path 216
The Imposter of the Soul 219
    Discerning the Imposter 223
    The Surreptitious Imposter 229
    The Two Types of Imposters 231
    The Imposter as Friend 234
    Self Evaluation 236
The Measure of Emotion 243
    Too Much Emotion 243
    Too Little Emotion 244
    Judiciously Applied Emotion 245
Astral Duality and the Middle Way 246

The Garment That Uplifts *249*
The Building of the Etheric Sheath 251
    The Etheric Field 252
Magic as Sexual Intercourse 254

A Question of Timing 256
Words of Power 259
The Midway Point 263
The Ancient Fires 269
In Search of the Enemy 273
Kundalini Magic 280

Part III

The Larger Agenda

Greater Life Shines Forth 285
The Effect of Divine Thought 287
      The Nature of Change and Evolution 291
      The Evolution of Societal Systems 292
      The Magical Nature of Logoic Thought 298
      Human Elementals 299
      Grades of Elemental Receptivity 302
      The Dual Edge of Social Systems 306
Final Remarks 309

Bibliography *313*

Index *317*

Index of Figures

Yin-Yang Symbol in Taoism	Figure 1	28
Monadic Sojourn	Figure 2	40
Vertical Extension (Plant Kingdom)	Figure 3	47
Horizontal Extension (Animal Kingdom)	Figure 4	50
Inward Extension (Human Kingdom)	Figure 5	55
The Human Constitution	Figure 6	117
Soul-Infused Personality (Partial)	Figure 7	221
The Emerging Imposter	Figure 8	222
The Imposter (Maturation and Diminishment)	Figure 9	230
The Two Midway Points within the Etheric Vitalization Cycle	Figure 10	265
Evolutionary Trend and the Lesser Cycles of Variability	Figure 11	297

Shine Forth

Preface

This book is rooted in the Trans-Himalayan system of philosophic thought. Sometimes called the Esoteric Tradition, it is a spiritual view of life that supports many of the core principles found in world religions today. Yet in itself, it is not a religious tradition. Rather, it is a collection of profound ideas that have application to every department of human existence. As such, it is a view of life that is inclusive of religion, but by no means limited to it. With regard to this book, it will be seen that the metaphysical principles it emphasizes have equal application to education, politics, science and the arts - to name just a few domains of human expression.

In particular, this book is directed to the process of spiritual creativity (magic), and the recognition that the soul is the higher creative agency within every human being. My intention is to give clarity to an otherwise obscure topic. Essentially, this book is divided into three parts. The first, entitled *The Foundation*, includes a variety of subjects that provide a base of support for understanding the magical process. The second part is the largest division, and is the central subject of the entire book. It is entitled *The Art and Science of Magic*. In it is presented an in-depth examination of the processes used by the soul to creatively express itself through an individual's outer personality. The intention is to provide the reader with not only an understanding of the magical process, but also the manner in which it can be more effectively utilized in his or her creative life. The final section, entitled *The Larger Agenda*, directs the reader to consider the creative processes of God. The nature of societal institutions are examined with an understanding that they represent a facet of God's creative intention manifesting through the human condition.

The teachings of the Master Djwhal Khul (as conveyed in the writings of Alice A. Bailey) are the primary sources that have guided me through years of spiritual study and practice. Though at times abstract and difficult to understand, I have found the wisdom and insights conveyed in these teachings to be deeply meaningful. In my view, these writings are well worth the time and mental rigor required in order to grasp their profound wisdom. They are governed by abstract considerations which demand that one think in unaccustomed ways. For many people, this can be challenging, yet it is also very growth inducing. Given the fact that the soul itself is found in the regions of the abstract mind, exercising the mind in this way supports movement toward the soul within. Of the many texts written by Alice A. Bailey, the one that has been the inspiration for the writing of this book is entitled *A Treatise on White Magic*.

Over the years, I have met many people who have been attracted to the Esoteric Tradition, but have expressed frustration at the obscure nature of its literature. As a result, people tend to back away from further study of this profound material. Given this fact, I have chosen to write in a way that supports the value and importance of abstract ideas, while simultaneously attempting to give clarity to them. Approaching this subject in an abstract fashion is unavoidable, for it is fundamental to the nature of the subject itself. Yet, it can be conveyed with less obscurity. It is my humble desire that this writing will provide such needed clarity.

How to Read this Book

This treatise is really two books in one. The main body of text provides the reader with an in-depth examination of the topic at hand. Terms that are unknown or obscure are defined, and it is written around the central goal of giving clarity to the subject. In addition to the main text, most of the pages have a brief passage to the side providing an important idea in an abstract and terse fashion. Generally, each passage has relevance to material presented on the page on which it is found.

This book can therefore be read in more than one way. For many, reading the main text will be most fulfilling. When this is the case, the passages can be read as summations of ideas presented on each page. For others, it may be more appealing to simply read the passages, and use the main text as a source of clarification and embellishment. In either case, it is my sincere hope that the reader finds the inquiry into this amazing subject to be rich and profoundly meaningful to his or her spiritual life.

Acknowledgements

I would like to acknowledge and thank my teacher, the Master Djwhal Khul. Through his profound wisdom, as conveyed through the Alice A. Bailey writings, I came to recognize that the note he sounded was a fiery truth sleeping deep within myself. It was he who reawakened this flame. In addition, may I express my deepest gratitude to my colleague and friend, Michael D. Robbins. It was his profound understanding of the esoteric philosophy that fanned this reawakened flame.

With regard to the writing of this book, I am deeply grateful to several people who were instrumental in its production. To Carole Beckham for her expertise and guidance in the many details of book publishing and editing; to my wife, Trina, for her unwavering support for its writing, as well as her many editing suggestions; to Sabine Barij, for the beautiful artwork she provided for the cover; to Regina Reitmeyer, for the knowledge and professional skill that she applied to its editing; and to Rick Prater for the years of encouragement he gave me in support of writing this book. Finally, I would like to convey my appreciation to my brother, Gary Meader, for the graphics he created to enhance various sections of the text.

William A. Meader
August 19, 2003

Introduction

Every human being is destined to become a spiritual magician. From the esoteric view of life, this is considered an indisputable fact. It is not a destiny as normally conceived, for we are referring to the fate of the soul, and not that of the ego—the personality. The soul evolves over vast periods of time, and its ultimate goal is to creatively express itself through a cooperative personality. By so doing, it influences the outer world through its power to magically uplift. This is the core purpose behind human evolution, and is the clue to the hidden yearnings of the soul. For this reason, each and every human being will eventually become a spiritual magician. The evolution of consciousness demands it be so. In this treatise, our attention will be directed to the soul as it evolves itself into the serving magician on behalf of humanity's upliftment. This is the destiny of every human soul, in this incarnation or another. It is to *shine forth* into form, and by so doing, contribute to the betterment of the larger whole.

The study of spiritual magic (sometimes called white magic) is really an investigation into how consciousness influences circumstance. Through the use of the human mind, ideas emerge. When acted upon, these thoughts shape outer events. This is magic. Though this may seem too commonplace to be called magic, it is in fact a creative event of supreme importance. This is because it involves converting something internally conceived into an outer effect. It is to transform an idea, created within the mind, into an objective reality. In the truest sense, this is magic, and it is miraculous. Relatively speaking, thoughts are intangible. Yet through a series of psychological processes, intangible thoughts lead to outer expression

The soul's magical destiny is to shine forth the fullness of its nature, and it does this as an act of service to the larger whole.

and resulting effects. As such, it is true to say that every human being is already a magician, for each is able to think thoughts that lead to action, thus generating outward effects (forms).

Thoughts can either give rise to outer forms that are supportive of life and evolution, or antithetical to it. The study of spiritual magic is an inquiry into the science of thoughtform-building in support of human betterment. Though most people build thoughtforms automatically, a spiritual magician builds them deliberately, and with an understanding as to the steps required to externalize them with power and transformative effect.

The art of spiritual creativity is really the magic of the soul. By this is meant that the soul is the originator of thought. Normally, thoughts are initiated by the human personality. Yet when the soul gives the impulse to thoughtform construction, it does so with the intention of creating an outer effect that will have uplifting value to a larger whole. This is the root intention of every soulful act of magic, in that the soul always seeks to transform something beyond itself.

As a generalization, we can state that soulful magic is less self-serving than personality magic. This is a distinction worthy of note. The soul is fundamentally a servant to the evolutionary intention of the large life of which it is a part. This large life could be referred to as God. Because God is evolving His consciousness through the human kingdom, as well as all other kingdoms in nature, the soul is a participant in that great evolutionary urge. White magic can therefore be defined as any creative action given impulse by the soul on behalf of the evolutionary Will of God.

When yearning to live according to one's inner divinity, the greatest challenge is to understand how the soul creates thoughts within the mind, and then translates them into action. Much of our inquiry into the

The soul outwardly serves through its power to shape thoughts that have uplifting effect.

art of magic will be centered upon this question. Though it is common for people to believe that the soul is creating our loftier thoughts, it is rare to question how one's personality may be distorting them. Spiritual magic not only encourages us to learn the process of thoughtform construction (as coming forth from the soul), but also to be vigilant to the dangers of distortion inherent within the process. These distorting forces are rooted in the personality's tendency to exaggerate, and thus disfigure, ideas received from the spiritual realm.

When the mind begins to engage itself around a soulful intuition, it will tend to distort it by adding *ahamkara* to it. Ahamkara is a Sanskrit term that means the tendency to imbue an idea with "I-ness." This tendency is often quite subtle and is usually not realized. Fundamentally, impulses coming from the soul are *not* intended to build the personal ego, but rather to selflessly uplift others. However, when the mind of the personality first grasps these descending impulses, it tends to claim ownership of them. Instead of realizing that the impulses are coming *through* the mind, the personality believes they are coming *from* the mind. Because the mind is a part of the ego-self, the personality naturally tends to make claim to its content. As such, the soul's descending insight is captured by the personality and becomes distorted through its identification with it. We will later discuss this tendency in much detail. For now, let it simply be understood that when striving to enhance soul expression, one's greatest enemy is his or her own personality.

White magic is both a science and an art. It is artful in that it requires a strong relationship to one's intuition and an ability to create forms that inspire and uplift others. When done well, that which is created is a demonstration of beauty in action. However, the magical process is also a science. It demands that an

The soul builds with purity, while its reflection, the personality, tends to distort that which has been sent forth.

Spiritual magic requires that one creatively build with measured consideration in order to offset distortion.

individual understand the step-by-step processes involved in building evolutionary thoughtforms, and how to methodically move these ideas through the various parts of the personality. For example, there is much to be understood when moving an idea into the realm of one's emotional nature. The question must always be asked, how do I give feeling to my idea to make it appealing to others? Such questions are crucial when trying to create according to the soul's intention. Adding emotion to an inspirational idea is important, yet it is also a source of great challenge. Emotions can exaggerate an idea beyond its intended value, and can therefore lead to excessive enthusiasm. This can be quite detrimental to the creative process through its distorting effects. Therefore, an understanding as to how we add emotion to thought is extremely important when trying to rightly create.

In this treatise, we will examine the creative process in order to comprehend this challenge and its remedy. Our goal in the study of this amazing and important subject is to deepen our understanding of how we better serve the living intention of the soul within. Nothing is more important than to live in such a way, for to express oneself according to the soul's wishes is to become the soul itself. Though we think that our soul is something transcendent to ourselves, it is actually who we are. The evolution of consciousness is founded on this understanding. This we will examine in much detail. For now, let it simply be said that the soul is our identity, and that our personality is merely its reflection.

Since the beginning of human existence, the soul has been seeking to manifest itself as an outward agent in service to life. As such, the evolution of consciousness is the evolution of the soul through form. Over aeons of time, the soul has slowly been shaping its relationship to incarnated life. The result is that it has slowly developed a measure of control over form. The fact that we, as human beings, are able to demonstrate behaviors contrary to our animal instinct is clear evidence of the enormous progress the soul has made over the ages. Consciousness had been encased within the animal kingdom for a very long period. During that time, instinct was the stride in consciousness that the spirit sought to develop. Yet, we now find that the evolutionary goal is to rise above the dominance of animal instinct alone, and therefore become the individualized human beings that we are. This is the great heritage of life as lived in the human kingdom. A human being not only knows the animal within, but is now beginning to sense his or her inner divinity as well.

Though the purpose of this writing is to convey to the reader a deeper understanding of the ancient principles of spiritual magic, the topic of evolution must necessarily accompany the discussion. The art of creative manifestation has direct relationship to one's place upon the great chain of evolutionary development. As an individual evolves over countless incarnations, there is a point at which the soul is inwardly sensed for the first time. Though this touch of the soul is fleeting, the individual is changed by the experience, for he or she now knows that the soul exists within. Up to this point, faith in the soul has been the assurance of one's immortality. Yet due to this fleeting glimpse, there is now experiential proof of the soul's existence.

For the next several incarnations, the soul increasingly infuses itself into the personality. Because of this, the soul's ability to influence thought and action grows proportionately. This is the foundation for the development of magical skills. As the soul becomes increasingly operative in life, there naturally develops a capacity to create uplifting effects within the outer world. Therefore, it can be seen that as one continues to

Magical capacity is proportional to where one stands upon the upward path of evolution.

evolve, so too does his or her capacity to magically create on behalf of human betterment. This is why it is true to say that all people are destined to become white magicians; it is an inevitable by-product of evolution itself.

Part I

The Foundation

Initial Ponderings

To fully appreciate the beauty of the magical process, it is important that a few prerequisites be first considered. An understanding of the great drama of evolution over the vastness of time, foundational principles governing existence and an examination as to the nature of soul will each act as springboards to our understanding of the magical process.

The Primary Principle

Within the Esoteric Tradition, there are a variety of principles that, when deeply considered, give profound understanding to the nature of life and creation. Of these, the cornerstone principle states that *all is one*. It is the simple notion that the universe, with all its diversity, is fundamentally an expression of One Life. This singularity of life can be called God, for nothing is more universally present. Not surprisingly, such a principle is recognized within most religious systems, though its implications are frequently not fully grasped.

When examining this principle a bit closer, it becomes readily apparent that it must, by definition, be applicable to all aspects of creation, including that which we call evil. This, for many, is difficult to accept. Yet if all is truly one, as this principle suggests, then how can anything exist as something independent of its all-inclusiveness? Complete oneness demands that nothing escape its embrace. Often, people of spiritual persuasion espouse divine unity, while overlooking the fact that such a view must include that which they most detest. Within Christianity, the idea that Satan is an expression of God is immediately rejected as blasphemous, yet in the same breath Western theology

Oneness manifests as multiplicity and is the Universe in its entirety.

speaks of God as the eternal all. This is a difficult hurdle for the Western theologian, for Satan has long been viewed as the adversary of God rather than a part of Him.

We have long been told that God is love, and that this love is the essence of all things. Yet, the notion that destructive will is also an aspect of God, equal to love, is difficult for many to acknowledge. If God is the One Life, then He must represent all attributes of force conceivable within the mind, or operative within human experience, including the forces of evil and destruction. These seemingly antithetical forces must also be viewed as aspects of God, and with as much conviction as when considering God as love.

Universal oneness is the most important principle needing to be grasped by anyone committed to the evolution of the soul and its magical ability to serve. To understand it is to come into relationship with the very nature and foundation of existence itself. We are each a particulate expression of One Life, and as such, nothing is free from its encirclement. From the esoteric perspective, no other idea is more crucial of acceptance. For the sake of emphasizing its primacy, we shall refer to this axiom as the *Primary Principle*.

The Primary Principle is a notion that is fundamental to understanding the many intricacies of the Esoteric Tradition. Indeed, it is the axiom that makes it possible to ultimately resolve all dualities experienced within one's consciousness—an essential prerequisite to full union back into the consciousness of the One. Every human being is conditioned to think and experience life within the context of dualistic perception. For every thought, feeling or intention one has, there is an opposite thought, feeling or intention that consciousness invariably holds as a potential. To conceive of happiness, one must also perceive unhappiness. In truth, it is

Nothing, not even that which is most despicable, can escape the all-pervasive embrace of the One Life.

through dualistic perception that we are able to derive meaning from our phenomenal experience. Good cannot be conceived unless evil is also envisioned.

Importantly, the Primary Principle is the axiom that states that transcendent to any duality is found a blending point where duality is synthesized into unity. In many ways, the upward path is a passage created by the resolution of various dualities found at any (and every) level of spiritual development. The resolution of any duality found within consciousness ensures that, experientially, one knows the truth of the Primary Principle. The synthesis of any objective or subjective duality is indication that a step toward the condition of oneness has been achieved. Upward mobility is therefore only possible through adjustments made within consciousness. Such adjustments are invariably founded on the unifying nature of the Primary Principle, relatively understood.

The resolution of duality leads to synthesis, and synthesis is the One Life void of fragmentation.

Resolution of Paradox

When working toward the resolution of duality, one is ultimately faced with the mystery of paradox. As spiritual beings, we must become accustomed to paradoxical truths. That is to say that paradox is inherent in every duality, and to resolve duality is to transcend it. Paradox is the product of consciousness when confined within dualistic perception. For instance, the idea that "life is inherently predetermined" is in opposition to the perspective that "life is based upon utter freedom." Yet, both these paradoxical perspectives, to be synthesized, must be perceived as fundamentally true. The Primary Principle is the cosmic precept that ensures that such a synthetic understanding will inevitably be achieved. From a much higher consideration, even the paradox of "existence and non-existence" must be resolved into a profound singularity. To the dualistic human mind, the resolution of such a duality may seem impossible and even irrational. However, from the vantage point of the Spirit, opposites within consciousness represent one truth expressed in two forms, and the evolution of consciousness incrementally reflects this realization.

The Primary Principle reminds the seeker that the adversities of life represent various aspects of the One Life attempting to achieve fusion. When an individual is confronted with difficult circumstances, such predicaments are not random occurrences. Rather, they represent various elements of this larger life interacting in an effort to establish right relationship. Elements of the One Life in interaction with each other have the potential to configure themselves in such a manner so as to become harmonized. When harmonization is achieved, then right relationship is established, and this as a preparatory step toward realizing inner synthesis. Any conflicted situation in one's life must eventually be understood in this light. The various elements found within any circumstance must be recognized as parts of a living whole (the individual person representing one of these parts) seeking harmonization as a prelude to inner fusion.

The experience of pain and suffering associated with a particular circumstance is the consequence of various misalignments existing between elements within that circumstance. Yet, these elements do not stand alone. They are, in fact, parts of a living whole. Though their misalignments create the pain evident within a situation, they are nonetheless seeking to configure themselves into harmonious accord. Again, the Primary Principle represents the foundation of this process, for any movement toward the fusion of diverse elements into a realized singularity is governed by this universal principle. Even when the human mind accepts the

Circumstance is hidden oneness struggling to express itself through the diversity of its many parts.

notion that the origin of all diversity is unity, these two ideas (unity and diversity) are not often considered as simultaneous realities. However, it is not an either/or proposition. Though the diversity of creation is abundantly apparent, it is simultaneously in a condition of oneness. Oneness is always present, even when all that we may sense at any particular time is the diversity of its parts. Therefore, unity and diversity are co-existent realities of creation—another paradox, to be sure.

Through various spiritual and meditative practices, an individual begins to sense the soul evident within all things. This then gives experiential validation to the truth of the Primary Principle. Technically speaking, it is a consequence of the opening of the third eye. Discussion about the awakening of this mystical eye from its historic slumber will be furnished later. Suffice it to say that through its opening, an individual is able to witness the unfolding purpose of the One Life, and this as it expresses itself through the diversity of manifested creation. In short, through the opening of the eye of the soul (third eye), one begins to see the living unity underlying the diversity of outer forms.

The mystical eye gives validation of underlying unity.

The Universal Fiat

We have been considering the Primary Principle as the foundational axiom proclaiming the oneness of all things. Yet on its own, this principle does not give insight into the incarnational intention of the One Life. It merely asserts its essential singularity, not the reason for its diverse expression. Admittedly, this first cause (as it is sometimes called) lies well beyond humanity's capacity to conceive it. It would certainly be presumptuous to proclaim the purpose of the One Life, for not even the life unit that informs an entire solar system (Solar Logos) possesses such knowledge. Even such an immense being as this is limited in its conception of universal first cause and the underlying purpose that gave impulse to cosmic manifestation. In truth, no entity at any level of existence can conceive the full intention that gave birth to cosmos. The ultimate purpose of creation is only known to the consciousness of the One Life, in its totality. All lesser expressions of life (which are cells within the One Life) are simply incapable of fully resolving this question.

Though this ultimate purpose is inconceivable, we can nonetheless speculate that one facet of God's purpose is related to His perfected expression within form. That is to say that the One Life, as it incarnates into substance (an aspect of itself), seeks to do so without loss of its identity in the process. In short, the One Life incarnates for the purpose of facilitating the expression of its full Being while in a condition of manifested existence. It seeks to *shine forth* within the field of duality. As such, the One Life is attempting to understand itself within the context of the subject/object experience. Therefore, any life unit within cosmos (which is God) is fundamentally guided by this same general objective. That objective is to rediscover oneself within duality, and by so doing, establish a perfect relationship between subject and object, spirit and matter. This is the *Universal Fiat*.

The Universal Fiat is a decree asserting the necessity that all units of life must learn to *shine forth*, and to do so with perfection. Such a proclamation is truly universal for it has equal application when considering an atom, a human being or the ensouling entity of an entire galaxy. All life must eventually demonstrate perfected relationship of spirit to substance, and this as a function of the Universal Fiat.

The Universal Fiat proclaims that the reason for being must be found, and that this reason is concealed within the interplay of spirit and matter.

Philosophically, there are many intricacies to be considered when contemplating the nature and purpose of universal life. An in-depth examination is not possible in the context of this writing. Even so, the assertion that the One Life seeks to express itself with perfection is both reasonable and intuitively sound. Its soundness comes from the power of analogy as we contrast the microcosm (human being) with the macrocosm (universal being). There is ample indication in the esoteric teaching that the goal of human evolution is the perfected union of life and substance, spirit and matter. Through the microcosm/macrocosm equivalence, the evolutionary goal for a human being must be related to the incarnational intention of the One Life. How could it be otherwise? All units of life, including human, are cells within the body of this universal entity. As such, the evolutionary goal of a human being must, by definition, be a minute reflection of the incarnational objective inherent in the One Life. The ancient Hermetic truism states that "as above, so below." Is it not therefore reasonable to say that "as below, so above?" It is in light of this view that we humbly, very humbly, speculate as to the purpose of universal existence.

All units of life, whether vast or minute, are cells within the One Life, and therefore carry a measure of Its incarnational intention.

The Original Condition

From the perspective of a human being, the Universal Fiat represents the guiding paradigm of one's spiritual development. To be what one is requires that the seeker constantly ask the question, who am I, and am I accurately expressing the thing that I am? Through this questioning process it becomes apparent that identity is a moving target. For most of a human being's incarnational history, the self is defined by the various mental, emotional or physical experiences he or she is having. Yet, these three categories of self-definition are eventually blended together. This blending is referred to as the integrated personality. When this integration occurs, the personality becomes the highest aspect of identity recognized by the individual. Later, upon the evolutionary path, the soul gradually emerges as the central point of one's realized identity. Still later, the monad (spirit) is experientially understood as who one truly is. This point of self-identity is endlessly changing. Yet even with such continuous change, the Universal Fiat remains operative and unchanging. It motivates an individual to continue the search for his or her true identity, then to express it with accuracy.

Self-realization must therefore be understood as a working hypothesis found upon a continuum of self-understanding and discovery. The Universal Fiat is what moves any unit of life upon this continuum. Taken to its final conclusion, this evolutionary movement draws all units of life back to the state of universal oneness, thus becoming the One Life once again. In the context of this writing, this state of cosmic synthesis is referred to as the *Original Condition*.

The Original Condition is founded on the understanding that, because all units of life within cosmos are expressions of the One Life, they each have within them the hidden memory of this unitive state of Being. It is the memory of this Original Condition that drives all units of life to evolve toward ever-broadening states of consciousness. This memory is the most fundamental paradigm found within evolving consciousness, for it indicates what was, and ultimately what is destined to again be. No greater spiritual demand is placed upon the seeker than to live by the Universal Fiat and *shine forth* continuously anew, and this, in an effort to recapture the Original Condition. As such, when discussing the various topics relevant to the magical process, we will peri-

The memory of the Original Condition exists within all units of life, and is the driving force of evolution itself.

odically be reminded of this fundamental tenet. Indeed, it serves as a foundational principle to all aspects of the esoteric philosophy.

Emergent Duality

It has already been stated that creation is the expression of One Life. This is true whether speaking of the visible or invisible worlds of existence. When considered from the Western perspective, this One Life can be referred to as God. If using terminology relevant to an Eastern view, It is called Brahman. The incredible diversity and distinctions evident within creation represent the manifestation of this One Life into a condition of multiplicity. Yet even as the One Life is manifesting in this way, it simultaneously exists in its pristine, unitive state.

When we see only diversity within creation, this is simply indication that, at that moment, we are unable to recognize the underlying unity that is ever present. In many ways, human evolution is based upon our growing capacity to consciously detect the unity that substands (underlies) distinctive forms. Because of this, it is important that we consider the nature of consciousness itself, for it is through consciousness that the realization of unity emerges. However, we must first examine the two principles in cosmos that give birth to consciousness. Specifically, the role of the Father and Mother Principles, as well as their interactive relationship.

When the One Life entered into a manifested state, a fundamental division developed within itself. This division is what can be called the Cosmic Father and Cosmic Mother. In the Eastern view, they are referred to as *purusha* and *mulaprakriti,* respectively. This cosmic

When the One Life manifests itself as multiplicity, it first emerges as cosmic duality, purusha and mulaprakriti.

division is crucial to one's understanding of esoterics, for in it is found the key to all dualities experienced within consciousness. Given the fact that the resolution of duality is the key to spiritual enlightenment, understanding the fundamental source of duality is indispensable.

At all levels of existence, the mother and father aspects of the One Life interact, and in so doing, consciousness emerges. This will be discussed with greater detail a bit later. For now, simply understand that these two creative forces (Cosmic Father and Mother) are projected from the One Life, and in their interaction, give birth to all states of consciousness. Yet to truly appreciate the beauty and majesty of the emergence of consciousness, it would be well to examine the essential qualities inherent within the Cosmic Father and Mother.

In many spiritual circles, people proclaim the importance of honoring the mother and father within creation, but such pronouncements are usually founded on an anthropomorphic view. In short, we tend to view these two principles in very human ways, and by so doing, miss their true cosmic significance. To truly understand these two sacred forces, we must remove our thoughts from the limits of male and female considerations. The Cosmic Father and Mother are far greater than the male/female distinctions that we tend to use when discussing such matters.

From the universal perspective, and therefore applicable at all levels of creation, the Father and Mother Principles represent energies that facilitate the evolution of consciousness. Yet, each embodies different aspects of the One Life as that life seeks to manifest itself *as* creation. Both are indispensable and equal in their support of evolution, but each plays an entirely different role in the process. While each

> *The interactions between purusha and mulaprakriti give birth to all categories of consciousness.*

represents different attributes of the One Life, at the highest level they are completely fused. Therefore, it is utterly true to say that ours is an androgynous God.

Having now sounded the note of sacred equality between the Father and Mother Principles, let us examine their differences, for equality does not mean sameness.

Attributes of the Cosmic Father

When examining the Cosmic Father, we find that there are three attributes or divine qualities that are inherently a part of its nature. The first is that the father aspect is ever correlated with Spirit. From it is expressed the *will to evolve*. It is this force that creates purposeful movement from one state of being to another. This is true no matter what magnitude of evolving life we may be considering. The cosmic masculine force is the mover of all things toward an objective. Broadly speaking, it does not find fulfillment in peace and repose. Instead, its satisfaction is achieved through effort directed toward something.

The Cosmic Father is the creator of purposeful change, and change is foundational to evolution itself.

The Father Principle is the dynamic energy within creation. In truth, it is cosmic will in motion. Because of this, it inevitably creates disturbance of some kind, for it will always leave a wake behind it. This trailing wake is experienced as distress and discomfort at all levels of creation. Therefore, this principle, working through any unit of life (subhuman, human or superhuman) is the force that causes change and its consequential pain. Yet when such a force is rightly directed, the pain experienced is that which facilitates evolution itself. Broadly understood, pain emerges when there is resistance to change, either positive or negative.

Because all things are evolving, and therefore destined to continuously change, pain is inevitable when resistance appears.

Secondly, the Cosmic Father houses the purpose of the One Life as it seeks to outwardly evolve within (and as) cosmos. This is the energy within creation that contains the imprint of what is to eventually be. As the One Life manifests and becomes the Universe, it gives to its masculine expression the secret of its evolutionary aim. However, as shall be shortly discussed, it is the Cosmic Mother that provides the intelligence to achieve this aim. We therefore see that the Cosmic Father is the agent that gives impulse to evolution, and this according to the divine purpose inherently contained within it.

Lastly, the source of identity is embedded in the masculine aspect of creation. Suggested by this is the occult truth that the root of selfhood is anchored within the Cosmic Father. This root is referred to as the *Principle of Identity*. Indeed, all entities within creation are at various levels of realized identity, and it is the Father Principle working within them that gives rise to this realization.

It is important to here note that identity is not the same as the self. The self is a construct. It is an assemblage of ideas that a human being (or any unit of life) uses in order to define its identity, but it is not identity itself. This Principle of Identity is an archetype (perfected design or prototype) depicting an attribute of God. The divine characteristic that this archetype reveals is the quality of *Being*. When considering it from a purely human perspective, this axiom concludes that the instinct to define oneself is essentially a masculine tendency. This is true regardless of gender. Whether an

The Principle of Identity is always governed by the Cosmic Father.

individual is male or female, the internal force that drives that person toward self-definition is ever understood as masculine.

At this point, it may be argued that since women define themselves as female, this axiom is erroneous. While it is true however that a woman defines herself as female, the unconscious force that creates the defining tendency is masculine nonetheless. Again, it is not the self-construct that is masculine, but rather, the instinctual tendency to build it.

Attributes of the Cosmic Mother

As with the Cosmic Father, the Cosmic Mother also has three attributes central to her nature. These characteristics are as sacred as those presented by the Father Principle, and as indispensable in facilitating the evolution of the One Life. Each of these attributes represents aspects of God bequeathed to the Cosmic Mother when the One Life divided into two at the beginning of cosmic manifestation. As such, they have relevance to all units of life within creation.

First and foremost, the Cosmic Mother represents the sacred substance within creation. However, to really appreciate this notion it must be understood that substance is present at all levels of manifested cosmos, not just the visible universe we see and touch. All planes of consciousness are really divine substance existing in varying grades of density. From the human perspective, thoughts, feelings and even intuitions are experiences of motherly substance assembled into forms. It is therefore crucial that when considering substance, we see it as something far subtler than matter as usually considered. Divine substance pervades all of cosmos and is the livingness within all forms, from the densest to the subtlest.

All planes of consciousness are layers of divine substance, and the livingness of that substance is the Cosmic Mother in expression.

Secondly, the Cosmic Mother is that part of the One Life that contains divine intelligence. It is within the Mother that God has placed the essence of all intelligence and instinctual knowingness. Through her, the intelligence needed in order to facilitate the evolution of consciousness is found. In truth, all atoms (elementals) of substance contain within them an infinitesimal measure of divine intelligence. The sum-total of God's knowingness is contained within the entirety of the substance manifested within (and as) creation. This is an occult fact of profound importance. From this we learn that the Cosmic Mother provides the divine intelligence needed in order for the Cosmic Father to manifest divine purpose.

The intricacies of this process shall be discussed later when addressing the magical work to be demonstrated by disciples in the world. Suffice it to say that the Father knows what must be done and the Mother understands how to do it. When the will and purpose contained within the Father interacts with the intelligence of the Mother, form and consciousness emerge. Whether we are discussing the consciousness of a human being or that of a galaxy, it is the interaction of the Mother and Father Principles that create awareness leading eventually to perfection of consciousness within form. Such is the evolutionary goal, at least as we can humanly conceive it.

The third attribute important to note is that the Cosmic Mother contains within her the Principle of Gestation. That is to say that divine substance holds the unique role as vessel for the incubation and maturation of consciousness. She provides the womb that nurtures life at all levels of consideration. From the purely human and biological perspective, we see that the female body is designed to provide gestation opportunity for the development of new human forms.

> *The Cosmic Mother is the custodian of all intelligence within creation. Through Her knowingness, the intention of the Father can be achieved.*

Yet on a higher level, the Mother Principle is also providing a container of intelligent substance that nurtures the seeds of human consciousness. Spiritually speaking, this is related to the causal body (the vehicle of the soul) within a human being. The causal body is composed of substance given by the Cosmic Mother. Through such a gift, the birth of individualized consciousness is made possible. Humanity's tremendous leap forward from the animal kingdom was facilitated through the Mother's intelligence contained within the causal body. Such is the marvelous role she plays, and continues to play in the evolution of the human species.

From this brief discussion, we see that the Cosmic Mother and Father both play an enormously important, though quite different, role in the evolutionary processes found within creation. Evolution of life at any level is truly impossible unless both these cosmic principles are operative. One provides direction, and the other gives intelligence to achieve this end.

The Cosmic Father and Mother Principles are equally sacred, yet their evolutionary roles are quite different.

Father Principle	*Mother Principle*
Spirit in Motion	Sacred Substance
Will and Purpose	Divine Intelligence
Principle of Identity	Principle of Gestation

The distinctions discussed here are given in an extreme manner. This is intended in order to highlight the differences between the Father and Mother Principles. However, it should be noted that, in actual fact, a bit of the attributes of the one are found in the other, at least in potential. The use of the yin-yang symbol of Taoism is a useful image in this regard (*see Figure 1, page 28*).

Figure 1

The sacred two hold deep within the memory of each other.

As is well known, the two sides of this image depict the masculine (yang) and feminine (yin) aspects of creation. The use of black and white visually gives distinction between these two cosmic forces. However, within the white portion of the symbol is found a black spot, and within the black, a white spot is present. These two spots indicate that there is always something of the masculine in the feminine, and something of the feminine found within the masculine. This can be said of the attributes we've been discussing as well. Though the Father energy in creation is primarily emphasizing divine purpose and identity, it does possess an elementary level of divine intelligence within it. Conversely, though the Mother is essentially the custodian of divine intelligence and substance, within this energy is found a rudimentary vibration related to purpose. Looked at more esoterically, each spot within this symbol represents the memory of the other when they were fused in a condition of at-one-ment. This memory is the basis and cause of the various forces of attraction within creation. Indeed, it is the memory of the Original Condition that the spots within the yin-yang symbol depict.

The unconscious memory of the Original Condition is what drives these two sacred streams of energy into relationship with each other. Through their interaction, consciousness emerges and the evolution of the One Life moves forward toward its destined state of perfection—a condition inconceivable to the human mind. All of cosmos is evolving toward this perfection of consciousness, for all of cosmos is the One Life in incarnation. This expression is twofold in nature. When these two energies, the Cosmic Father and Mother, establish right relationship with each other, perfection of expression is achieved. The One Life will then enter into a state of cosmic rest and abstraction (*mahapralaya*). Such is the destiny of all things.

The Masculine Pronoun

We now come to a subject that is important, though sometimes challenging for people. It has to do with the fact that in most esoteric, philosophic and religious literature, the use of the male pronoun is commonplace. There are several reasons for this, not the least of which is the fact that many early writers were essentially disrespectful of women and anything related to feminine attributes. Certainly, it is without dispute that humanity has historically been gender biased in favor of males. From this author's perspective, society's movement toward gender equality and egalitarian patterns of behavior is a positive development, and I find much encouragement in it. Yet, equality is not synonymous with sameness. From the esoteric point of view, masculine and feminine attributes are equally sacred, but serve entirely different divine functions. Because of this, a deeper and non-sexist reason for the use of the male pronoun can be realized. I would like to provide two profoundly important reasons for using the

The use of the masculine pronoun has historically been abused, though it is rooted in a sacred truth.

masculine pronoun when trying to teach or influence others. Both have to do with the nature of the Cosmic Father and Mother as we have been discussing.

To begin, it must be understood that the use of words such as "he," "him" and "man" are in no way intended to discriminate against women. Rather, the reason for such usage is that it is the masculine aspect of a human being that the esoteric literature is seeking to influence. That is to say that, because it is the Masculine Principle that initiates movement in consciousness, it is that part of consciousness that the great spiritual teachers of the past and present are seeking to educate and influence. This is true regardless of one's gender. Esoteric literature is speaking to the masculine part of the reader, not his or her feminine side. As a reminder, the feminine aspect of consciousness is the divine intelligence found within substance. This therefore includes the substance that makes up one's physical, emotional and mental bodies, as well as the causal body of the soul.

In truth, the feminine within each of us is doing fine just as it is. It contains divine knowingness and makes that intelligence available when called for by the masculine within each of us. It is the masculine in every human being that gives impulse to action of any kind, and it is this that the spiritual teachers of the past and present are seeking to influence. Spiritual literature is designed to create insight and understanding that will stimulate the masculine side toward action in support of continued spiritual development. It is the masculine, not the feminine, that must move to create change. However, it is the feminine within each of us that provides the intelligence and understanding that must accompany change, and it will do this automatically as change occurs.

> *Esoteric literature is speaking to the masculine side of every human being.*

The second reason for the rightful utilization of the masculine pronoun has to do with the Principle of Identity earlier discussed. You will recall that within cosmos, the Principle of Identity is rooted in the masculine side of the One Life (God). As such, it is the masculine side of our nature, not the feminine, that is central to the formation of the self-construct. Yet, it is the feminine aspect that provides us with the thoughts, feelings and intuitions that define who we are. Importantly, the self-construct is a structure within consciousness that *represents* one's true identity. It is the gate to pure identity (Being), and identity is a quality of God inherent in the Father Principle. Because the esoteric teaching is seeking to address the part of us that is "identity," it is quite appropriate to use the masculine pronoun in such an effort.

It should be noted that this is also the deeper reason for God being identified as a "he." Such an expression in no way suggests that God is male. Quite the contrary, God is the perfect expression of both masculine and feminine energy, and is divinely androgynous. Yet when we reference God as an "entity," the use of the masculine pronoun is occultly correct. In other words, when considering the spiritual beingness of God (or of a human being), the male pronoun should be used because the Principle of Identity (Being) is assigned to the father side of creation. When we speak of God as divine intelligence (such as the wisdom and beauty inherent within nature, or that contained within the human soul itself), God is best understood and described as a feminine expression.

Having laid out the reasons for utilizing the masculine pronoun, as an author I am obliged to honor this. In the writing of this book, and from this point forward, I will utilize the masculine pronoun when necessary. It should be stated that there are opportunities

The One Life is androgynous. As entity, It is always masculine, and as attribute, always feminine.

Out of the one universal flame come the sparks that are the "units of life." They evolve through form, and consciousness is their reward.

in the writing of this work when using neutral or dual-gender terminology works well. When such is the case, I shall certainly do so, and this will be my creative preference. However, there are times when using such terms can be detrimental to the integrity of the idea being conveyed. It can create an awkwardness of expression, particularly as it pertains to the cadence and power of the idea being conveyed. When such is the case, I will then utilize the masculine pronoun without hesitation. As shall be later presented, the art of creative magical work has much to do with the power of words to transform and uplift others. As such, cadence is a crucial component of magical work, and must not be forfeited for the sake of political correctness.

Though the reader may not yet fully grasp the reasoning behind the correctness of using the masculine pronoun, it is hoped that through a considered reading of this book the understanding of this idea will become clearer. Please understand that when the masculine pronoun is used in this book, it does not indicate male bias for the reasons I have here discussed.

Monadic Sojourn

In the previous discussion, the expression "units of life" was used. Yet, what are these units of life? Within the esoteric tradition they are called monads. As the One Life extends itself into manifested expression, points of light emerge. These points of divine radiation are the essential atoms of the One Life's livingness. Metaphorically, if God is a flame, monads represent the countless sparks shooting forth from that flame. In point of fact, it is the monad that is slowly evolving through form. The monad is the ultimate being that each of us is. If the soul is considered the *higher* self, the monad could be called the *highest* self. It is the ever-present eternal entity at the very core of one's essential being. It transcends that which we call the soul, and it is the real "I" at the heart of one's existence. From the Judeo-Christian perspective, the monad is synonymous with pure spirit.

Because the monad may be a new concept to those who read this work, a simple analogy may lend deeper understanding. For the moment, let us say that the One Life (God) is symbolized as a cloud. With this in mind, the monad then represents a drop of water that is condensing within that cloud. By way of condensation, this drop of water has developed a measure of individuality within the cloud, yet is still deeply connected to it. This is precisely what can be said of the monad. It is individual in its potential, but is still deeply connected to the universality of the One Life. More than any other structure within oneself, the monad characterizes both individualness and universalness simultaneously. It is the monad that is slowly evolving through time, and does so through all of the kingdoms in nature sequentially. By so doing, it gradually discovers that it is, paradoxically, the whole and the part.

It may be asked, what is the experience of monadic consciousness before evolution begins? In truth, this is a mystery not yet solved. Within esoteric lore we are given to understand that the origin of the monad is lost in the mists of time. We really do not know from where the monad came, nor when. Having stated this, it is useful to assume (for the sake of pedagogic discussion) that the monad's major developmental gains are occurring here on our earthly sphere.

We can begin by postulating that before the monad began its fall into matter, it resided in a condition free from pain and discomfort. Essentially, it experienced unconditional ecstasy, and this without waver. Yet, it is a kind of bliss founded on ignorance, for knowledge is not

The monad exists beyond the soul and is pure spirit itself—its origin a mystery, profound.

possessed by the monad at this phase. The only thing it is capable of perceiving is the joy of union with all that is, for it senses itself as boundless and eternal. Through such perception, it knows only bliss and contentment of being. Most importantly, the monad is not yet conscious of itself. Its only experience is bliss and boundless existence. To it, blissful ecstasy is all that is. The capacity to know itself as an entity within the larger whole is simply not possible.

Referring back to the previous metaphor, though the monad is an individual drop of water, it is only so in potential. It has not yet actualized its individuality. At this stage, it knows only the Boundless All, and this it realizes with utter naiveté. It is a state of Being void of the ability to understand, reason, intuit and feel. Its experience is broad and universal, not narrow and particular. It sees only the whole without the capacity to perceive the part.

By analogy, the immature monad is like an infant. There is a joyful simplicity to newborn children, due to their non-discriminative relationship to life. An infant is not able to clearly distinguish between itself and that which is not of itself. From this state of naïve innocence, an infant perceives the world as if it were an extension of itself. So, too, the monad knows itself without discriminative faculty. In its beginning phase, it sees itself as the entire universe, and nothing else. The long incarnational journey it is about to embark upon will teach the monad to make such discriminations, and it will take uncounted millions of years for this faculty to be fully actualized.

The monadic spark knew only bliss and the peace of boundless life. Ignorance reigned, though the spark knew it not.

Entrance into the Mineral Kingdom

From the state of blissful innocence, the monad begins its descent into matter. The objective of this downward journey is for the monad to gradually acquire knowledge of reality, and to discover its individual nature. The push toward incarnation is not one initiated by the monad itself. Rather, it is the incarnational will of the One Life that forces all lesser units of life (monads) to incarnate into substance. As a reminder, this substance is part of the One Life as well, and is essentially the Cosmic Mother providing a container for monads to take outer form. Thus, matter acts as the intelligent substance that, when organized into form, teaches the monad precisely what it needs to eventually gain full knowledge of reality and itself. Through millions of years of interaction with divine substance, the monad will slowly develop the attributes needed to truly know itself as a part within the larger whole. As such, the descent into substance necessitates that the monad forfeit its fused relationship with the Boundless All, at least seemingly so.

From the Christian angle, this is metaphorically revealed in the story of the prodigal son who leaves the father's home. In essence, the monad leaves the condition of union with God and enters into a state of bewilderment. It is to be lost in the wilderness of form and substance, far from the place where union with the One Life was known. This incarnational descent into substance requires that the monad travel to the bottom of the arc of life, then slowly work its way upward, back to the place of its original home—a place in consciousness called the Monadic Plane. The bottom of this arc is the mineral plane, for it is the densest of the seven planes of consciousness (*see Figure 6, The*

Without choice the spark falls into the density of matter; imprisonment is then its lot. Allness seems to vanish.

Human Constitution, page 117). We therefore find the monad beginning its incarnational existence on the Physical Plane, and within the mineral domain.

It is important to recall that all kingdoms in nature are really expressions of life. So it is with the mineral kingdom. That which we call mineral is really the physical expression of rudimentary monadic life. Minerals are organic, contrary to what contemporary science would suggest. All aspects of creation are understood as expressions of life. That which we call inorganic is actually teeming with life if we could but recognize it. And how could it be otherwise? For if all is truly the expression of the One Life, then there can be nothing in the visible and invisible worlds that escapes that oneness. All things therefore live, and minerals are no exception.

The livingness of all things is fundamental to occultism (study of that which is hidden), and is often referred to as the *Doctrine of Hylozoism*. It is a philosophic precept that advocates the inseparability of life and form. This is an essential idea to keep in mind when trying to heighten our understanding of the ancient esoteric philosophy. It is an axiom applicable to all categories of form, the mineral kingdom simply being the most elementary. Therefore, it is not surprising that the monad will incarnate into the mineral kingdom in its initial phases, for life within that kingdom will give to the monad its first basic etchings of experience.

The monad will live within the mineral kingdom for millions of years. As it does so, it gradually learns how to benefit from the rudimentary intelligence conveyed to it by the dense substance it is contained within. This intelligence slowly makes it possible for the monad to construct mineral forms with greater levels of perfection.

> *For aeons, the spark evolves through mineral form. Slowly do the basic etchings take shape and emerge.*

As with any domain of life, including the human, wide developmental differences exist within each kingdom. Within the mineral kingdom, the vast array of mineral forms represents the varying levels of evolutionary development found within that kingdom. Beginning with the basic minerals, such as granite and limestone, life evolves upward through various categories of mineral structures. Eventually, the life contained within these basic mineral forms will evolve into the metals, leading finally into the category of precious stones and crystals.

When speaking of the evolution of the mineral kingdom, please keep in mind that we are talking about the development of monadic life within that kingdom. From the esoteric perspective, it is consciousness that evolves. Physical forms evolve as well, but only as a reflex response to the evolution of monadic life developing within and through them. This is true for the mineral kingdom and all domains of life, including the human kingdom. When we say that limestone is lower on the evolutionary scale as compared to jewels, we are simply making reference to the fact that the consciousness (sentiency) of the former is not as developed as that found within the latter.

Each kingdom in nature gives to the evolving monad certain attributes essential to the evolution of its consciousness. Though rudimentary, there are two primary traits that the monad acquires while it slowly evolves through the mineral kingdom. They are:

1. Geometric symmetry
2. Radioactivity

The first has to do with the structural makeup of the form. Crystals are considered an example of the highest developmental forms within the mineral kingdom. The

The evolution of physical form is understood as mere reflex.

geometric symmetry evident in crystalline structures demonstrates its evolutionary status. It indicates that the monadic life working within crystals has developed a perfected relationship to substance, and demonstrates this perfection through its regularity of proportion and symmetry. Within the human kingdom, the higher correspondence can be found in the amazing organization and symmetry of the human body. Also indicative of this legacy is humanity's power to organize life and societal forms for efficiency. Though we human beings take such things for granted, it was while residing in the mineral kingdom so long ago that the seeds of organization and symmetry were planted within us.

The second attribute to be developed in the mineral kingdom is *radioactivity*. Indeed, elements such as uranium represent lofty monadic development within mineral form. Such substance is advanced in that it demonstrates its capacity to radiate its inherent power. Radioactivity reveals that the indwelling life is no longer confined by its encasement. Essence is power, as is monad. When the monad is able to radiate itself through mineral substance, it indicates triumph within the mineral kingdom.

The principle of radiatory life is important at any level of development. For example, when the human soul is able to radiate itself through the mental, emotional and physical bodies without distortion, enlightenment and liberation is then achieved. Indeed, as human beings, we are trying (consciously or unconsciously) to enhance our radioactivity. When mineralization was our lot, the first etching of this capacity was chiseled into the very foundation of our existence.

> *Radiation indicates triumph within mineral form. The power of monadic life is liberated from its mineralized tomb.*

It is interesting to consider these two advanced categories of mineral life—crystalline and radioactive elements. In the ancient esoteric teaching, we are given to understand that the mineral kingdom evolves through the influence of the First Ray of Power and the Seventh Ray of Organization *(see Soul as the Quality of Divinity, page 73)*. This fact is most interesting in light of these two advanced mineral forms. In the case of radioactivity, it is the inherent power of the monad that is radiated. This certainly corresponds to the First Ray, with its essential nature rooted in power. Crystalline structures represent organizational perfection and symmetry, which correspond to the influence of the Seventh Ray, sometimes called the Ray of Organization. As such, it is apparent how important these two rays are as agents of transformation within the mineral kingdom. More will be said about the seven rays when we discuss the nature of the soul and the ray that it's found upon.

The kingdom that the monad is working through is crucial in that each kingdom provides it with an important dimension of experience. That is to say that each kingdom provides the indwelling life with the opportunity to experience a state of being that has dimension to it. In the case of the mineral kingdom, this dimension can be referred to as *isolated location*.

When the monad was in its non-incarnational state of bliss, it knew itself to be the All—a condition of unencumbered Being. In such a condition, it experiences itself to be everywhere simultaneously while being incapable of knowing itself to be somewhere. This state is symbolized by a "circle," representing boundless existence *(see Figure 2, Monadic Sojourn, page 40)*. Yet, when incarnated into the mineral kingdom, the monad is forced to experience the antithesis of what it had previously known. It is a condition of complete imprisonment within substance

The density of the mineral prison shuts out the Boundless All. Isolated location then reigns.

Monadic Sojourn

**Densest State
(Bottom of the Arc)**

- Forfeiture of Universal Being
- Mineral Encasement and Imprisonment
- Seed of Individualized Awareness
- Isolated Location

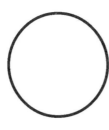

**Pre-Journey State
(Top of the Arc)**

- Identification with Universal Being
- Blissful and naive state
- Naive existence
- Non-Individualized Awareness
- Boundless Location

**Post-Journey State
(Top of the Arc)**

- Identification with Universal and Individual Beingness
- Perfection Achieved, Enlightenment
- Individual Realization of God Consciousness
- Isolated Boundless Location

Figure 2

without even the capacity to demonstrate mobility. As earlier stated, the dimension learned is that of isolated location. This new dimension is symbolically represented as a "point." The monad now experiences its existence somewhere, but no longer everywhere.

Symbolically considered, when the monad departs from its blissful state and enters into mineral form, it forfeits the circle in order to slowly learn of existence as a point. It is a lesson learned after millions of years of mineral confinement. The experience of isolated location is the root of what will lead the monad to eventually discover its individualness, which is life as a point in the truest sense. In truth, individualization doesn't occur until the monad enters into the human kingdom. Nonetheless, isolated location within the mineral world serves as the foundational matrix for the individualization process to occur after human existence has been earned over distant aeons.

When movement into the plant domain occurs, the etchings that were earlier achieved serve as needed foundation.

Entrance into the Plant Kingdom

Great ages pass before the monad liberates itself from the mineral kingdom. Such liberation must be earned, as is the case for all evolutionary development within creation. As has been said, there are no shortcuts in cosmos. This is most certainly true. The journey is long and seemingly endless. Yet every incarnation, no matter which kingdom of life we consider, provides the monad with an incremental advancement from its previous level of development. When it finally earns the right to move out of the mineral category of life, it is the plant kingdom that offers the monad its next field of learning.

As we consider life within this second kingdom, it is well to remember that at this state of development the monad still has no conception of itself. It does not perceive itself as a distinct entity. Rather, it only has a gross sense of location and isolation. The capacity to compare its experience with anything is not yet possible. At this stage, the monad has only the most rudimentary instinctual sense of place and inertness of being. This is the major quality of awareness bestowed to it during its mineral epoch. Entrance into the plant domain will provide the monad with a new set of experiences, each of which will build additional attributes into its nature. These new attributes require that the dimension of isolated location be already established.

During the monad's long sojourn through the plant kingdom, there are three major qualities that it is seeking to develop. They are:

1. Magnetic Appeal
2. Harmonic Relation
3. Upward Yearning

The first quality for us to consider is *magnetic appeal*. The plant domain holds the key to developing the power to draw life unto itself. It is therefore not surprising that human beings are enormously attracted to plant life. This kingdom draws humanity to it by the power of its magnetic radiation. Because of this, humanity has historically used plants as symbols of affection. For example, the rose has long been used as a symbol of love when given to another person. Without the need for words, there is something about this magnificent flower that speaks to the human heart. This is true of many forms of plant life.

Inherent in the radiation of plants is an energy that softens the outer world and reveals the unity of life. Esoterically considered, love can be understood in this way. It is the divine force within creation that enlivens us with the vision that we are all truly one. Love invites

> *The power of magnetic appeal emerges when the monadic spark resides within flower and verdure.*

us into a unitive field where oneness can be felt. When handing a rose to someone dear, is this not a symbol of recognized unity conveyed in the giving? Such is the power of plant life to create love and magnetic warmth. Plants are inherently attractive. They draw life unto themselves via the quality of magnetic appeal radiating in and through them. To a bee seeking sweet nectar to produce honey, it is the flower that magnetically attracts. Indeed, the flower represents a fountain of life to the bee.

We see therefore that magnetic appeal is first etched into consciousness when life resides within the plant kingdom. As human beings, this quality is still with us today and has been further developed. It is recognized in our capacity to magnetically attract people and circumstance into our lives. Interpersonal love, and our capacity to sense the oneness of humanity, is rooted in this ancient lesson learned when we (as monads) evolved through the plant kingdom uncounted aeons ago.

The second quality to be developed within the plant kingdom is *harmonic relation*. This is recognized in the harmony and beauty associated with this domain of life. Humanity has long marveled at the splendor of creation, particularly as it is expressed within plant forms. It is clearly evident that the harmony existing in nature is astoundingly beautiful, and when not disrupted by humankind, demonstrates perfect interrelational poise and balance. Plants synchronize themselves according to the greater rhythms in nature, such as the seasons and the cycles of day and night. People who tend gardens often speak of it as a means to achieve inner peace and harmony. We also see this harmonizing force manifesting in the magnificent color display of plant life.

Harmony of relationship is shaped when life manifests in vegetative form. Divinity bursts forth as beauty.

Beauty and harmony are inseparable companions.

Through the harmony expressed within the plant domain, beauty emerges in its splendor. This is a point of major import when considering this kingdom of nature. It is within the plant kingdom that the development of divine beauty first emerges with clarity. From the esoteric perspective, beauty is considered an attribute of God, and is an essential quality that must take root within evolving consciousness. The relationship between beauty and harmony is crucial in this regard. It is when various forms within an environment harmonize with each other that beauty emerges. Beauty therefore depends upon harmony for its recognition. It is the inevitable consequence of the harmonizing force displayed through vegetative forms. It can be argued that mineral forms also display beauty. This is, of course, true and indisputable. However, from the esoteric perspective, beauty in mineral expression is incidental to the primary attributes to be developed within that kingdom. In the vegetable kingdom, the manifestation of beauty is not incidental but deliberate and ordained.

Though plant consciousness is rudimentary (as compared to animal and human), these attributes serve as the foundation for the development of higher orders of harmony to be refined later within the animal and human kingdoms. Within the animal kingdom, we see that harmony is further developed, resulting in the natural interplay that exists between various species and their environment. In the human domain, this rightful interplay with nature is only now being recaptured. This we can see in the growing environmental movement occurring in the world today. However, this harmonizing force is also seeking to evolve still further in this, the fourth kingdom in nature. As human beings, our capacity to create harmony within the complexities of human living is evidence of this fact. Humanity's ability to create art forms that have the power to uplift the human spirit is further indication that harmony and beauty are continuing to be refined within us. This energy is also creating the conditions that lead to the harmonizing of the human soul with its lower reflection, the personality.

The third attribute built into the consciousness of plant life is the yearning for light. Generally speaking, this urge is revealed in the tendency of plants to upwardly reach toward the sun and its nurturing rays. To the plant kingdom, the sun provides the most essential radiation in support of its sustenance and growth. No other category of life is as dependent on direct sunshine as are plants. From the esoteric perspective, the plant kingdom is most receptive to the energy of *prana* emitted by the sun. Prana is the name given to the sun's hidden energy (behind and within the sun's outer display of light), and is considered the true life-sustaining force in our solar system. Indeed, it is a spiritual energy that provides living vitality to all that is upon our planet.

Interestingly, it is the plant kingdom that is best able to utilize and transform prana with efficiency. The lower reflection of this intimacy can be seen in the process of photosynthesis uniquely operative within the plant domain. From the occult perspective, this is the main reason why spiritually minded people are encouraged to live a vegetarian lifestyle.

Interestingly, most people are under the impression that vegetarianism is based upon a repulsion to the killing of animals for human consumption. However, this overlooks the fact that plants are manifestations of life as well and are equally as sacred. The reason for making the plant kingdom one's primary source of nourishment is related to the question of prana. Because prana is best absorbed and assimilated through plants,

Upward yearning toward the source of life begins. The seeds of aspiration are planted.

its life-sustaining power is greater than that offered through animal flesh. This is the deeper occult reason behind the emphasis on a vegetarian diet.

There is actually a second reason that occultism promotes vegetarianism. Within their range of development, plants are the most evolved forms of life on our planet. To understand this, the phrase "within their range of development" must be kept in mind. When considering the entire kingdom, plant life is nearing its apotheosis of evolution. Therefore, its forms of life demonstrate the greatest purity and perfection of expression. To consume the Earth's verdure is to take into oneself a sacred vibration of purity and sustenance.

The tendency to upwardly yearn, though initially carved into consciousness when living within the plant kingdom, is clearly present and operative in our lives today. This is particularly true when we consider people who are trying to live according to their highest values and spiritual aspirations. Our yearning for the light of the soul is a higher rendition of the plant's yearning for the light of the sun. Often in esoteric literature, there is reference to the light of the soul and its correspondence to the sun's radiance. Indeed, the soul is the sun within each of us. Our meditative strivings are motions in consciousness that were initially developed in the plant kingdom. Such inward and upward tendencies are simply higher order refinements of the same sacred principle developed so long ago.

It is through the tendency to upwardly yearn that the monad in the plant kingdom begins to relate to a second dimension of existence. *Vertical extension* now becomes evident within its nature. No longer is the monad viewed as simply an inert point of concentrated existence as it was in the mineral kingdom. Now, it is able to move vertically, and in both directions. There is the striving toward the sun, as well as a downward thrust as it

To live the life of soul, one must inwardly sense the vertical dimension of being, a quality implanted when the physical sun was life's highest striving.

plunges its roots into the soil of the Earth. As such, the vertical line is a useful symbol for this added dimension of existence and experience *(see Figure 3, Vertical Extension, below)*.

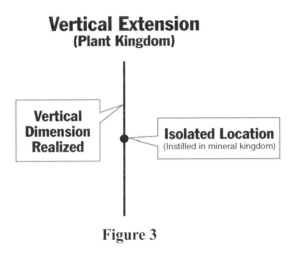

Figure 3

In the esoteric literature, we are given to understand that the plant kingdom is developed through the influence of three divine rays. Though called by various names, these rays are the Second Ray of Love, the Fourth Ray of Harmony and Beauty, and the Sixth Ray of Aspiration and Devotion *(see Soul as the Quality of Divinity, page 73)*. These rays are emanations of God, and condition all units of life within this second kingdom. Each provides the energetic attributes that must be conditioned into the sentiency of those monads residing within the plant kingdom. As can be seen, these rays clearly correlate to the attributes to be developed by monads evolving through this kingdom.

Entrance into the Animal Kingdom

When the monad has come to the end of its journey within the plant domain, it transfers itself into the third kingdom, the animal. Here again, we find a domain of life demonstrating a wide range of developmental grades. The monad will spend countless millennia working its way through this kingdom. By so doing, it will gradually gain additional attributes preparatory for entrance into the fourth kingdom, the human.

The added dimension realized in the animal kingdom is that of *horizontal extension*. It is here that the monad learns to free itself from its immovable rootedness in the Earth. By so doing, it discovers a new aspect of its existence through greater freedom of movement. Unlike a plant, an animal has the capacity to move parallel to the horizon. This expanded mobility gives tremendous versatility and adaptability to the monad's experience of life. It is a new dimension of existence to be added to the previous two dimensions earlier realized. This can be symbolically presented as the horizontal line *(see Figure 4, Horizontal Extension, page 50)*.

Horizontal movement now finds its place. Versatility of experience is thus enhanced.

The animal kingdom is governed by two divine rays, each conditioning the monad with an essential quality. They are the Third Ray of Intelligence and Adaptability, and the Sixth Ray of Devotion *(see Soul as the Quality of Divinity, page 73)*. Through the energy of the Third Ray, the monad develops the *instinctual mind*. Over vast periods of time in animal form, monadic life establishes and coordinates the rudiments of mind through the maturation of various instincts, all of which contribute to its survival. As it does so, it becomes identified with the consciousness of the species of which it is a part. Importantly, instinct represents the first etchings within the mind that give the monad a basic sensitivity toward collectively defined states of consciousness. In one sense, this is a way to understand animal instinct. It is a collection of behaviors defined by a species and governs all animals within that species.

Instinctual mind serves evolution well, for when life eventually enters into the human kingdom, instinct becomes the foundation upon which human thought and reason are built. The power to reason is an attribute acquired within the human domain, and animal instinct provides the basic intelligence and adaptability for its development. In addition, one of the evolutionary goals of human life is to acquire the faculty of intuition. Metaphysically considered, intuition is viewed as a higher rendition of the instincts developed when the monad journeyed through the animal kingdom so long ago. The distinction between intuition and instinctual consciousness (the root of psychism) is important to consider. We will later examine this when discussing the nature of astrality (emotion) and its role in the magical process.

Within animal is found the matrix of future thought. Instinctual mind emerges, though individual it is not.

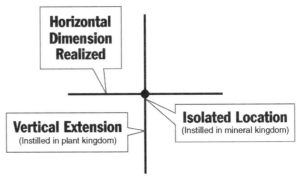

Figure 4

The second key attribute to emerge for life within the animal kingdom is the quality of *devotion*. This relates to the Sixth Ray *(see Soul as the Quality of Divinity, page 73)*. This ray is particularly influential when we consider the most evolved of the animal types, those that have been domesticated. These animals have had close association with the human kingdom, and as such, have benefited from humanity's radiation and influence. Because of this, they will be the first category of animal forms to enter into the human kingdom when the cycle of opportunity occurs.

Because of their devotion to mankind, many species of animal have been trained in behaviors that go beyond their instinctual nature. Indeed, domestication prepares animals for their eventual transition into the human kingdom. Animal devotion (desire to please), coupled with an ability to be trained, builds important substructures in an animal's consciousness. These rudimentary structures will eventually be needed in order for the monad to develop individualized mind when it enters into the human kingdom in the distant future. Admittedly, a domesticated animal is far from being an independent thinker. Yet as a result of its devotion to a human being, the first etchings of independent mind begin to take form. Indeed, this is a prerequisite for entrance into the human kingdom. From these initial etchings, intellect will someday be built.

The quality of devotion evolves still further when life enters into the human kingdom. Humanity's devotion to God is simply a refinement of the devotion developed when experiencing life within the animal domain. Keep in mind that, from the esoteric perspective, God is a relative term. Any entity is a god in relation to forms of life less developed than itself. Therefore, in relationship to animal life, human beings are indeed gods. As such, the importance of wise husbandry toward all animal life cannot be overstated.

I Am!
No other mantram is more relevant to the monad's human journey than this.

Entrance into the Human Kingdom

When the monad finally enters into the fourth kingdom, the human, it has stepped into a domain of experience unlike anything previously lived. The events that occurred within the previous three kingdoms set the stage for the monumental event that is to occur during the human epoch, for it is in the human kingdom that individualization occurs.

Within this fourth kingdom, the monad is given the equipment needed to become truly an individual, thus rising above its instinctual animal nature. The equipment referenced here is an individual *causal body*. The causal body is a vehicle of substance existing for the purpose of developing individualized consciousness within a human being. Prior to entering the human kingdom, the monad utilizes the causal body that governs the species of animal or plant within which it happens to be housed. The consciousness (or sentiency) of an animal or plant is therefore defined by its species. Yet in the human kingdom, the monad is given a personal causal body, and as a result, it learns of its individualness.

Over time, the monad must learn to utilize and mature its causal vehicle. As the container of soulful consciousness, the causal body is a fascinating topic, and we will examine it in detail a bit later in our discussions. At this point, it is important to simply understand that the destiny of human development is to unfold the causal body, and by so doing, make possible the expression of its innate divinity and potential. The completion of this process is what we commonly call enlightenment. Enlightenment occurs when the full nature of the causal body radiates through the personality without distortion or encumberment.

When the human spark begins its inward turn, duality of self comes into view. A struggle for synthesis will eventually ensue.

Occultism teaches that there are two rays that primarily govern the development of the human kingdom. They are the Fourth Ray of Harmony through Conflict, and the Fifth Ray of Concrete Knowledge and Science *(see Soul as the Quality of Divinity, page 73)*. Because the human kingdom is the fourth, it seems fitting that the Fourth Ray would be pivotal in human evolution. Whenever examining this ray, it must be understood that it always relates to a struggle between two things, the resolution of which leads to harmony and beauty. In this case, it is an inner duality that is at issue. The soul/personality duality becomes abundantly apparent when life matures within the human kingdom. It is an inner recognition of two contrasting forces within us, that of the animal and that of the divine.

For the first time, the monad is now able to introspect, and by so doing, discovers itself to be an essential duality in manifestation. The recognition of this is what eventually drives the individual to begin to walk a deliberate spiritual path in hopes of resolving this duality. However, resolution does not imply the elimination of the animal nature, but rather the subservience of it to the soul. It is the Fourth Ray, operating within the human kingdom, that energetically stages this internal struggle, leading eventually to complete harmony between these two forces. Success for the monad will come when the soul is able to triumphantly master and guide the personality and animal passions. This is the destiny and hallmark of full attainment within the human kingdom. Therefore, one of the attributes to be realized by the monad in this kingdom is *internal duality*.

The second influential ray guiding the evolution of humanity is the Fifth Ray of Concrete Knowledge and Science. Through its radiation, humanity is stimulated to develop the mind. In many ways, the emergence of the individualized mind is the hallmark of human evolution. The monad acquired the foundations of mind through the development of instinct while residing within the animal domain, prior to the human stage. However, as previously noted, instinctual mind is not individualized mind. The Fifth Ray is the divine radiation that animates the mental plane, and also governs the maturation of the causal body (the container for soul consciousness).

What is being suggested here is that the expansion of the individual mind is crucial within the human kingdom. This is not to suggest that intellectualism is advocated. Rather, it is the capacity to think clearly and without distortion. This requires a keen awareness of one's individuality, realized through clear thought rather than by the persuasions and opinions of others. It is to think abstractly and concretely with independence and certainty, and not be swayed by mass consciousness (a

To know thyself requires one have faculty of mind.

remnant of animal instinct). This is what it really means to develop the mind principle within the human being, and it is an evolutionary necessity to do so. Therefore, the second major attribute to be developed by the monad while in the human kingdom is *individualized mind*.

As was the case when traveling through the previous three kingdoms, in the human kingdom the monad is exposed to a new dimension of existence and experience. This dimension is *inward extension* resulting in conscious awareness of subjectivity *(see Figure 5, Inward Extension, page 55)*. For the first time, the monad now has the capacity to move inwardly through the power of introspection. Using the individualized mind, it can observe the nature of its subjective experience. It sees what it is inwardly, and by so doing, gradually begins to know itself. This requires that one be internally attentive, for self-knowing is only achieved when the monad is able to discern how thoughts and feelings are separate and independent from that which is outside itself. The monad must learn that it has the power to individually create thought and feeling, and this without environmental pressure or the persuasions of its instinctual heritage. Individualized mind, having the capacity to inwardly gaze, makes this possible. Therefore, the fourth dimension of experience emerges through the monad's capacity to explore the inner realms of subjectivity, and to then contrast the subjective self with that which is not of itself.

> *Pure thought must reign, and this, independent of instinctual urge and the collective persuasions of the human herd.*

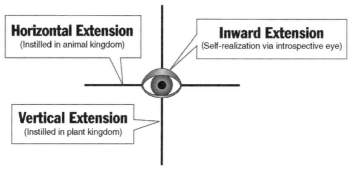

Figure 5

From this point forward, the monad is self-conscious, an achievement that represents its major mission when beginning its evolutionary journey. With steadiness of effort, it then continues to refine its sense of selfhood. Toward the later stages of human existence, the monad gradually becomes interested in recapturing the sense of universality it possessed before it began its long journey aeons ago. When this occurs, an individual is said to have entered onto the probationary path, leading to a series of initiations that will eventually earn him rite of entrance into the fifth kingdom in nature. These initiations will be discussed later. Suffice it to say that each initiation represents a milestone of evolutionary development to the soul seeking mastery over its reflection, the personality.

While on the spiritual path, an individual (now disciple) gradually establishes rapport with the consciousness of the larger life within which he is a cell. This therefore represents the first attempts by the monad to begin regaining the consciousness of the One Life. Yet, this process takes many incarnations to achieve.

The sense of universal awareness (relatively speaking) occurs through the gradual development of group awareness. The more one is identified with the soul, the more that person will sense inner group unity. Group consciousness must always be developed as a needed prerequisite to universal awareness.

There comes a time on the path, specifically at the third initiation, when the light of the monad is consciously touched. The key word in this last sentence is "consciously." Indeed, the monad has been operative through the entire evolutionary journey, for it is the monad itself that is evolving. However, it is at this initiation that one becomes consciously aware of the monad within. Up to this point, the monad has been working behind the scenes, and has therefore been unconsciously operative. Yet at the third initiation, the soul is fully expressive in one's life. This therefore makes it possible for the monad to come into view, esoterically considered. When this begins to occur, the initiate faintly starts to sense universal consciousness, and is often astounded at its implications.

By the time the sixth initiation has been reached, the initiate has returned to the original abode of monadic life. Essentially, the monad has come home. It now has returned to the place (plane of existence) where it began its terrestrial journey so long ago. However, now it is much more than it was when it began its descent into form, for it has garnered the experiences of life lived within all kingdoms of nature. The spirit is now fully conscious of its individual Beingness, and is an intelligent agent on behalf of God. Indeed, the monad now exists in a paradoxical condition. It realizes itself to be the All, while simultaneously knowing that it is an intelligent part within the All. A heightened state of

As one deliberately walks the spiritual path, separateness gives way to inner group awareness. When complete, universal mind is then touched, though not seized.

enlightened Being has therefore been consummated. To the monad, this is both its honor and its reward. Such is the great sojourn of the Spirit through time.

The Nature of the Soul

We have thus far been considering the evolution of consciousness as it pertains to the monad's journey through the many kingdoms in nature. From this, it becomes clear that the evolution of consciousness is incremental, covering vast periods of time. As such, when we restrict our study to the human kingdom, and the evolution of the individualized soul within that kingdom, this notion is also operative. That is to say that the individualized human soul incrementally develops its capacity to manifest itself through form. Each human incarnation sees the soul more effectively express itself through its lower reflection, the ego (personality). Its goal: to fully radiate its nature through the personality, and this without distortion.

It is important to note that the human personality is triple in nature, being composed of mental, emotional and physical attributes. In the esoteric view, these aspects of the lower self are considered vehicles of outward expression to be used by the soul. Over countless incarnations, the overarching challenge of the soul is to manifest itself (and therefore its will) through these vehicles. When done completely, an individual is said to be fully soul-infused.

Soul infusion suggests that one's personality is well developed, yet completely subservient to the soul's creative intention. This marks the time in the soul's long journey when true spiritual magic is possible. At this time in history, there are comparatively few people who can be called true white magicians. Few there are whose

The evolution of the human soul is incremental. Its status is measured by its ability to radiate through its triple reflection.

causal bodies are fully opened, which is indication that the soul completely dominates the personality life. Even so, their numbers are growing with each passing decade, and it is the destiny of all to reach such heights, in this incarnation or another. Many of the greatest people in human history have demonstrated such developmental status. When soul infusion is complete, one's ability to shape and uplift the human condition has global and historical implications.

White magic is essentially rooted in the creative urge of the soul itself. As such, an understanding of soul is an important step in comprehending the magical process. The soul is the creator, at least as it is considered within the human energy system. However, it is important to realize that from the larger perspective, it is not the soul that is the ultimate creator, but God. When viewing it in this way, we then understand that the soul is acting as a creative agent on behalf of Divinity. As such, it is best to consider spiritual magic to be a co-creative process. The soul co-creates according to the will and intention of the larger life of which it is a part. The soul is therefore *seemingly* initiating the creative process, and does so through the utilization of its threefold personality. Indeed, successful co-creative magic is proportional to the personality's cooperative stance in this regard.

The personality is essential if soul-inspired magic is to occur. This is because it represents that part of us that is accustomed to relating to the outer world. Spiritually considered, the personality exists for the purpose of interacting with the external aspects of life. Why is this so? The answer is that it is of the same nature as the outer world. It has a natural affinity with most forms, and this because it is largely composed of the same substance. Personality is essentially consciousness defined by concrete thought, emotional feeling and

White magic is best understood as a co-creative effort.

physical sensation, all of which are esoterically understood as substantial forms. As such, the personality will have a measure of rapport with the outer world that the soul does not naturally have.

Importantly, the soul resides upon the plane of abstract mind. It therefore needs a vehicle in order to have influence within the realms of normal human experience. Because an aspect of the personality is composed of mental substance, the soul can utilize this aspect when seeking to influence the outer world of thought. When the soul needs to make emotional contact with the environment, it does so via the emotional body contained within the personality. Finally, the soul utilizes the physical body as a conduit for expressing itself in terms of outer physical activity. Therefore, white magic is rooted in the soul's capacity to express itself through the threefold personality.

In the esoteric tradition, it has long been understood that there are several aspects to understanding soul. As such, we can define soul in many ways, each of which adds deeper insight into its nature. We shall therefore consider soul from six perspectives. They are:

1. Soul as universal matrix
2. Soul as the principle of love
3. Soul as sentiency and consciousness
4. Soul as the organizing principle
5. Soul as individualized identity
6. Soul as the quality of divinity

The soul is the agent of God's creative intention, and the threefold personality gives outer expression to that intention.

Soul as Universal Matrix

We begin by looking at soul from its most fundamental perspective, as a principle inherent in all expressions of manifested cosmos. To understand this, we must first recall that creation itself represents one entity in manifestation. When this One Life manifests (as cosmos), It does so by way of expressing Itself through diversity. As a result, the seemingly endless variety of forms within creation emerge. Yet even as the One Life is contained within a field of multiplicity, It is nonetheless a singularity in Its essence. It is all that is, and nothing can exist independently of It. In truth, everything in existence is merely a fragmented expression of the One Life as It emanates Itself into an endless variety of forms.

The Universal Being emanates Itself into form. The One becomes the two, and the two become the many.

When we consider soul, and its root beginnings, we must consider the moment when the One Life mysteriously began to manifest Itself, thus creating the universe in its entirety. Though the beginning of this process is shrouded in occult lore, it can nonetheless be stated that as this One Life began Its movement into multiplicity, It did so by first transforming Itself into two. In short, the One Life created out of Itself a reflection of Itself, and by so doing, duality came into existence. These two aspects of the One represent, from our human perception, the expressions of the Cosmic Father and Mother (*purusha* and *mulaprakriti*). All lesser dualities, as recognized within the human experience, represent lower reflections of this universal duality. Indeed, this great duality is the cosmic prototype for all lesser dualities evident within creation, objectively and subjectively considered.

As the One Life becomes the two, something else emerges simultaneously, and it is this that represents the foundation of soul. Where there are two, there always emerges the principle of relationship between them. When the Cosmic Father and the Cosmic Mother come forth from the One Life, they immediately are in relationship, for one cannot exist independently of the other. Therefore, soul (cosmically considered) is rooted in the relationship that emerges when the One Life becomes two.

Sometimes referred to as the Middle Principle, soul is always understood as a force that unites. It is the *principle of relationship* that emerges, and its existence is based upon the memory of the Original Condition. That is to say that relationship (or the force that unites polarity) is based upon the fact that the Mother and the Father have within them the memory of their original state of oneness. This memory serves as the force that creates their binding relationship.

From this universal consideration, we can rightly say that soul is the Middle Principle between opposite poles at every level of creation. As such, it serves the role of reminding any and all dualities that they are one in essence and origin. This is a broad idea, but it is truly foundational when considering the nature of soul. Soul ever serves as the representative of oneness, but is not oneness itself. In other words, soul consciousness is not governed by oneness, but is the gate that leads to it. When considered from the highest and purest perspective, the principle of relationship *is* soul. Yet as the One Life continues to fragment itself into greater density and multiplicity, relationship becomes the root matrix for the emergence of soul, and is no longer understood as the soul itself.

When the One becomes the two, magnetic polarity springs forth. Thus does the matrix of soul emerge.

The Trinity of Creation

When trying to learn occultism, the nature of these three expressions of the One Life need to be understood. They are often referred to as the Three Aspects, and have correspondence to the trinity noted in both Western and Eastern theological systems. To avoid confusion, please realize that the original two (Cosmic Father and

Cosmic Mother) are referred to as the first and third aspects, respectively. Relationship, though it seems to manifest last, is nonetheless called the second aspect. This is because it is the Middle Principle and unites the original two. Below is a breakdown of this sacred trinity, and a variety of correspondences worthy of note.

Where there are two, a third will always be.

First Aspect	*Second Aspect*	*Third Aspect*
Father	Son	Mother
Life	Consciousness	Form
Being	Relationship	Activity
Monad	Soul	Personality
Will	Love	Intelligence
Thinker	Thinking	Thought
Life	Quality	Appearance
Father	Son	Holy Spirit
Shiva	Vishnu	Brahma

To illustrate the Middle Principle (second aspect), we can examine the relationship between two people. When first meeting, a relationship is established, be it positive or negative. In either case, it is still a relationship. Assuming that it evolves in a positive manner, an intimacy begins to emerge between these two people. As such, this emerging intimacy draws them closer together, and a commonness of vibration correspondingly emerges. In point of fact, such unified vibration represents the birth of soulness between them. The point to keep in mind in this example is that this emerging soulness is built upon the principle of relationship. This analogy, though clearly mundane, does nonetheless convey the notion that relationship forms the matrix of soul.

When considering this idea within a human context, as just done, such an idea may seem simple and obvious. Yet, it becomes more interesting when relationship is understood universally. When it is considered as foundational to every facet of diversity found within cosmos, such ideas begin to weigh more seriously in our minds. It must be understood that relationship is a principle inherent in all things, large or small. It is a living principle, and within its embrace is found the memory of the Original Condition. This great cosmic principle ever holds the power to unite things by bringing all parts into right relationship within a systemic whole. As such, unity established through right relationship is an inescapable prerequisite to the eventual realization of essential oneness.

It may be a bit easier to grasp the principle of relationship if we confine our considerations to the human kingdom for a moment. In the esoteric tradition, the oneness of the human family is a fact in nature. Indeed, humanity is considered a single entity incarnated into a myriad of separate expressions, and each expression comes forth as an individual human being. Though the number of people on our planet is enormous, they are collectively understood as one living entity manifested through a multiplicity of forms. Our evolution, as a species in nature, is to eventually rediscover this inherent oneness. It is oneness that transcends unity, for it is a fusion best described as a synthesis of Being.

As earlier stated, unity is the gate that will eventually lead humanity to discover its oneness. Indeed, it is the Principle of Relationship (as a cosmic law) that gives birth to the urge to unite. In practical terms, this suggests that all people have a divinely ordained place within humanity's oneness. This sacred principle is thus driving mankind forward in order that

Within any living system, its parts evolve by finding their rightful place within the larger whole. Intelligent synthesis can then be realized.

we each find our destined place within the organism of humanity as a living whole. To use an analogy, every cell within a person's physical body is equal and divine, and in their totality, the health and oneness of the body is realized. For this to occur, each cell must be in its rightful place, for place and function are mutually dependent. So it is with the human family. In our totality, we are a singularity of life. Yet within that oneness, we each have a place and function which supports and gives sustenance to this singularity. Indeed, it is the memory of our oneness (experienced aeons ago) that drives human evolution forward. Deep within each of us is the memory of the Original Condition, and our striving to unite is merely an unconscious effect of this ancient memory.

Returning to the topic at hand, let us recapture the thought that the principle of relationship governs the soul within all forms of life. The universal expression of soul is sometimes referred to as the *anima mundi*. Defined as the soul within all things, the anima mundi is a living energy functioning within all units of life, large or small. Indeed, it is true whether reflecting on the life contained in a blade of grass, a human being or the entity that ensouls a solar system. All units of life, from the simplest to the most complex, have soul. In point of fact, there is nothing in existence that is void of soul. For cosmos is the out-picturing of the Mother and Father in relationship to each other, and relationship is the universal matrix for the birth of soul.

Soul as the Principle of Love

Because the soul is essentially the power that unites, it is not surprising that it has an association to love. Love is the cosmic principle that unites all things through its power to reveal the underlying oneness in

From relationship the anima mundi emerges. Nowhere is found a place where it is not.

creation. Love does this through its ability to see itself in all facets of manifested existence. It can be said that cosmic love has the power to recognize all things as within itself. As noted earlier, relationship holds the memory of the Original Condition, and it is love that is that memory. Not often is memory associated with love. Yet from the cosmic perspective, there is only one thing to be remembered. It is the memory of being the All, and love has the power to mimic such existence, thereby drawing all things back to it. Herein is revealed an important occult law. It is the *Law of Attraction*.

The Law of Attraction is universal, and love is the quality that emerges from it. Always, we will find that love is magnetic, and this is true whether we are considering human or divine love. By its nature, love contains the quality of magnetic appeal. For example, when we proclaim that "God is Love," what we are really saying is that God is the living energy in creation that has the power to draw all things back into a unitive state of oneness. From the human perspective, love between two people does the same thing. It is an energy that causes two people to be magnetically drawn to each other resulting in a sense of union. As such, interpersonal love gives indication that a united soul is in bloom.

For centuries, the soul has been described as an expression of selfless love. In the human being, the soul represents the intermediary (Middle Principle) between the monad (spirit) and form (personality). Essentially, its role is to unite the two, and the experience of such union is love. When pure and unfettered, it is registered within consciousness as something revealing greater unity. Interestingly, when clouded by selfish tendency, love is still experienced. However, it is tainted by this selfish vibration, and is thereby less able to reveal the larger field of unity that is its mission to make known. Though

The soul unites through its power to attract, and love is this power. The two are never apart.

we think of love in these rather human terms, it must be understood in its abstract implications as well. For example, can we fathom that the force of gravity is simply another expression of the Law of Attraction? Therefore, it too is a manifestation of love.

Soul as Sentiency and Consciousness

Universally considered, soul is rooted in the relationship between the two poles, spirit and matter. Yet, the principle of relationship serves simply as its underlying matrix. We must also understand that soul is the agency of experience. That is to say that soul not only unites, but through such unity, interaction between the poles also emerges. This interaction results in the development of sentiency. By this is meant that soul makes it possible for any life unit to *experience* something. Sentiency is therefore synonymous with impressionability.

Sentiency is characteristic of all manifestations of life. Even life contained in an atom of substance is sentient. It too has soul and is therefore impressionable. Though this appearance of soul is infinitesimal in its scope and development (compared to a human being), it still exists and is capable of recording impressions of some kind. Minute as it may be, an atom has a rudimentary sense of aliveness. It is sometimes difficult for people to fathom the implications of this notion. Clearly, it is an idea that reaffirms the occult axiom that all things in creation are essentially organic. All things live because soul is found innate within everything. Even a stone is living, inasmuch as it is possessed of soul. While it is true that modern day science perceives minerals as void of life, from the occult perspective, all things live, including the stone.

> *All evolutionary categories of life are sentient, even a stone.*

There is a small distinction between sentiency and consciousness. In many ways, these two definitions of soul can be considered synonymous. Even so, there is a subtle differentiation worthy of note. Sentiency is very much related to the quality of impressionability. As such, consciousness can be viewed as an addition to sentiency. Added to impressionability is the capacity to react to what is being impressed. Consciousness therefore governs an entity's capacity to register vibration (coming from that which is external to it), and is the agency that creates internal and external reactions to such stimuli.

It is important to remind the reader that all prehuman expressions of life are conditioned by a collective, rather than an individual soul. For example, unlike human beings, animals do not have individual souls. More accurately, animals do not possess individual causal bodies. Instead, their experience of soul is related to the soul of their particular species. For the animal, consciousness is primarily experienced as instinct, which is defined by the species to which it belongs. Therefore, soul is experientially revealed through instinctual responses. In truth, an animal does not truly know itself to be separate from the instinctual behaviors it has inherited. Such a capacity only emerges when considering the human kingdom and beyond.

One may logically ask, why is it that there seems to be unique personality traits within certain species of animals? Anyone having a pet knows well that animals vary widely in their temperament. The reason for this is that animals are the category of life to individualize next and thus become human. As such, the rudiments of individual behavior naturally develop in the animal kingdom. Perhaps it would be better to say that the underlying matrix for individual behavior begins its development in animals. However, this matrix does not

Out of primal sentiency arises consciousness. Reactivity then is.

need an individual causal body (a necessary vehicle for individualized consciousness) in order to emerge. Individualness in animal is based upon temperamental distinctions that naturally arise from biological and environmental variables. Such individualness is not based upon self-consciousness, as is the case with humans. This is an important point to ponder.

A slight exception to this notion relates to the consciousness of domesticated animals. They have benefited from their close proximity to individualized human beings. Through training, these animals demonstrate behaviors that transcend their instinctual nature. As a result, domestic animals (as compared to those in the wild) will be the first to enter into the human kingdom when the door to such movement opens again in the future.

An example of this preparatory conditioning of a domesticated animal can be seen in one's relationship to a pet dog. When a cat runs in front of a dog, the dog's instinctual response is to chase it. However, if the owner of the dog is nearby and calls out a command for the dog to stay, it will usually stop (if well trained). This is an important indication that the quality of individualism is beginning to form in its consciousness. Why is this so? Simply because the dog was able to avert, if only temporarily, its instinctual nature. The ability to rise above instinct is the hallmark of individualized existence in the human kingdom. Because of the dog's intimate relationship to its human caretaker, a template for individualized consciousness has been built. However, this doesn't mean that the dog has an individual causal body. Still primarily governed by animal instinct, it hasn't the ability to introspect. As we have seen, introspection is a capacity that first emerges within the human kingdom, and this because an individual causal body makes such a process possible.

Domestication implants the seeds that can resist instinctual urge.

Nonetheless, the underlying matrix for individual behavior is slowly developed by animals, and this is the explanation for their varying temperaments.

Sentiency is the nature of soul as it expresses through all categories of form. Consciousness, on the other hand, is an attribute that emerges out of sentiency, and is that which eventuates in individual and universal realization. When individual consciousness comes into view, a human being emerges onto the stage of life, and when the universal is realized, a god is born.

Soul as the Organizing Principle

Because the soul is the Middle Principle, its role is to relate intelligent substance (inherent within the Mother) with divine purpose and will (intrinsic to the Father). The soul therefore brings divine will and intelligence together. This union is an interesting one when fully considered. The will of spirit utilizes the soul to assert its developmental intention, while substance provides the intelligence necessary for divine will to be fulfilled. The soul then is understood as the agency that organizes the intelligence of substance in accordance with the will and purpose of spirit. The result of such coordinated action is that forms emerge. Forms therefore represent the intelligent organization of substance as defined by purpose and will.

Understanding the organizing function of the soul is crucial. It doesn't matter at what level of entification (existence of an entity) we may be considering. Whether discussing the soul contained within a plant, or the soul manifesting through a solar system, its organizing power is primary. For example, when considering a tree, we can see the drama between will and intelligence taking place. All of the atoms of a tree contain a profound (though minute) measure of intelligence. Yet,

The soul gives organization to living intelligent substance, and this, according to higher purpose.

The incarnational will of the human monad interacts with intelligent substance, and thus emerges the outer person.

it is the life force evolving through it that has organized these atoms so that they collectively take the form of a tree. In this simple example, the will of an entity (spirit seeking incarnation through a particular species of tree) interacts with intelligent substance (matter), resulting in the formation of the tree itself. The tree is the assemblage of organized substance. Its many attributes (color, size, shape and so on) are the expressions of this intelligence. Indeed, the intelligence to create a specific type of tree comes forth from the sumtotal of intelligence contained within the matter used in its construction. Yet, it is will that impulses the incarnation of the tree and the assemblage of its substance. The point to be highlighted here is that this interaction *is* the consciousness of the tree.

Naturally, this pertains to the human experience as well. The monad (spirit) seeks to incarnate into the human kingdom in order that it may learn of itself through its interaction with divine substance. As such, it combines with substance. The soul emerges as the uniting principle within. It then organizes substance to create the mental, emotional and physical vehicles needed for full incarnation to occur. In this example, it must be realized that the will of the monad (Father) is to incarnate into a given form and circumstance (in this case a human form), and it is motherly substance that has the intelligence to assemble such a form. The soul unites monadic will with divine substance and forms then emerge in response to this union. Human form (mental, emotional and physical) represents the intelligent organization of substance in accordance with purpose and is the product of the soul's organizational endeavor. Later, we shall see that this process is foundational to white magic, for magic is the art of building thoughtforms out of intelligent substance, and this according to the will of the thinker.

Soul as Individualized Identity

As we have discussed, soul is the force that unites the monad (spirit) with divine substance (matter). This is simply a lower reflection of the cosmic duality of Father and Mother, for the monad is the father within each of us, and intelligent substance is the mother. However, when it comes to the soul found within a human being, there is a new factor to be considered. As compared to subhuman categories of life, human beings have individual souls.

A human being is not only conditioned by the soul that animates the human kingdom, but also by the individual causal body (vehicle of soul consciousness) that he possesses. It is this fact that makes it possible for a human being to know himself to be an individual, separate and distinct from others. The causal body gives us the capacity to think, ponder and introspect. Our reasoning capacity is what lifts us above the realm of our instinctual heritage. The causal body provides individual containment for the wisdom garnered through experience, and facilitates the development of our reasoning and introspective minds. Thus it is possible for a person to experience a sense of identity quite separate from the herd. Indeed, the experience of I-ness emerges in the human kingdom, and because of this, the grip of animal instinct slowly gives way.

Essentially, the causal body is a representative of the Father and the Mother Principles in cooperative rapport. At its center is found the so-called jewel in the lotus. This jewel is the monad in extension. It is the center of identity and purpose within the causal body, and therefore correlates to the Father. However, the form that encases the jewel represents the Mother, for this shroud is essentially substance of an extremely high

Identity is realized when soul takes root upon the fourth tier. I-ness emerges, first as selfishness, then as selflessness.

grade. It is substance that is divinely intelligent, and acts as a vehicle for the gestation of individualized consciousness.

The important point to keep in mind is that the causal body exists as an actual form for each and every human being. No life below the stage of human can make this claim. The monad uses the individual causal body to focus itself. By so doing, it then has the capacity to concentrate its attention, and thus become aware of itself in contrast to that which is not itself. In short, because it now possesses an individual causal vehicle, the monad has what is required in order to realize its individualness, and to mature itself into an effective thinking entity.

It has been said that consciousness (as typically considered) can exist only if there is an object (form) to perceive. This is most certainly true, particularly when we consider that thoughts and feelings are forms as well. Because of our individual causal bodies, we as human beings have the ability to know ourselves. Yet, even this is an experience in consciousness that is dependent upon form. Our sense of individual identity is governed by a wide array of thoughts and feelings related to who we think we are. As human beings, we can never truly be conscious of our absolute identity; we can only be conscious of the mental, emotional and physical forms we internally use to symbolize that identity.

As earlier mentioned, introspection is a capacity not possible to the monad before it enters the human kingdom. It is the individual causal body that gives to a human being this introspective capacity. In addition, the causal body houses every thoughtform used to represent an individual's higher sense of self. Essentially, these thoughtforms serve as useful tools. They are mental symbols that give representation to the many aspects of the identity being inwardly sensed. They lead us toward

> *Beingness is ever transcendent to the mental forms used to symbolize it.*

absolute identity, which is a state transcendent to consciousness as we know it. Such a state is perhaps best described as a condition of Beingness. In truth, until one has risen above the human kingdom, it is impossible to experience Beingness directly. It can only be sensed indirectly, and this through the utilization of the many thoughtforms stored within the causal body, for they give symbolic form to the formless essence of Being. This will become clearer when we discuss the formation of the causal body a bit later.

Soul as the Quality of Divinity (Seven Rays)

There is a tendency to believe that all souls express the same essential quality. Such an assumption is however only partially true. Though all souls are inherently conditioned by love, beyond this important commonality, significant variations exist. In the Esoteric Tradition, it is understood that there are seven types of souls, each of which represents an essential quality of God seeking manifestation through the human kingdom. As the One Life (God) manifests as cosmos, Its radiation is *qualified*. This is what is meant by the statement that the soul represents a quality of divinity. Each soul, by its nature, accents an aspect (quality) of God, and as such, is destined to reveal that quality in the outer world.

Before describing each unique soul type, it is important to briefly comment on the nature of light, for it provides an important analogy that will help in our understanding of soul variation. When white light is projected through a prism, it divides itself into the seven colors of the visible spectrum. Each color is unique unto itself. Each affects us a bit differently. Each prismatic color expresses a specific aspect of the white light that gave it birth. Interestingly, when we examine the various

The One Life shines forth in prismatic display. Upon one of its rays is found the human soul, its quality thus defined.

religions throughout the world, we see that light is frequently used as a symbol for God. The "Light of God" is a phrase commonly used by those who are spiritually inclined. Just as white light divides itself into seven colors, so too does the Light of God express itself in seven unique qualities. In the ancient Esoteric Philosophy, these seven divisions of divine light are referred to as the Seven Rays. Most importantly, every human soul is an expression of one of these Seven Rays.

Each ray represents an aspect of the One Life seeking to evolve itself through form.

Ray 1	The Ray of Divine Will and Power
Ray 2	The Ray of Love and Wisdom
Ray 3	The Ray of Abstract Intelligence and Activity
Ray 4	The Ray of Harmony through Conflict
Ray 5	The Ray of Concrete Knowledge and Science
Ray 6	The Ray of Idealism and Devotion
Ray 7	The Ray of Ceremonial Order and Magic

There is much that can be said of the Seven Rays. They represent the essence of divine energy within creation itself. From them emerge all that is found in the universe, both objective and subjective. These rays condition all aspects of evolution, and are cyclic in their expression. When considered in the context of Christianity, they have correlation to the archangels. In Hindu mythology, they are represented by the seven *Rishi Lords*. In music, the seven rays characterize the nature of the musical scale, and in chemistry, they relate to the seven periods (categories of elements) found within the periodic table.

When considering the magical process, the ray of the soul will characterize the types of effects that a person will create in the outer world. As such, it is well for us to briefly examine the Seven Rays, and the divine role they each play in the evolutionary drama of humankind.

Ray 1

The Ray of Divine Will and Power

The intention of this type of soul is to reveal the *Purpose of Divinity* within the human kingdom. All life is evolving, and it is the objective of this ray type to supply the power and direction to this evolutionary movement. Therefore, the function of the First Ray soul is to express the power of divine purpose through loving strength and synthetic vision. Its role is to shatter those forms that no longer adequately express the Love of God. This great stream of life is best understood as a liberating force. It frees life from its encasement within outworn forms, thereby allowing it to seek new and higher forms through which to express itself more radiantly. It is therefore not surprising that the First Ray is deeply associated with death and rebirth. Esoterically speaking, death is nothing more than the liberation of life from inadequate forms of expression.

Today, there are many souls found upon this ray. Their responsibility is to wield will and power, and to do so within the context of love. First Ray disciples are uniquely sensitive to the larger spiritual principles seeking to evolve through human society and environmental circumstance. As such, they tend to commit their lives in support of such principles, even when destruction of certain societal forms may be

Divine purpose is held by those upon the First Ray of power. Love and synthetic vision must accompany its expression.

required. Leadership comes naturally to this type of soul, for they see what must come to be and will naturally assert power on its behalf.

Societally, the First Ray animates and vitalizes the institutions of politics, government and international statesmanship. Fundamentally, this ray represents the purpose and will of God, and is the energy within society that forces humanity to move forward in its growth and development. Evolution itself would not exist but for the driving forward motion that this ray demands.

Ray 2

The Ray of Love and Wisdom

The Second Ray is the ray that conditions life with *Divine Love*. Its role is to reveal the unity that underlies all apparent diversity within creation. Love, expressed through compassion and understanding, is how this ray manifests for those whose souls are conditioned by it. It is the ray of inclusiveness and relates all things to each other by revealing the love and wisdom underlying outer events. Spiritually speaking, love is understood as an energy that attracts all unto itself. As such, the Second Ray is truly the emanation of God's love, and is the magnetic power found within all aspects of creation.

For disciples upon this ray, wise and loving thought is considered the antidote to all human malady and misfortune. Such people tend to commit their lives to promote love and wisdom in all that they see and do. In truth, wisdom is a form of love, and it demonstrates itself through understanding and tolerance.

From the larger perspective, this ray governs the educational efforts found within all human societies. It is also the force that animates the healing arts, whether

> *Inclusiveness governs those upon the second stream of life. Love is the force that joins through unitive vision.*

traditional or alternative in nature. Because humanity is in transition from the Piscean to the Aquarian Age, this soul type has a large incarnational presence at this time. Because of their innate capacity to illumine, people with Second Ray souls are able to skillfully disseminate the new and emerging ideas that will shape human society during the Aquarian era to come.

Although all the rays are crucial to humanity's development, none is of greater import than this, the Second Ray. For according to ancient record, it is this ray that governs the life of the entire solar system. Our Solar God (Solar Logos) has a Second Ray soul, we are told. As such, and regardless of ray, all efforts on our planet must be accomplished on behalf of divine love.

Ray 3

The Ray of Abstract Intelligence and Activity

The Third Ray is the energy most related to *Divine Intelligence*. Essentially, it is this ray that provides the underlying knowingness in all of nature. With respect to the human kingdom, it is the force that animates human thought. Its purpose is to reveal the Mind of God within the consciousness of humanity, as well as to give spiritual understanding to all human activity.

For those souls upon the Third Ray, their purpose is to demonstrate the interconnectedness of ideas. The Mind of God is as sacred as God's Love. Many Third Ray disciples therefore dedicate themselves to serve humanity by using their minds to fathom the mysteries of existence. This objective is accomplished via the manipulation of ideas, particularly abstractions. The power of manipulation is understood as an essential and sacred attribute of this ray, for through the rearrangement of ideas, eternal truth will surely emerge.

The power to manipulate form is the hallmark of the Third Ray worker. Ideas and material resources both feel the effect.

Interestingly, some Third Ray disciples are given to serve humanity through the world of business and finance. Business is understood as a sacred force in the world of human affairs. Indeed, this expression of the Third Ray centers upon the manipulation of resources, rather than of ideas. The divine role of business and finance is to utilize money and materials in ways that support humanity as a whole, rather than just the select few. Many Third Ray disciples demonstrate their "calling in Christ" by promoting an equitable distribution of material and financial resources in support of the one humanity.

The holy trinity is now revealed, its sacredness well known.

From this we can see that the Third Ray governs the institution of business and all forms of exchange. It is also the ray that is responsible for the many philosophic presentations of truth conceived and promoted throughout human history. In addition, this is the ray most associated with karma, for it holds the memory of what was, as well as the archetype of what is to be.

It may be well to briefly state that the first three rays somewhat correspond to the sacred trinity found within both Eastern and Western theological systems.

<u>Ray 1</u>	<u>Ray 2</u>	<u>Ray 3</u>
Father	Son	Holy Spirit
Shiva	Vishnu	Brahma

Ray 4

The Ray of Harmony through Conflict

The Fourth Ray is the force that creates a sense of equilibrium and beauty within creation. When considering the *manifested* universe, all existence is perceived dualistically. In truth, cosmos is the outward manifestation of an endless array of dualities. By its very nature, the human mind perceives dualistically. For every thought, feeling, idea or intention that we experience, there is an opposite thought, feeling, idea or intention that the mind entertains as a potential. For example, war is a meaningless concept if peace is not also conceived. Happiness has meaning only when contrasted with sadness. As such, the function of this ray is to find balance and resolution to the many dualities ever present within the human experience.

People upon the Fourth Ray tend to immediately see both sides of opposing perspectives and will persistently search for the means to harmonize them. As such, they are normally quite skilled in the art of compromise. The *Beauty of Divinity* is what is sought, for when harmony is achieved, beauty spontaneously emerges. This is what is known and searched for by people evolving upon this ray. To such people, spiritual truth is considered synonymous with beauty. Beauty is realized as the gate into the mysteries of life. Through this gate, God is realized. For when the heart and eye are bathed in beauty's splendor, divinity proclaims itself through awe and wonder.

From a global perspective, the institution most associated with the Fourth Ray is the United Nations. Its charter and mandate is to act as a mediating force in international affairs. Finding "harmony out of conflict" is clearly seen here. This ray is also connected to artistic expression. Art is occultly intended to lift the human spirit and to aid humanity in its recognition of the sublime. Though all seven rays have relationship to humanity's artistic yearnings, it is the Fourth Ray that holds the deepest association.

From the two a deeper harmony must be sought. So says the Fourth Ray worker. In his eyes, beauty and truth are seen as one.

Ray 5

Ray of Concrete Knowledge and Science

The Fifth Ray is the energy that reveals the *Clarity of Divinity* through the pursuit of correct knowledge. Its role is to create within consciousness the ability to distinguish truth from fiction. The difference between this ray and the Third Ray is important to consider. The Third Ray gives to humanity the ability to use the mind with creative adaptability and to deepen our understanding of reality through the connecting of ideas. However, it is the Fifth Ray that disciplines the adaptable mind, so that the distinction between truth and falsity can be more clearly discerned.

For those upon the Fifth Ray, life tends to be dedicated to finding solutions (truth) to the many problems facing humanity. Through the use of clear and precise thought and analysis, the Fifth Ray disciple reveals cause and effect relationships that are not initially known or recognized. As such, this type of individual will be unbending in pursuit of truth, and will not yield to unsubstantiated theory or speculation. From a still deeper perspective, the spiritual purpose of such a disciple is to demonstrate that the function of knowledge is to reveal the spiritual essence behind all forms within creation.

When considered from a societal perspective, science is the manifestation of the Fifth Ray. It is the one institution within society that most demands accuracy in its pursuits. Science is completely dedicated to the precise examination of reality. Through the use of scientific investigation and experimentation, much of human suffering has been eliminated. Advances in medicine, physics and chemistry all give testament to the transformative power of this ray. Indeed, because of

Separate that which is true from that which only seems to be true. Such is the motto of those who seek knowledge through Fifth Ray means.

its influence (as it works through the more enlightened representatives of the scientific community), the existence of the soul will someday be established as a scientific fact.

Ray 6

The Ray of Idealism and Devotion

This is the ray that brings spiritual sight to all evolving forms of life. Essentially, its purpose is to bestow the *Vision of Divinity* within consciousness. This vision gives to one an inner sense of direction by revealing the inward abode where spirit can be found. As the sacred energy of devotion, it instills within us a willingness to dedicate our lives to something transcendent to ourselves. The Sixth Ray gives us the capacity to intuitively sense the spiritual ideals to live by, and to strive toward them with unwavering devotion.

People whose souls reside upon the Sixth Ray are moved to devote their lives in support of the ideals they inwardly sense. Such disciples have the power to lift humanity into the realm of Spirit. They live their lives as sacrificial examples of commitment to the causes for which they stand. This energy eventually leads one to realize that the path to enlightenment is found through the renunciation of desire. Human desires are recognized as anchors that prevent us from inward and upward ascent. For the Sixth Ray disciple, the power to serve lofty ideals can only be accomplished when the desires of the personality are overcome.

Through its influence, humanity gradually comes into a realization of the spirit within. The Sixth Ray teaches us to inwardly and upwardly gaze, and to know that something much greater than life as we know it awaits those who aspire toward the inner light. This

Aim for the ideal; a banner held high by those with Sixth Ray vision, true. Sacrificial service is their means to achieve.

divine ray is the energy that animates religion within the many cultures of the world. It is also the energy that governs all social welfare movements. In addition, the Sixth Ray characterizes the worthy causes for which people passionately fight, such as the protection of the environment, the amelioration of world hunger and the trumpeting of universal human rights. Lastly, this ray of idealism is largely responsible for the manifestation of war within the human kingdom. This is not surprising when one considers the fact that war is most often an out-picturing of clashing ideals.

Ray 7

The Ray of Ceremonial Order and Magic

The Seventh Ray is best known for bringing order out of chaos. Its purpose is to provide the energy needed to translate spiritual ideas into tangible effects. Through the influence of this ray, the *Manifestation of Divinity* is made possible. This ray influences humanity to outwardly create according to divine intention. It represents the quality of God that gives form to divine essence. In this regard, it is the creative force expressed by the One Life. The evolutionary purpose of form is to give containment to spirit. Form is therefore destined to reflect the divine essence that seeks to evolve through it, and it is the Seventh Ray that makes this possible.

Disciples with Seventh Ray souls are said to be true magicians, for they are naturally able to create positive change in the world. Most often, this is achieved through the power of the spoken or written word. This person understands the magical potency of language, knowing it to be an instrument for creating new forms through which Spirit can express itself.

> *Forms should be built true to the patterns they are destined to reflect. The Seventh Ray worker knows this well when creating outer effects.*

As a generalization, Seventh Ray people are inclined to view things in practical terms. Their organizational abilities are normally quite good, which is one of the reasons that they are able to manifest what they intend. They are frequently attracted to business, politics or educational environments. They also may be involved in the arts, particularly when the elements of ceremony or ritual are involved.

The Ray of Organization, as it has also been called, seeks to give good form to societal structures and institutions. All administrative efforts are animated by it. As the energy responsible for creative manifestation, this ray is intimately relevant to our study. White magic has been called the science of thoughtform-building. It is the Seventh Ray that teaches us to build thoughts that are efficient in their design, while remaining true to the archetypes they represent. Consciously or unconsciously, the Seventh Ray magician believes that God is revealed through the creation and perfection of outer forms. Such people are dedicated to building structures (mental and/or physical) that can efficiently serve the cause of human betterment.

The Formation of the Causal Body

The formation of the causal body is a fascinating account, as given to us in ancient occult lore. By and large, its beginning is said to go back to the middle of the Lemurian epoch of human existence. At that time, we are given to understand that mankind experienced individualization. It was a time when humankind developed the ability to lift itself from perceptions and actions governed exclusively by animal instinct. We began to develop the capacity to think individually, no

The seeds of individualized mind were planted long ago, and thus a new kingdom was born.

longer impulsively responsive to instinctual urge. This development was only infantile in expression, but the seeds of this capacity were planted nevertheless.

The formation of the causal body, as conveyed in occult lore, occurred twenty-one million years ago, and was the result of a great intervention of angelic life upon our planet. Legend of this event suggests that a very high order of angels (devas) came to Earth to implant the spark of mind within animal-man of that time. These solar angels, as they are called, provided infant humanity with the substance necessary to develop individual causal bodies. From that time forward, all people have had an individual solar angel overshadowing them. These great angelic beings are deeply connected to the soul and loosely correspond to the guardian angel notion espoused in the Christian faith.

The solar angel is extremely important to a human being in that it provides the substance and structure of the causal body itself. Most important, it is the innate intelligence, inherent within causal substance, which makes it possible for humankind to develop the quality of manas (mind). The causal body is therefore a container of intelligent substance of an order far higher and more refined than the substance composing the mental, emotional and physical bodies of the personality.

The use of the term "causal body" is important to consider here. It is said to be a person's body of causes. That is to say that the causal body is a container of forces within oneself that ultimately brings forth outer effects. It is the source of the incarnational urge, as well as the root of one's life tendency toward activity. The causal body stores the memory of one's incarnational history, and therefore frames each incarnation to work out past karma. It is the cause of life circumstance, and

Solar angelic life streamed forth in distant ages past. Through their gift, the causal body came into being.

gives birth to outer effects within circumstance. In this sense, the causal vehicle represents one's body of causation.

Interestingly, when spiritually sensitive people speak of experiencing their souls, such a claim is only partially true. This is because part of the experience is not of them at all. Instead, they are inwardly sensitive to the intelligence and wisdom of their overshadowing solar angel. What we often think is an experience of soul is actually an awareness of the wisdom coming forth from the substance of the causal body. Because this substance is of the solar angel, this angelic entity, rather than oneself, is actually the origin of the wisdom we inwardly sense. The part of intuitive experience that is of oneself is the deep and silent *presence* lying behind the soulful wisdom we possess. Apart from the sense of this presence, all aspects of soulful experience are largely the out-picturing of the intelligence contained within the causal body, and therefore the solar angel.

Admittedly, this concept is rather difficult to grasp, at least initially. The presence we are considering here is the monad, which is one's true and eternal self, whereas the solar angel is an assisting agent to it. This is why the solar angel is sometimes called the *angel of the presence*. "Beingness" is the term that perhaps best defines the natural state of the monad. Yet, anything *experienced* in consciousness (which always implies internal movement and the creation or manipulation of form) is really phenomena qualified and conditioned by the solar angel, and not the indwelling highest self (monad).

The monad is the ever-present center of Being that gives impulse to events within consciousness, but is not consciousness itself. Given this fact, most spiritual experiences (within consciousness) are not directly of oneself, but are instead of the solar angel. At their

Beingness lies behind the content of consciousness. The angelic shroud hides its presence, and thus it exists unseen.

formless root, such experiences are impulsed by the Presence (monad) but the experience (as it is registered in consciousness) is solar angelic in origin. Again, this may seem a difficult idea to grasp. Until the personality is mastered, internally discerning the monad from the mediating solar angel (soul) is well nigh impossible. For most spiritually aligned people, the monad is not yet in view, and thus the distinction is not realized. For those likely to be considering these ideas, the distinction is not important, though someday it will be. Nonetheless, it is crucial that one understand the principle. Transcendent to the soul (though unrealized) is found the spirit-self, the monad. What we consider a soulful experience is really the consciousness of the solar angel acting as surrogate to the monad.

It must first be recalled that the monad is truly the magician within. Yet, for the purposes of this work, considering the soul as the creator is right and appropriate. It is the soul that is seeking to create according to divine intention as sent forth from the monad. It is also the soul within us that acts as agent on behalf of the Hierarchy of Masters. These beings represent those elder brothers and sisters on the path who have shown us the way, and as such, provide humanity with the wisdom and experience necessary to move forward in evolution.

The masters are the members of the fifth kingdom in nature, the kingdom of souls. Theirs is the task of impressing the minds of certain members of humanity with the insights and ideas needing to be externalized in the outer world. This process is what slowly yet surely moves humanity forward in its growth and development. By divine mandate, these great beings have the responsibility of taking humanity's evolutionary needs

> *The soul is a willing surrogate in service to the monad's intention. Their distinction is well-veiled until the former has mastered its reflection.*

in hand. As such, they selflessly dedicate their existence to this effort, and utilize disciples (via their individual causal bodies) to this end.

When an individual has some measure of soul infusion, that person can be rightly considered a disciple. It indicates that he is being guided by the wisdom of his causal body, at least to some extent. The Masters of Wisdom are then able to transmit to such a person the ideas needing to eventually be brought forth into the outer world. This they do by using the disciple's causal body as a conduit for their transmission. As such, they hope that the disciple will properly register the ideas sent forth, then find ways of externalizing them into the outer world of human need. This is largely what the magical process is about. For the disciple, it has to do with his capacity to sense the intuitive impression sent forth from the Hierarchy of Masters, then to translate it into an outwardly useful form. If such effort is successful, the form created will invariably have the power to environmentally uplift. Soul-inspired magic results in such an effect. The soul always seeks to serve a larger whole. A focus on the whole will always take precedence over creative acts motivated by personal want. This is ever the litmus test of true spiritual magic.

Disciplic living requires that consciousness be receptive to the promptings of the soul. Then can the Masters use that soul in service to world need.

Through these preliminary discussions, a foundation for the study of white magic has been laid. We have examined a variety of principles related to the esoteric philosophy, and have established an understanding of the soul and the causal body. In addition, a brief consideration as to the seven types of souls has been offered, as well as the unique methods of service they each render in support of human upliftment.

As is often the case, to study a particular subject requires that one have a measure of familiarity with several tangential topics, each of which is essential in order to grasp the primary subject at hand. To a small extent, this has now been accomplished, and we can therefore proceed with our inquiry into the art and science of white magic. Our study is divided into three parts, each corresponding to the particular vehicle the soul is utilizing at various stages of the magical process.

Part II

The Art and Science

of Magic

The Point of Light Emerges

- *Magic Upon the Mental Plane* -

When considering white magic, we must examine the process from several perspectives. As the soul attempts to transmit its ideas into the outer world, it must do so via the threefold personality. The human personality is the instrument needed by the soul to successfully externalize its wisdom and essential nature. The great challenge for the soul is to convey wisdom in such a way that it is rightly received and interpreted by the personality. This is a formidable task, for the personality is often colored by various impurities. For example, within the mind will be found thoughtforms that are unwholesome. These thoughts have the capacity to distort the truth sent forth by the soul, and hence can be detrimental to the creative process.

In addition, when the descending idea reaches the plane of emotions, the soul is then challenged by the lack of stability that is often present within the emotional body. Here are also found impurities, but of an emotional kind. Therefore, the emotional body can often be an obstacle to the soul's creative work. As shall later be seen, emotions give much to the thoughtform that the soul intends to externalize. Yet, they are also a threatening source of distortion and misapplied magic.

Even the physical body must be used as a transmitter of the soul's evolutionary message. When correctly engaged, the soul will be able to effectively externalize its impulsed thoughtforms. However, here too are found impediments to successful magical work. Lack of a

> *The human personality is destined to become a willing servant on behalf of the soul's magical intention.*

healthy physical body, or an inability to properly relate to the physical environment, are examples of such impediments. Yet when they are rightly used, each of the personality instruments (mental, emotional and physical) adds a needed and beautiful ingredient to the wisdom sent forth by the soul. We shall therefore consider the magical process as it pertains to these levels of expression within the personality field. As we examine each, we will attend to three considerations. They are:

1. The purpose of magical work upon a particular plane of consciousness.

2. The methods used by the soul as its interacts with the substance of the plane under consideration.

3. The hazards to be avoided as one creates upon a particular plane of consciousness.

Spiritual magic is always viewed as a top-down approach to creative expression. The beginning point of the process is the soul itself. Remember, the soul, not the personality, must direct the entire creative effort. As we consider the magical work upon the mental plane, keep in mind that the causal body is found upon that plane. Importantly, it is the higher mental plane, the plane of abstract ideation, where the soul finds its abode.

For those new to such an idea, it is often received with surprise. This is because the soul is most commonly considered as the embodiment of spiritual love, and the mind is considered antithetical to such love. For long, the spiritual community has tended to see the mind as the "slayer of the real," and therefore as

The soul is the true magician, and finds its abode upon the plane of abstract mind.

having little or no connection to divine love. It is true that the soul is essentially a great center of divine love within the microcosm (a human being), for it acts as the middle principle between the monad and the personality. Yet, the soul is intimately related to the principle of mind as well. Found upon the higher mental plane, the soul is essentially destined to evolve into a perfect expression of loving mind.

When the mind acts as the slayer of the Real, it simply means that it is being used in support of separative thought. However, the Son of Mind (the mind of the soul) always engages in thoughtforms that support unitive vision. Because the soul is located on the abstract levels of the mental plane, its ponderings will be correspondingly abstract. This is an important notion to remember. The soul engages the higher mind in such a way that broad principles of divine ideation are realized.

Higher consciousness represents the field of *manas* (mind) capable of manipulating mental substance so that patterns of truth can emerge in one's awareness. This is fundamental to the soul's nature as it generates thought. It is true that the soul is a center of love, but it reveals such love through its innate relationship to the mind that thinks in abstractions and sees larger principles of truth.

Broad and abstract is the language of manas when uttered by the soul. Still, love is ever present.

The Direction of Soul Communication

It may be supposed that the soul is always seeking to communicate its magical intention within the lower worlds of the personality. Though it is easy to understand why such is believed, this is not actually the case. Generally speaking, the soul has the capability of focusing its attention in three directions. Frequently, it is attending to the affairs relevant to its own plane of existence. That is to say that it spends much time in contemplative rapport with the group of souls to which it has energetic and karmic relation. Because the soul is rooted within the consciousness of its group, much of its outgoing attention is communally focused in this way.

Secondly, the soul is at times upwardly oriented. On such occasions, it is communing with the larger life to which it is a part. When doing so, it is usually in a state of passive receptivity. The soul seeks rapport and guidance from a vaster and more evolved field of life than itself. Generally speaking, this vaster field relates to the Hierarchy of Masters, and their influential radiation.

Lastly, the soul becomes mindful of the personality, the vehicle it uses to interact with the world of thought, feeling and physical reality. This is when the soul downwardly gazes at its reflection (personality). When in this condition, it is usually in a state of active positivity in preparation for communicating with the personality. Indeed, it is when the soul downwardly gazes that white magic is made possible.

Because there are times when the soul is attentive to the personality and other times that it is not, the magic of the soul is considered rhythmic in nature. This idea may shed light on the seemingly inconsistent experiences of soulfulness that people report. For most disciples, there are times when a sense of the soul's presence is readily recognized, while at other times it seems fleeting and difficult to establish rapport. At times, a sense of spiritual connection and purpose is easily perceived, while on other occasions it seems to have disappeared, leaving the individual bereft and disconnected. Though there are several reasons for such experiences, the explanation offered here is the most common. Essentially, the soul pulsates. There is a rhythmic ebb and flow of soul-personality alignment. Understanding this rhythm is crucial in order for the

Triple is the soul's view, and rhythmic its attention.

personality to sense the moment of magical opportunity. The magician must learn to rightly perceive these internal rhythms and utilize them advantageously in the magical work. The details of this will be given later. Suffice it to say that correct timing can make the difference between effective magic on behalf of the soul and creative work void of soulful guidance.

It should be here noted that this rhythmic tendency is a condition inherent in disciplic life. However, this is not so for the initiate. When one has achieved initiate consciousness (beginning at the Third Initiation), the soul is then able to gaze in all three directions simultaneously. Though there are many distinctions to be made between the consciousness of a disciple and an initiate, this is one of the most important. When the transfiguration occurs, the personality is completely infused by the soul. No longer does the soul need to gather its power in order to downwardly gaze. In addition, initiate consciousness indicates that the causal body has now fully matured, resulting in the elimination of its vacillating tendency. As such, it is able to simultaneously hold its union with the personality, the inner group and the larger life.

When the soul downwardly gazes, a time of magical opportunity is then at hand.

The Downward Gazing Soul

Having an understanding of the soul's pulsating nature, we shall now consider the soul as it readies itself to downwardly gaze at the personality. This gaze is really the downflow of creative intention. Because the personality contains a variety of impurities, the soul's attempt to communicate with it is often challenged. To compensate, the soul must gather unto itself all of its energetic resources to accomplish the task of properly impressing the mind of the personality. This is the downward gaze. Its purpose is to instill in the

Penetration into form requires the gathering of power to counter the deflections of impurity.

personality an evolutionary idea needing expression in the outer world. As such, the gathering of power requires that the soul draw to itself the energy it has extended elsewhere, and by so doing, accumulate the force necessary to assert itself within the darkness of its lower reflection.

You may recall that the soul is the structure within the human energy system that makes it possible for one to become conscious of anything. Yet, during our day-to-day experience, the soul is *inattentively* extended into its lower fields of expression, namely the threefold personality. This extension of soul is what animates every thought, feeling and physical sensation that we experience. In actuality, what we call the lower self (personality) is simply the soul attenuated into the mental, emotional and physical planes of substance. More specifically, the personality represents those extensions of soul that have forgotten that they are extensions. Personality is that part of the soul that is lost in the lower three worlds. As a consequence, we tend to identify ourselves with our thoughts, feelings and physical sensations. In short, the soul confuses itself with the threefold garment that it is wearing. Personality is therefore best defined as the attenuated and misdefined soul.

In many ways, this gathering activity of the soul (prior to asserting its divine idea into the mind of the personality) is largely related to the accumulation of surplus energy associated with the day-to-day extensions it has projected into the personality. When this surplus has been gathered back to a central point of focus, namely the causal body, the soul is then ready to consciously project its idea into the waiting mind of the personality.

From one perspective, this is an event of heroic proportion on the part of the soul. An act of daring is required in order to magically impress the mind, given the risk that what is projected may be misinterpreted and/or misapplied by the personality. The soul is always subject to the karmic aftermath of a distorted personality response. Yet, as mandated by cosmic law, it must take such a risk. By so doing, and over the course of many lifetimes, it then learns how to increasingly purify the personality so as to make it less likely to demonstrate a wayward response. The soul therefore begins the magical process by gathering itself into a concentrated point of power. This it does in preparation for communicating with the personality, which is, as earlier mentioned, the confused part of itself.

In truth, this gathering process is a form of meditation done by the soul on its own plane. This is often a point overlooked. Such a meditation is not that done by the earnest individual seeking to experience transcendent states of consciousness. Rather, it is the soul itself that meditates, and does so throughout the duration of an incarnation. This is true whether we are considering the soul when it is focused upwardly or downwardly, as well as when it is attentive upon its own plane.

The nature of the soul's meditation will be different depending upon its directional focus. When upwardly aimed, the soul is receptively meditating in order to invoke response from the greater life. When directed to relations found upon its own plane, it contemplates the purpose of its ashramic group. When downwardly gazing, the soul seeks to establish communion with the personality, and this in preparation for transmitting a divine idea in need of embodied expression. The soul is therefore always in a state of meditation of some kind. It is a meditative process of which we (as personalities) will have little or no realization, for it is a super-

Transcendent and enduring is the soul's meditative life. The direction of its attention defines the nature of its ponderings.

conscious event lying beyond the normal range of awareness.

The Alignment of the Personality

Thus far we have been considering the activities of the soul as it prepares for its magical orchestration. This involves an accumulation of energy, as well as the transmission of that energy via the soul's own meditative dialogue with the personality. The next phase of spiritual magic has to do with the needed preparations of the personality itself.

Because the personality is essentially consciousness identified with organized form, its natural tendency is to be outwardly oriented toward the world of objectivity, rather than inwardly directed toward realms of subjectivity. That is to say that the personality will have a natural proclivity to relate itself to the world of thought, feeling and physical experience. Like attracts like. Because the threefold personality is composed of mental, emotional and physical substance, it will have a normal association to substance of the same kind. Because of this, the personality has an innate tendency to resist developing rapport with the soul.

Essentially, the causal body is of a different substance, and its vibrational influence upon the personality is therefore foreign to it. At times, the persona will even view the soul's radiation as threatening and ominous. Of course, as the individual becomes increasingly soul-infused, this resistance wanes over time. The soul-infused portion of the personality is that aspect of the lower self that has willingly yielded to the soul and its radiation. When such is the case, the heightened vibrations of the causal body are no longer viewed as threatening to the personality, but are instead welcomed.

Magic cannot occur unless the personality is aligned with the soul. The measure of soul-infusion determines the ease of this alignment.

The Role of Meditation

At this point in our discussion, it is well to ponder the importance of orienting the personality so that it is able (and willing) to receive impressions sent forth by the soul. For this to successfully occur, the personality needs to make right alignment with it. The work of soul-inspired magic can proceed when this is accomplished, but not before. You may ask, what is the alignment required? The answer to this question invariably leads us to the subject of meditation. We are not referring here to the meditation performed by the soul on its own plane. Rather, we are referencing meditation as we commonly consider it. When well incorporated into one's life, the outer practice of meditation (performed by the personality) gradually teaches the personality to commit to the soul's magical agenda.

The inclusion of a disciplined meditation practice in one's life is an absolute prerequisite to becoming a magician in the truest and highest sense. Daily meditation makes possible a proper and effective line of communication between the soul and the personality, thus providing a necessary conduit for the soul to transmit its intention and wisdom. Regular meditation aligns all three bodies of the personality so that they are all placed into a condition of magical receptivity. As such, the importance of meditation cannot be understated. It therefore would be of value to discuss the additional benefits of meditation, particularly as they relate to the magical process:

1. Meditation brings about a state of equilibrium within the threefold personality. Various mental and emotional states are harmonized, making it possible for the soul to successfully *impress* its agenda upon the lower self. Once equilibrium has been reached, a

Meditation builds a communicative bridge between the soul and its outer garment of form. Alignment is the result, and magical capacity is sure reward.

higher vibration can be imposed upon the personality, making it possible for the soul to effectively transmit its creative intention. This is an essential prerequisite. In short, the personality must be hushed, so that the voice of the soul can be heard. It is the *voice of silence* (a seemingly paradoxical statement) that is internally registered when the mind remains quiet and steady in the light.

The voice of the silence is heard when meditation is woven into the fabric of life.

2. When done consistently, meditation provides the individual with experiential evidence that he is something transcendent to his thoughts, feelings and physical sensations. The personality then realizes the existence of the soul, and a *conscious* relationship between the soul and personality can commence. From the point of view of the magical process, this realization is crucial, for it marks the moment when an individual begins to meditate with regularity. By so doing, intimacy between the soul and personality will grow with increased rapidity, and likewise will the magical effectiveness of the soul be enhanced.

3. Meditation conditions the individual with the ability to detach from thought. This is done when the disciple learns to internally distinguish the thinker, thinking and thought. The thinker is the being that is transcendent to thought, while thinking is a process of the mind. Thinking is governed by motion, and the thinker is its implementor. When the thinker engages the mind in thinking, thought is its product. As such, meditation gradually conditions one with the capacity to experientially distinguish these three internal aspects of consciousness. It is a needed ability in the magical work. The magician must consciously remain detached from the motions of

his mind (thinking), and also from the thoughtforms that are created by these motions.

4. Meditation facilitates the opening of the third eye, the eye of the soul. As this eye gradually opens, the soul is able to see more clearly within the three lower worlds (mental, emotional and physical). This "eye of vision" is an important spiritual organ used in creative manifestation, for it directs the entire magical process. It makes it possible for the disciple to sense the unity underlying the multiplicity of forms in the outer world, and to discern the deeper purpose behind them. This will be discussed in greater measure as we proceed further into our study of the magical process.

The antahkarana is the inner bridge. Through it, the voice of the silence is heard, and the eye of vision awakens.

In the ancient texts, the communication medium between the higher and lower self is referred to as the *antahkarana*. The antahkarana is the energetic bridge between one's soul and personality, and its construction is facilitated by the practice of regular meditation. This "bridge of light" is the conduit by which the soul interacts with the personality for the purpose of guiding it in the creative work. In this regard, when meditation is practiced over many years, all aspects of the lower mechanism are gradually reoriented toward the light of the soul. Through its practice, the life energy of the threefold personality is vertically redirected, and in due time, submits to the soul's regime.

To understand this process, it must be realized that the substance of the personality is composed of divine light at its core. When the personality is fully aligned with the soul (in meditation deep), this indicates that the personality's light has conformed to the greater light of the soul. More specifically, the fiery light inherent within the three lower vehicles (the mental, emotional and physical bodies) is lifted in supplication to the light of the divine self within. Solar fire (light of the soul) thus irradiates the three lower vehicles.

By yielding to the soul's agenda via meditation, the mind becomes a cooperative agent on behalf of the soul's magical work. Indeed, the mind shifts from simply being an independent generator of thought to an instrument receptive to the soul's ideation. In addition, the aspirant's emotional body becomes tranquilized so that it can effectively give vitality to the idea impulsed by the soul via the mind. No longer does the aspirant's emotional body demonstrate uncontrolled volatility. Granted, emotional swings will still occur, but the aspirant is no longer led by his emotional reactions. Lastly, through years of meditation, the aspirant's physical appetites are tamed, thus providing the soul with a pure and cooperative physical body through which to work.

When the mind is receptive, the emotions tranquilized and the physical appetites well governed, then the soul can effectively use these lower vehicles to magically create. What was a solitary effort on the part of the soul now becomes a cooperative undertaking between four aspects of the magician's nature. The soul has developed partnership with the mental, emotional and physical bodies of the personality. In fact, this collaborative arrangement between the one and the three is indispensable to spiritual magic. The soul needs these three aspects of the personality in order to carry out its creative will. However, this united endeavor can only go forward when these lower vehicles give way to the superior light of the soul. Meditation trains the threefold personality to acquiesce its internal flame to the solar fire coming from above. It is therefore not surprising that in occultism the number four is related to the creation of forms. The one (soul) utilizes the threefold

> *By way of the lower three, the soul creates its desired effects. Magic is always a quaternary affair.*

personality, and forms emerge. As such, magic is understood as a quaternary endeavor.

The Cave

As has been stated, the personality must be in a condition of readiness before the magical work can be done. Though meditation is the primary means to this end, the right understanding and utilization of "the cave" is also crucial to successful magic. The cave is actually a reference to a place within the magician's head. More specifically, it is located at the very center of the head and is composed entirely of etheric substance. To the white magician, the cave is the place (within his etheric system) where the magical work must be carried forward. As such, we will examine this magical place within the head and the manner in which it facilitates the creative process. The cave serves three functions in this regard. They are:

1. The standing place of the magician
2. The anchor point of soul-inspired thought
3. The origin point of creative projection

The secret of magic has much to do with the correct use of the cave, a place deep with the etheric head.

The Standing Place of the Magician

The key to successful creative work has to do with the place of centralized activity and the origin point of creative expression. As such, the cave is the place where the magician must isolate his identity in order for the creative work to be done correctly. By this is meant that the sense of self must be placed within the cave, deep at the center of the etheric brain cavity. To understand this, we must remember that at any given moment a person's sense of self can be isolated. Always, the magician must be asking himself, where am I right now? Though we can ask this question in relation to thoughts and feelings, in this context we are actually considering the physical placement of one's sense of self.

For the average individual, the self is found where one's external attention is directed. The outer world is constantly presenting us with stimuli that draw our attention. This attention to outer stimulation will often carry the self with it. For example, if one is in a heated argument with another person, the self is likely to be found in the midst of the argument itself. As I mentioned, this is true for the average individual, but it still can have relevance to the intelligentsia of the world, and even disciples at times. It's quite easy for the personality to lose itself in the outer interactions of life, even for just a moment.

For the intelligentsia and disciples of the world, the physical self is not as likely to be captured by external stimuli. Rather, it tends to remain anchored in the region of the face, or the forward part of the head. Our dominant senses, such as sight and hearing, are found here, and we most often monitor and attend to the outer world from the face. In other words, the integrated and intelligent people of the world are usually able to hold their central point of personality focus, and when considered physically, this corresponds most to the region of the face. The fact that the ajna chakra is located between the eyebrows gives further support to this idea, in that it is the etheric location where the personality integrates itself.

Yet to the magician, neither of these placements of self are appropriate. Effective magic occurs when the self can be drawn back into the central region of the brain cavity. Here is where the sacred cave is found, and here it is where truest alignment with the soul is made possible. Therefore, the magician must learn to draw the self (usually located at the ajna center) back into the

To the magician, the cave provides the place wherein his feet are set.

cave. The cave is not something that is easily found. In fact, it may take several years of meditative effort to gradually become fully cognizant of its existence and place. This is another reason for meditation; it is the discipline that eventually leads to the discovery of the magical cave within.

When the self is drawn back into the cave, an interesting transformation is slowly realized. This transformation has much to do with an alteration that occurs to the magician's identity. By correctly drawing oneself back into the cave, the self becomes transformed into the Self. Stated differently, when the personality self is pulled back (and correctly finds the cave), it becomes radically transformed in the light of the higher self (soul) which is irradiating this etheric cavern. This is a fundamental concept to be pondered. The cave is in the center cavity of the etheric brain, and is directly below the crown chakra. It therefore is the place for the soul's direct line of descent. As such, the cave is where the magician can truly sense the higher self, as well as transform the lower self so that it blends with the higher, thus establishing cooperative rapport.

The Anchor Point of Soul-Inspired Thought

White magic is truly the art of giving tangible form to creative thought impulsed by the soul. As such, the study of soulful magic is said to be top-down. That is, white magic is the art of bringing subtle wisdom from the intuitional plane (top) into the denser fields of the magician's mental and emotional bodies in order to give it form. When successfully done, the form created is then externalized into the physical world as an act of service. To say that it is a top-down process simply means that magic is the art of bringing the subtle into dense form in order to create outer transformational

The cave is the place of interface between the soul's radiation and the outer world of form. The first is governed by the world of causes, while the latter conforms to the world of effects.

effects. What is important to realize is that though it is top-down, the bottom is what needs to be prepared first. Specifically, the magician must establish correct relationship to the cave, and this as a prerequisite to all that follows in the creative process.

It shall be seen later that all intuitions, thoughts and feelings are funneled through one's etheric body before being registered in consciousness. In short, nothing can be experienced (and registered in the brain) without its vibration first influencing the human etheric field. The etheric vehicle is said to be the energetic sheath underlying the dense physical body. In some sense, it can be considered the interface between the subtle intangible world (in its many divisions) and the dense physical form. As such, all that is perceived in human consciousness (as we understand that term) is made possible through the etheric vehicle.

Having said this, we now see why the first efforts of magical work are related to the magician's relationship to the cave. The cave is a field of etheric substance in the center of the head, and densely corresponds to the ventricles within the brain. The magician must not only find the cave, but must never leave it. To stand in it is to be placed at the very location where soul-inspired thought makes entrance into one's etheric field. Establishing this placement of self is crucial, for it ensures the highest alignment with the soul and its expressive purpose.

It should be stated here that the self is not located only in the cave, for it has other important dimensions of existence as well. It is only the form-based dimension of the self that is anchored in the cave. In actuality, the self is found on a continuum of consciousness. When we speak of placing the self within the cave, it simply denotes the bottom of the soul's expression, and it is there that the magician finds anchorage for the self.

White magic only occurs when the soul's radiation is extended from top to bottom. The high point is the causal body, while the lower is the cave itself.

From this central point within the head, the magician then projects himself through the cave into the subtler dimensions of consciousness. In this regard, the cave can be called a portal of sorts. It is a gate through which the magician travels in order to establish his relationship with the causal body (vehicle of the soul found upon the higher mental plane), as well as realms beyond. This projection is, in fact, the extension of the self toward its higher pole. The idea to keep in mind is that the true magician must be able to experience full-spectrum consciousness. He must be able to hold the self within the cave (without waiver), while simultaneously projecting himself into the causal body—the natural resting place of his higher consciousness. In short, the magician must learn to be in two places at once. When he is able to do this, then the downflow of insight and wisdom can be transmitted without distortion or encumberment.

The Origin Point of Creative Projection

The creative manifestation process has much to do with the power of visualization and the ability to correctly direct an image or idea toward the outer world. It is one thing to sense the soul's wisdom and creative intention, but it is quite another to effectively project that intention as an act of service. This process of directing (or projecting) thought will be discussed later when considering the role of the third eye in the creative process. Nonetheless, at this juncture it is well to know that the use of the third eye is only effective if the cave in the head is continuously held by the magician.

From this, it can be ascertained that the role of the cave is bidirectional. First, it is the sacred location where the inspirations of the soul are properly registered. In this capacity, the cave is negative and

The cave is a portal through which inward and upward movement can occur. Thus is the higher pole found. The creator then knows the heights and depths simultaneously.

receptive to the downflow of the soul's radiation. Secondly, it is the initiating point for projecting the soul's creative wisdom into the world of form. In this role, it acts as a positive center of purpose and assertion, and it utilizes the third eye as guide to this projection. When done correctly, the effect is that something external to the magician is transformed, and therefore freed. The cave represents the pivotal point where the soul meets the outer world and seeks to express its creative intention as an act of uplifting service.

Meditation for Finding the Cave

The cave within the head is not easy to ascertain. It is something that often takes years of meditative effort to find and creatively utilize. Yet, it is inevitable that all spiritually committed people will develop a relationship with the cave, in this life or in a future incarnation. The cave is not something that is simply found. In actuality, it is something that needs to be created as well. It exists within the head, but at first, only as a potential. One of the many functions of disciplined meditation is to gradually transform the potential cave into the actual cave. As such, occult meditation is designed to contribute to this actualization process.

The method of slowly awakening the cave can be included in virtually any meditation one is using. The following meditation can assist in this process. As you work with this meditation, realize that the imagination is your greatest tool. To imagine the cave is what slowly will awaken it in due time. The picture-making faculty of the mind is always the force that leads to the actualization of that which is imagined. This is an occult principle of deep import.

> *Slowly does the cave get built, imagination its means. Destiny decrees that it be used for love that surely frees.*

Cave Meditation

1. Begin by focusing on the breath cycle. The intention is to regulate this cycle so that both the in-breath and the out-breath are of equal duration. This will harmonize the etheric vehicle, and give poise and stillness to the emotional body.

2. Gently shift your attention to the heart center, located between the shoulder blades. See it as a vortex of compassionate and loving energy. Then, imagine that this energy is in motion from the back to the front of the body. Feel it radiate outward (from your heart chakra) into the environment. For a few moments, simply hold the awareness of this radiating love.

3. Now lift your attention to the crown chakra, just above the head. Here is where the will and intention of the soul makes entrance into one's life. For a few moments, allow yourself to quietly imagine and feel the quality of higher will.

4. Next, gently shift your awareness to the ajna center (the chakra between the eyebrows). Believe that you, as the self, are focused at this place. Without undue effort, try to concentrate your place of being at this point.

5. From this point of focus (ajna center), very slowly draw the attention back to the central region of the etheric brain cavity. It is in the center of the etheric head, and not the dense physical, where the attention is placed. This is done imaginatively, as well as factually. Do this for about one minute, and no more.

6. From the central point of attention (within the etheric head), lift the awareness vertically into the causal body, the vehicle of the soul. If effectively done, there should be a feeling of expansiveness. When you have found the quiet place of soulfulness (above and within), silently

sound the sacred word, the OM, to firmly establish the sense of soul alignment and focus.

7. Now try to hold a sense of the expansive soul quality within you, while simultaneously holding the sense of self within the etheric head (the cave). You are trying to hold your self in two places at once.

8. While trying to hold these two aspects of your self, contemplate these words: *"Having pervaded my body with a fragment of Myself, I still remain. I am."*

9. After contemplating this seed-thought for a few minutes, reaffirm that you are still able to sense the quiet soulful point within, as well as the self that is anchored within the cave.

10. Finally, close the meditation by chanting the OM, imagining it first being sounded from the high point of self. Then chant the OM again, this time imagining it to be sounding forth from the self that resides within the cave.

The Emerging Point of Light

We have thus far seen how the soul prepares itself for the magical act. We have also discussed the meditative work required by the personality in order that right relationship can be established between it and the soul. Our next consideration is the soul and personality relationship itself. It is in their communicative interplay that the first indications of something new to be revealed and expressed shall come forth within the magician's mind.

In the esoteric literature, we are given to understand that at this stage in the process, a "point of light" emerges within the mind. This point of light is really the product of the circulatory energy flowing between the two centers (soul and personality) due to successful alignment in meditation. As the personality meditates, a heightened vibration is developed within its threefold nature. When this vibration becomes attuned to the note being sounded by the soul (as it meditates on its own plane), the link is established, for the soul and personality are then in harmonic resonance. This indicates that the causal body and the cave are interconnected and reflective of each other. As a result, the interplay between personality and soul is free flowing, and from this flow emerges a point of light.

At this juncture, the magician is not yet aware of an actual thought coming forth from the soul. Rather, this point of light represents the blueprint of the thought that is to be. Indeed, it is the precursor to a soul-inspired thought. This can sometimes be recognized when an individual senses within his mind that there is something near to consciousness but not yet realized. Those who meditate are usually familiar with this experience. It is the sense that there is something almost ready to be seized by the mind, though there is nothing

Dynamic rapport between the soul and personality has been achieved. Energy circulates between the two and a point of light emerges.

yet available for the mind to latch onto. It is a feeling that something is internally churning, yet there is no movement occurring in consciousness, for the mind remains steady in the light. These descriptions may seem rather paradoxical, but such is the case when considering this phase of the magical work.

Though what is sensed is not yet a thought that is consciously recognized within the mind, it is nonetheless the intuitive germ that will eventually mature into a consciously perceived thoughtform. As this intuitive light grows and matures, it will eventually clothe itself in substance of the mental plane. When this occurs, a thought is experienced in the creator's mind. He then has a realized insight, or a flash of mental understanding. In truth, this is the first phase of the magical work. It is the *"a-ha"* experience that we all have had when a new and insightful thought pops into the mind. Yet before this occurs, an intuitive germ (point of light) is planted by the soul into the soil of the waiting mind, and it is this that will eventually mature into an enlightened thought.

The point of light is the intuitive germ of a thought that is to be.

The Nature and Composition of Thought

At this point in our discussion, it is important that the nature of thought be examined. What is a thoughtform, and how does it really come into being within the mind? Such questions may seem unimportant to some, but it is in their answer that many deep mysteries about life and experience are revealed. Furthermore, the understanding of the nature and formation of thought is essential if one is to truly co-create in accordance with the Will of God. To make an uplifting contribution to the betterment of humanity, one must really understand how thoughts come into being within consciousness. In this regard, the most important axiom to always keep in mind is that *thoughts are things*. We tend to view a "thing" as a tangible and recognizable form within the outer world. Though far subtler than physical objects, thoughts are things as well, and are found within the mental body of the thinker. Just as forms found on the physical plane are composed of substance contained within the physical world, so too are mental forms composed of substance found upon the mental plane.

All planes of consciousness are really strata of substance. This stratification is differentiated by the various characteristics and qualities inherent within substance itself. For example, the substance that makes up the mental plane is of a nature and quality that is particularly suitable for the construction of thoughts. This particular strata represents atoms of fiery intelligence. On the other hand, the substance of the astral (emotional) plane is best used in the creation of forms that support the experience of feelings. This strata of substance is particularly attuned to the quality of desire, an attribute foundational to all feeling states.

Whether lofty or profane, thoughts are living things.

Most important is the fact that all substance, regardless of its category, is essentially living. The atoms of substance found on any plane, though indescribably minute, are nonetheless imbued with life. How could it be otherwise? If everything that exists is an expression of the One Life, as occultism maintains, then how could anything escape the livingness of that One Life? All things live, including the thoughts within our minds.

When we examine the origin and formation of thought, we are really entering into a consideration of the life found upon the plane of mind. Atoms of substance found upon that plane (as well as any plane) are called *elementals*. When a thought is experienced within the human mind, it is because myriads of mental elementals (atoms of mental substance) magnetically join together, and the end result of their union is the creation of a thoughtform. Indeed, a thoughtform is the assemblage of countless elemental lives, geometrically configured in accordance with the nature of the idea that was intended by the thinker, the soul. In other words, a thoughtform comes into being because the will of the thinker energetically influenced these elemental lives to assemble themselves in a certain way so as to accurately reflect the intended idea sent forth by the soul. Therefore, every thought experienced within the human mind is in reality a geometric construction of uncounted atoms of elemental life.

It is crucial that the reader not conclude that these assembled elemental lives produce thought. Rather, their bonded relationship to each other *is* the thought being experienced. When really pondered upon, this idea is quite remarkable. Even now, as you read this paragraph, each idea registered in your mind is perceived only because an aggregation of elementals have come together to be the thoughts you are now having. To reiterate, thoughts are things, and represent an aggregate of elemental lives that have coalesced according to the will of the thinker.

When considering the magical work, we can see why it is important that the disciple understand the process of thoughtform construction. As the soul asserts its creative idea into the personality, it first emerges as a point of light. Yet from another perspective, it is a sound that the soul emits. Esoterically understood, sound is said to be the great manifesting force within creation. In the Eastern tradition, we are told that Brahman sang the universe into being. From the Christian angle, much of its doctrine centers upon the "Word of God." In both cases, these ideas are referring to the great creative

> *Like moths to a flame do the myriads gather round the point of light. Because of their assembly, a thoughtform comes into being.*

Sound that gave birth to cosmos. With this understanding, the sound of the soul is equivalent to the point of light previously discussed. The One Life breathes itself outward via sound, and the resultant effect is the manifestation of all that exists. This is also true when considering the microcosm, man. The soul of the human being breathes outward while sounding its note, and as such, the forms of the personality come into being. Incarnation thus occurs. Importantly, the same can be said of the incarnated soul that is creatively trying to influence the mind of the personality. When the personality is aligned with it, the soul's note can be detected, and a thoughtform then emerges within the waiting and receptive mind.

How this occurs is quite interesting, for it too is based upon an outbreath of sound, symbolically considered. The elementals are essentially passive. These infinitesimal entities live strictly for the purpose of constructing forms according to the vibrations they sense. When the soul sounds its magical note, mental elementals are attracted to the vibration of that note. They then move toward the sound and begin to construct a material edifice around it. When completed, a thoughtform has been constructed, and the thinker has a realization of the thought within his mind.

When contemplating the nature of these elemental lives, it must ever be borne in mind that they, in their myriads, are of different grades and levels of evolutionary development. Some mental elementals are of lower development than others. In the Esoteric Tradition, it is taught that each of the seven planes of consciousness are actually divided into seven subplanes. Each of these subplanes is representative of a differing quality or grade of elemental life. When the soul is effectively working within the mental plane, it is attempting to build thoughtforms made of living

The One Life breathes Itself forth via sound, and galaxies come into being. Herein is the basis for the soul's incarnation and creative work.

substance found upon the higher subplanes of that plane, particularly the highest three. When the personality builds thoughtforms, it will tend to utilize elementals found within the lower four subplanes of the mental plane *(see Figure 6, The Human Constitution; note Plane V).*

This is a broad generalization, but nonetheless denotes a common distinction between thoughtforms built by these two centers of consciousness, soul and personality. As such, elementals will tend to respond to differing rates of vibration sounded forth by a human being. When a personality entertains gross or perverted thoughts, such tendencies represent a sounding of a note as well. But it is a sound of low vibration, and will consequently attract mental elementals of lower grade, those found upon the lower subplanes of the mental plane. The quality of the vibratory note being sounded (either by the soul or personality) will define the type or grade of elementals that will be attracted to that sound. When the will of the thinker is motivated toward the construction of thoughtforms that are progressive and uplifting, then a correspondingly higher grade of elementals will be attracted to the lofty note sounded. The result will be the construction of evolutionary thoughtforms.

Through this discussion, we have seen that there is an unwavering correspondence between the will of the thinker and the elementals that assemble into thoughtforms in accordance with that will. As most thoughtforms have some type of environmental effect, it becomes clear that monitoring one's thoughts (and the underlying motives behind them) is a wise habit to foster. Every human being is responsible for the consequences of his thoughts. This is basic to karmic law. It therefore behooves one to be mindful of the process of thoughtform construction. The true magician

The quality of the note sounded defines the grade of elementals attracted to it.

The Human Constitution
- Also is the Cosmic Etheric-Physical Plane of the Logos -

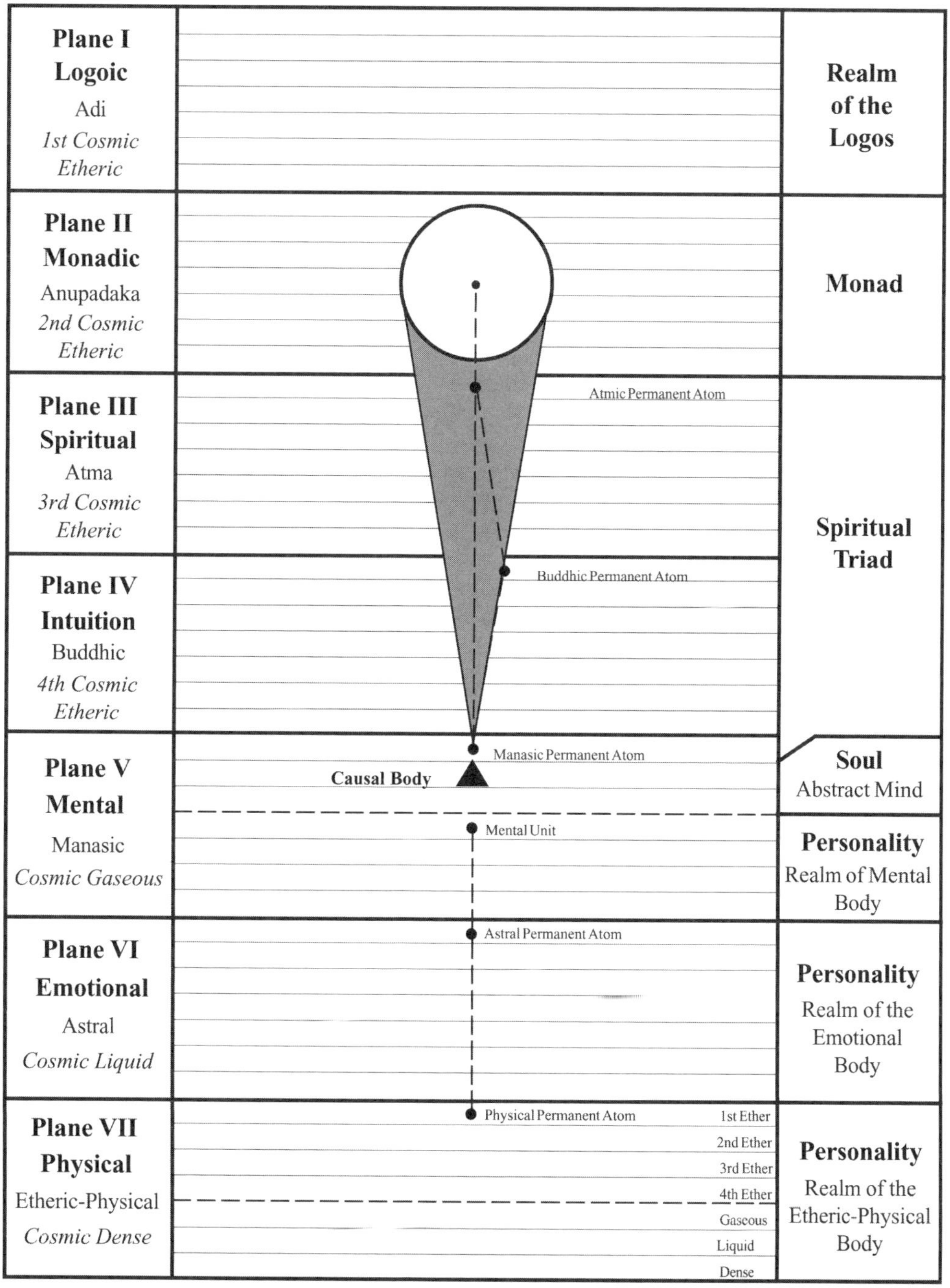

Plane		Realm
Plane I **Logoic** Adi *1st Cosmic Etheric*		**Realm of the Logos**
Plane II **Monadic** Anupadaka *2nd Cosmic Etheric*		**Monad**
Plane III **Spiritual** Atma *3rd Cosmic Etheric*	Atmic Permanent Atom	**Spiritual Triad**
Plane IV **Intuition** Buddhic *4th Cosmic Etheric*	Buddhic Permanent Atom	
Plane V **Mental** Manasic *Cosmic Gaseous*	Manasic Permanent Atom **Causal Body** Mental Unit	**Soul** Abstract Mind **Personality** Realm of Mental Body
Plane VI **Emotional** Astral *Cosmic Liquid*	Astral Permanent Atom	**Personality** Realm of the Emotional Body
Plane VII **Physical** Etheric-Physical *Cosmic Dense*	Physical Permanent Atom — 1st Ether 2nd Ether 3rd Ether 4th Ether Gaseous Liquid Dense	**Personality** Realm of the Etheric-Physical Body

Figure 6

is one who is intimately aware of this and is conscious of the responsibilities of thoughtform-building. He must ever be aware of the true motives lying behind his thought processes and the effects his thoughts have upon the outer world, either for the good or ill.

The Synergy of Thought

Let us, for a moment, examine the process of thoughtform construction a bit further. It must be remembered that elementals are a part of the Mother Principle of creation. As such, they are the building blocks of intelligence found within all things. Elementals act as custodians of this divine intelligence, and each contains a minute measure of it. They can be looked at as cells storing basic information. To use a simple analogy, we need only look at the physical cells of the human body. Such cells are amazingly intelligent, in that they contain important DNA information imprinted within them. On a much subtler level, the same kind of thing is found with regard to the elementals of the mental plane. They are minute atoms of living substance, each containing an infinitesimal measure of divine intelligence. When these elementals collectively assemble themselves, synergy takes place. To use an old adage, the whole becomes greater than the sum of its parts. By this is suggested that a thoughtform is more than the sum total of the atoms of intelligence that go into its making.

Perhaps another simple analogy would be helpful to highlight this notion. Let us say that an automobile has been completely disassembled, and all its parts are spread upon the floor. For the sake of analogy, we shall say that each part is an elemental, and that its unique design represents the intelligence inherent within it. As such, even in its disassembled condition there is much

A thoughtform is greater than the sum of intelligence contained within its elemental parts.

intelligence that is present, for there are thousands of intelligent parts laid out to see. Yet, it is when the car is reassembled that synergy becomes evident. The parts augment each other when they are all assembled correctly, resulting in a working automobile. Synergy then emerges because the car is much more than the total of the design (intelligence) inherent in each of its parts.

The same can be said of a thoughtform. A thought is a grouping of elementals that have organized themselves into a particular form according to the will of the thinker. The by-product of this organization is that the intelligence contained within the elementals is collectively enhanced by their assembly. When we have a thought, we are actually experiencing a synergistic phenomenon, for the thought is more than the sum total of its intelligent parts (elementals). It is the synergy of meaning that arises through their cooperative rapport.

It may well be asked, does the construction of a thoughtform have any effect upon the elementals that go into its assembly? The answer is most certainly yes, particularly when the thought is lofty and profound. Synergistic thoughtforms give to each participating elemental an experience of knowledge transcendent to its own intelligence. Indeed, it is through such experience that the elementals themselves evolve. This is one of the means by which the human and deva kingdoms support each other in their respective evolutions. Each uplifts the other. Humanity gives to the elementals (lowest expression of devas) the opportunity to assemble themselves into thoughtforms, thereby providing them enhanced realization. Conversely, devas give to human beings the intelligence necessary to manifest higher purpose.

The synergy that occurs within a thoughtform is the force that uplifts the elementals that compose it. They thus evolve.

The Diminishment Factor

When the soul sounds forth its creative note, a thoughtform begins to assemble within the magician's mind. There is however a great paradox associated with this phase in the creative process. When a thoughtform first emerges within the mind, it is already an indication of its diminishment. Stated differently, when an individual has a soul-inspired thought, it is at that same moment that the original idea becomes less than it was. Something has been lost simply because the mind thought it. Why is this so?

The answer lies in the fact that spiritual magic is oriented toward giving tangibility to that which is boundless and without form. When the soul initiates a magical act, its intention is to give form to a formless truth. This formless wisdom is revealed through *buddhi*. Buddhi is the intuition. Divine archetypes to be expressed in the outer world come forth from the buddhic plane. This plane is located above the mental plane, and its content is relatively formless *(see Figure 6, The Human Constitution; note Plane IV, page 117)*. Essentially, the soul is a conduit for impressions coming from the buddhic plane. Its intention is to transmit these formless intuitions into the mind of the personality, and by so doing, give form to them. However, whenever something formless is brought into a condition of form-boundedness, limitation ensues. The formless idea, as conceived by the soul, is given structure, and as a result, a thought emerges within the mind. Yet because the thoughtform itself is a limitation, some aspect of the original intuition will invariably be sacrificed in its construction. Such is the nature of spiritual magic. The magician must always remember that a soul-inspired thought is a *representation* of a formless truth. Because of this, it is never as true as that which it represents.

> *The moment a person registers a soul-inspired idea within the mind, that thought is indication of its diminishment.*

This diminishment continues as the created form descends into denser planes of consciousness. When the thoughtform begins its plunge into the emotional body, a further abatement will then surely occur. The same can be said when the physical expression of the thoughtform begins to take form. Each step of the journey leading toward the externalization of a soul-inspired idea is increasingly restrictive to that idea. The purpose of spiritual magic is not simply to translate divine truth into an outer reality. It also mandates that this be done while not adding diminishment beyond that which is naturally and unavoidably occurring within the magical process itself.

It may well be asked, what has become of the sound and the point of light? Do they too give way to something lesser? The answer to this question is surely yes. As the mental elementals construct themselves around the point of light (which is the sound being emitted by the soul), the light then grows increasingly dim, and the sound becomes muffled. The light of truth, which is the formless point of light, takes on a tinted hue, and the sound no longer rings its original tone. Essentially, it has been modified by the form that has encased and muted it. The sound then becomes another tone, similar to the note originally chanted by the soul, but stepped down. In the ancient esoteric writings, this has sometimes been called the "second sound." The second sound is therefore the first sound after being modified by the mental sheath that now encases it. This new note represents a diminishment of the original sound emitted by the soul.

When the modified sound is still harmonically in tune with the original note (contained within the point of light), then it will serve the purpose for which it was intended. Indeed, it has a power and vibration to it. It has the power to influence the environment, as most

The soul's creative note is sent forth, and the second sound comes into being. May this new tone resonate to the sound that inspired it.

innovative ideas do. Yet, it is not as powerful as it was when it was originally sent forth by the soul. This represents its diminishment, as earlier discussed. It is less than it was, but is nonetheless useful to the soul as long as this lessened vibration (note) still retains the essence of truth that was originally present.

Sound as the Creator of Effects

As already mentioned, sound is fundamental to the creative process. When considered at its most basic level, we only need examine the nature of speech and its power to transform an environment. It is through the power of speech that the magician is able to initiate environmental upliftment, which is the primary objective of all spiritual magic. Every thought uttered forth has an effect upon the environment, and this either for good or ill. It will tend to give unity and understanding to outer events, or it will support further fragmentation. In either case, a new form has thus been created.

In truth, every effect is a form. Therefore, the true white magician is one who gauges his effects upon others, and does so with constant vigilance toward creating and expressing only those forms that support the evolution of the larger whole. Human society is virtually the product of thoughtforms sounded forth over the ages. Words contain within them the power to build and transform the world. Nothing within the realms of human existence can escape this principle. Everything created by humanity is the product of human thought sounded forth over time within the confines of space. This is not a principle simply limited to human application. Rather, it is the root of all manifesting processes within creation, including that initiated by God. For instance, the Laws of Nature represent the

All thoughts expressed through the sounds of speech have an effect upon the outer field. This the magician knows well.

external effect of God's thought expressed through divine utterance. The magician must see this principle clearly, and know that the words chosen (and how they are expressed) will define the environmental effect, as it does with all units of life within cosmos. Sound governs all that comes into externalized existence. Such is the nature of divine creativity.

Also important are the sounds coming forth from the fullness of the disciple's form life. Every vehicle within the personality emits a sound within the environment, as does the personality as a whole. A human being is emitting vibrations into the outer world via his mental, emotional and physical bodies, and this unceasingly so. Without words spoken, this sounding forth is occurring. Each must therefore assess the environmental effect of his form presence in the world. This assessment will give the magician deeper understanding as to the nature of his personality forms. As a result, he gains insight into how to rightly utilize these forms on behalf of the soul's creative agenda. We can see therefore that the esoteric understanding of sound is something beyond the type our ears have grown accustomed to hear. Occultly considered, sound emerges whenever there is movement within time and space, including the motions evident within the threefold personality itself.

The personality sounds a chord of three, and the outer world feels its vibration.

Dangers of Thoughtform Construction

The wise building of thoughtforms is fundamental to the magical process, yet such activity is not free from peril. There are dangers associated with the assembling of ideas within the mind. If the thinker is not mindful of such obstacles, it is likely that he will be their victim, and this unknowingly so. As such, it would be well to note the most perilous of these dangers.

The Danger of Obsession

The first great danger has to do with the problems of mental preoccupation. Often a person will become fixated on the thoughtforms that he has been building within his mind. This focus, though essential to build the form correctly, is also an obstacle. It can result in a tendency toward a fanatical attachment to the ideas conceived. If he is not careful, this can lead to a dangerous obsession. When this occurs, it often renders the aspirant creatively paralyzed, at least for a time. When severe enough, obsession can literally shut down the magician's creative faculty for the remainder of his life.

Not surprising, attachment to one's sense of individual identity is at the root of obsessive thought. Inadvertently, the magician becomes so fixated with an idea that the thoughtform becomes associated with his personal sense of value and self-worth. Obsession is ever caused by the thinker's inability to remain detached from the thoughtform being created.

Such events are commonly witnessed in everyday life. Many people become obsessed by an idea or a single viewpoint, yet never seem able to externalize it. Instead, they hold onto it begrudgingly and live out the remainder of their years blaming others for its failure to manifest. Projection of fault onto the environment is simply a defense mechanism used by the personality to justify this failure. Sadly, such a person will frequently live out his life unwilling to see the folly of his ways. Many potentially effective people have been victimized by this problem. Even advanced disciples are prone to obsession's fatal grip.

Identification with cherished ideas is the source of obsession's evil grip. Caution is well advised.

The Danger of the Vacuum

White magic is the art of moving a soul-inspired thoughtform into the outer world of effects. It involves transferring a subjectively realized truth into a condition of objectivity. After the magician has built a thoughtform (according to the formless inspiration of the soul), the next step is to move that thoughtform through the personality vehicles. The goal is to push the thoughtform outward in hopes of creating tangible effects. As such, magic is always related to the movement of an idea (or set of thoughtforms) from a subjective to an objective condition.

The first step in this process is to move the thoughtform into the emotional body, thus adding a feeling quality to it. It must be remembered that the emotional body is of greater density than the mental body, and therefore more objective. This therefore means that when moving a thoughtform into the emotional realm of the personality, such movement is toward greater objectivity. The same phenomenon occurs as the externalization process continues. The thoughtform (now tinctured with feeling) is pushed into the etheric/physical part of the personality. This too is a motion toward greater objectivity.

There is a danger that the magician must recognize when moving a thoughtform toward greater objectivity, for such movement leaves a wake behind it. This wake is really a vacuum in consciousness, and it can be a menace to the magical effort. It is a vacuum created by the displacement of the thoughtform from its original place. When the magician moves the idea toward greater objectivity, this vacuum will tend to be filled by something. Unfortunately, it is the identity of the magician that usually gets pulled into this void.

Danger menaces as a thoughtform outwardly moves. A vacuum trails its motion, and the Self becomes its unintended victim.

Ahamkara makes impure one's soul-inspired thought. Full-spectrum consciousness gives perspective and defense.

Within each of us is found a self-construct. The self-construct represents the many thoughts and feelings that we internally use to define who we are. In truth, there are countless threads of mental and emotional associations we use internally to establish our identity. They are constructions within consciousness that we use to define the attributes of self. Fundamentally, these associations are useful in that they provide us with the forms we need to realize who we are. Yet, they are only temporary constructs. In truth, identity is actually something transcendent to thought, feeling and physical sensation. Nonetheless, the tendency of the mind to create threads of thought that reinforce the self-construct can be detrimental to magic. It is this tendency that is activated when the vacuum emerges in the creative process.

When we move a thoughtform through the threefold personality, there is an automatic tendency to use it as something to strengthen our sense of identity. Though this occurs unconsciously, the end result is that we begin to believe that we are the thought we have conceived. Herein lies the crux of the problem. The magician must learn to remain detached from his thoughtform.

We have been told by science that nature abhors a vacuum. As can be seen, this idea has application to consciousness as well. When moving a thoughtform toward objectivity, the self is frequently pulled into the vacuum created by this motion. One's attachment to an idea is sure indication that it has become contaminated. The energy of *ahamkara* (self-reference) has subtly been added to the divine idea, and this leads to the distortion of what was originally intended.

The primary antidote in overcoming the dangers of the vacuum involves a reverse movement within consciousness. As the magician works at externalizing his thoughtform, he must simultaneously draw himself inward. It is to experience two movements of consciousness at the same time. While the thoughtform is being pushed toward externalization, the sense of the self must be pulled back. Though one can look at this spatially, it is more accurate to view it as an inner dimensional movement. The pulling back of one's sense of identity is really a movement toward greater subtlety of being. This is opposite to the motion being applied to the thoughtform, for it is being propelled toward gross tangibility. Admittedly, this skill is difficult for the would-be magician to develop. Yet, it is crucial to the creative manifestation process. Invariably, we must all learn to be in two places at one time. The subjective end of this polarity is always considered the quiet point of Being, while the objective end is the place of form and activity. This is full-spectrum consciousness. It is to be high and low simultaneously.

The Danger of Unbridled Thought

A third danger when building thoughtforms has to do with the speed and degree of mental proliferation. When the building of an idea is too rapid, there is a risk that it will cause undue distortion. Enthusiasm can construct a thoughtform (or series of thoughtforms) with such rapidity that the original intention of the seed that gave it birth becomes obscured. In other words, the light of divine purpose that gave impulse to the idea has been lost by the ungoverned tendency of the mind to multiply the form. Indeed, the magician loses sight of the soul. The original idea may have been rightly impressed upon the mind, yet his subsidiary constructions of thought are ill-conceived. This is a danger.

To understand why this phenomenon occurs is the first step in avoiding it. The source of this problem has to do with the forfeiture of accuracy for the sake of

When the activity of thinking takes precedence over its accuracy, the light of the soul fades from view. The selfish path then looms near.

mental rapidity. When the mind is enthusiastically engaged, it will sometimes become less precise with each of the connecting thoughts that it adds to the original idea. This imprecision is compounded when inaccurate thought is built upon inaccurate thought. Rapidity of thoughtform construction will often cause this effect. The end result is that the light of the soul is blotted out, and the thinker is left with a miasma of distorted thoughtforms.

When extreme, this phenomenon can mistakenly lead an individual down the path of selfish magic (sometimes called black magic). There are several steps in the process where the disciple may inadvertently step onto the path of selfish magic. One of these perilous steps relates to the unbridled construction of subsidiary thoughts as they expand outward from the original idea. Caution is therefore well advised.

The Danger of Astral Neglect

Before the creator begins moving his thoughtform into the field of emotions, it is important that an assessment of his emotional condition be done. Too often, an individual will add to a thoughtform an emotional component without properly considering the "condition of the waters." Water is the symbol for emotion (and emotional body), and its status must be examined in the light of mind. It is the mind that must discern the stability (or lack of it) present within this watery sphere. When the magician's astral body is deemed tranquil, adding emotional coloring to the thoughtform is good. When agitated, danger lurks.

When the emotional (astral) body is overly stimulated, adding feeling to the thoughtform is a grave mistake. Emotional turbulence will surely distort a soul-inspired idea, rendering it ineffective, at least from the

Emotion will eventually be added to the thoughtform held steady within the magician's mind. The condition of the waters must first be well surveyed.

soul's point of view. Also detrimental is fear or negative emotion of any kind. If such emotions become attached to the thoughtform, the consequences can be harmful to its manifestation and can even run counter to the good. Emotions related to desire are also insidious to the form that the soul seeks to manifest. When desire is present, the emphasis of the magical work shifts from selfless service to themes of self-satisfaction.

The most common form of distortion is caused by the over-stimulation of emotions. For this reason, vigilance toward assessing one's emotional condition is important *prior* to adding feeling to the idea conceived. Interestingly, the personality will usually view this differently. From its perspective, astral enthusiasm is considered validation that a thoughtform is correct and is coming from the soul. This is of course an erroneous conclusion. In addition, such emotional surges tend to provide the lower self with a feeling of ego-worth. Remember, at this stage in the creative process, the magician is still working with mental substance. The thoughtform has not yet descended into the emotional realms. Here the magician is simply encouraged to pause and examine the state of his emotional body to ensure that it is serene before continuing the creative process, and thus avoid this pitfall of astrality.

Needless to say, this is by no means an easy skill to acquire. Emotions seem to rise up automatically, and regulating them seems well-nigh impossible. Yet, this is what is required. When the emotional body is unregulated, there is the risk that it is governing the creative process, rather than being a tool used in the process. This is what often happens to well-meaning people without them realizing it. They believe that a lofty feeling state (emerging spontaneously in response to an idea) is indication that the soul is in control. Frequently, the truth is quite the opposite. As we shall

If the watery sphere is agitated, a pause is well-advised. The stormy seas must give way to the peace of tranquil day.

later discuss, the emotional body is an incredible asset to the soul's creative agenda, but only when it is harnessed. When unbridled, it indicates that the magician lacks mastery of it, and the risk of distorting the descending thoughtform is consequently great. Therefore, the need to assess the condition of the waters is crucial, and must initially be done *before* adding feeling to the thoughtform created.

The Contemplative Antidote

A period of contemplation ensues, and the intuitive root is once again sensed. Formlessness and form are then compared.

The four perils just explained represent very real dangers that can thwart the creative effort. Being watchful of our thoughts and feelings is crucial to ensure that the work remains aligned with the soul's intention. Importantly, when considering these dangers, there is another remedy that must be employed as well. It is the process of steady contemplation.

Contemplative meditation is an effective antidote to all four dangers that we have been discussing. It is designed to help the magician reestablish a relationship with the formless buddhic (intuitive) realm. As a reminder, it is from the buddhic plane (via the soul) that the archetype of what is to be created comes forth. This meditative step requires that the magician cease building his thoughtform for a period of time, then move back into an inner place of contemplation. By so doing, he reconnects with the formless source that gave birth to the thoughtform he holds within his mind.

Admittedly, it is difficult to describe in words the results of this phase. When holding the mind steady in the light (contemplation), the magician is able to inwardly sense the rightness of the thoughtform(s) he has thus far built. The function of this technique is to re-imbue consciousness with a sense of the intended idea to be manifested. He must then reexamine the thoughtform, and by so doing, become inwardly aware of its integrity, or lack of it. By so doing, a kind of inner vision is established. Essentially, it is the eye of the soul, the third eye, which provides the disciple with this comparative sense. This spiritual eye has the capacity to weigh the difference between the archetype intended (intuitively sensed), and the thoughtform(s) that has been built. From this inner realization, a decision can then be made as to whether or not to go forward in the manifestation process.

The Etheric Triangle of Magic

In all magical work, three etheric chakras are employed. They are the heart, throat and ajna centers. Together, these three centers have the capacity (when rightly employed) to manifest the soul's intended idea, and with minimal distortion. When cooperatively allied, they ensure that the four dangers can be overcome.

The heart, throat and ajna unite in service to the soul's creative intention.

Heart Center
This is the etheric center that links a person to the soul most directly. When fully open and operative, the heart center will generate within consciousness the quality of selfless love. It is a love transcendent to any sense of *ahamkara* (self-reference). As such, its radiatory effect upon the environment is unconditional. In the magical process, this chakra ensures that the magician constructs thoughtforms built upon a platform of unitive love.

Throat Center
This is the center within the etheric body most responsible for the thoughtform-building process. Through it, the soul projects its creative intention, and forms are built in accordance with that intention.

This center generates the thoughtforms needed for the wisdom and insight of the soul to be expressed. In addition, it is the structuring center for the soul's creative work. It shapes formless ideas into rightly configured thoughtforms that have the power to environmentally uplift. This center therefore has an intimacy with the mind.

Ajna Center
This is the center where the vision of the soul finds its etheric outlet. Seated between the eyebrows, this chakra makes it possible for the soul to guide the creative process along intended lines. Here is where the third eye is expressed. Its function is to ensure that the thoughtform will be directed to where it is needed and at precisely the right time. This center makes it possible for the soul to gauge the subtle energies operative in the three worlds (mental, emotional and physical), and to direct the creative process in accordance with this vision.

The heart bathes the field in love, while the throat shapes words that uplift. Both are well directed when the inner eye is open.

If this *triangle of magical endeavor* is active in the magician's etheric body, the perils earlier mentioned can be avoided. When the heart center is fully operative, the emotional waters have been tranquilized. It indicates that the solar plexus center (the chakra that activates emotion) has transferred much of its energy to the heart center, thus giving tranquility to the emotional waters. The heart center also puts the disciple en rapport with the buddhic plane where the magical archetypes are found. It is this plane where the love of God can be authentically felt. Thus, a human being's etheric heart center, when open and vital, gives him access to the buddhic plane of divine love. When it is suggested that the magician reestablish contemplative rapport with *buddhi*, such an act not only makes it possible to retouch the archetype, but also to reunite him with God's love.

When the throat center is operative, the magician is able to build thoughtforms true to the soul's intention. The problem associated with unbridled proliferation of thought is tempered by the soul's ability to regulate the rapidity of thoughtform building. It does this when it is able to rightfully engage the throat center.

Finally, the dangers of obsession are overcome when the eye of the soul, the third eye, is operative in the magical process. In turn, this suggests that the magician is able to stand steady within the cave. When such is the case, the soul is able to direct the creative effort by remaining detached from the thoughtforms it has created. Therefore, these three centers, when united in triple service, become the remedy to the obstacles inherent at this stage of spiritual magic.

The Reversal of Etheric Polarity

The awakening of these three chakras involves a transference of energy from three corresponding centers within the lower portions of the etheric vehicle. These correspondences are as follows:

Lower Centers	Higher Centers
Base Center	Head Center (Crown/Ajna joined)
Sacral Center	Throat Center
Solar Plexus	Heart Center

In many ways, the key to evolution is related to an energy transfer between the three lower centers and the three higher centers. For purposes of clarity, it is perhaps better to state that this transference is based upon a reversal of polarity. Human beings have long

Discipleship has much to do with repolarizing the etheric sheath. The lower triangle must give way to the higher three.

been polarized within their lower centers, and understandably so. For aeons, the emphasis on survival (base center) and the instinctual urge to perpetuate the species (sacral center) have weighed heavily in humanity's collective consciousness. These things, coupled with the ancient emergence of human desire (solar plexus), speak of the profound role these three lower centers have played in the evolution of humankind. Even so, due to the comparatively advanced standing of today's humanity, the higher chakras are in need of awakening. This suggests that a reversal of polarity is required. Such repolarization involves a shifting of emphasis from the lower three to their higher corresponding centers.

The degree of repolarization achieved indicates where one stands on the path of evolution.

For uncounted ages, the higher centers have been negative to the positively charged lower centers. In other words, the lower centers have historically been more influential in shaping human behavior and activity. Yet, the time has come when this must change. The lower chakras must become negative to the higher, and therefore quiescent. Indeed, this transference is destined to occur. In many ways, the measure of one's spiritual development can be gauged upon the degree to which this shift has taken place. As such, it is a gradual process, occurring over the course of many incarnations.

The higher centers are far more subjectively based as compared to the lower centers. These upper three (heart, throat and head) make it possible for humanity to move beyond issues related to the mere survival of the form nature, and to develop the higher qualities of selfless love, divine intelligence and spiritual will. When examined closely, it becomes apparent that these higher qualities represent the same properties attributed to the lower centers, but on a higher turn of the spiral of significance. These correlative attributes are as follows:

Base and Head Centers
Both of these etheric centers relate the human being to the nature of will. In the case of the base center, it is the will to survive that emerges. This energy conditions human consciousness to focus on issues pertaining to the physical body and its maintenance. Conversely, the head center is responsive to the soul and/or monad, and manifests within one's life as the *will-to-be*, spiritually considered.

Sacral and Throat Centers
These two centers both manifest the creative power inherent in life. The sacral center wields energy through the human sexual drive. Its divine mandate is to ensure the continuity of the species via the perpetuation of human forms. On the other hand, the throat center gives to a human being the power to create evolutionary ideas, and this as a function of expressing the soul's urge toward creative service.

Solar Plexus and Heart Centers
Each of these centers energetically gives birth to the quality of attraction within a human being. The solar plexus demonstrates the principle of attraction by stimulating the desire to possess. There is always self-reference evident, and it is fundamentally based upon attraction to form. Attraction expressed through the heart center conditions consciousness to selflessly draw toward itself that which supports the unitive nature of spiritual love and life. It does this without any tendency toward self-reference.

When walking the spiritual path, it is crucial that one examine the nature of these energies. Always the question must be asked, how is will, attraction and the creative urge experienced in my life? For the majority,

The two triangles are similar, yet different. When considered over time, the lower has historical advantage.

an honest assessment will lead to the conclusion that mixed motives often govern our actions. Much of our behavior is impulsed by the three higher centers, yet in most cases, the lower centers still have undue influence. This will be so until the disciple becomes transfigured.

Transfiguration marks the stage in which the lower nature is completely under the control and governance of the soul. When mastery of the animal appetite is achieved, the light of divine countenance has dominion over all physical actions and reactions in life. To be transfigured also indicates that emotion no longer controls one's life. Even mastery of the mind is required for transfiguration to be earned. For most, such a state has yet to be achieved, but will in due time. This can be depicted as follows:

Disciplic life represents an inner struggle between competing forces. Freedom from the lower three will one day surely be.

Average Person:	The lower chakras dominate and are unconsciously operative. When stepping onto the probationary path, the higher centers come into view. Repolarization then consciously begins, often superficially.
Disciple:	Repolarization is consciously occurring. A variety of disciplines are adopted to facilitate the process. The battle between the soul and personality reflects the struggle to repolarize.
Initiate:	Repolarization is largely accomplished. The lower triangle no longer exerts undue control. Transfiguration is thus achieved.

The destiny of human consciousness is for the soul to take full dominion over the ancient tendencies of the lower etheric triangle. This is transfiguration, and is the long-term goal for all, either in this incarnation or another. Given this fact, it may be well to discuss the initiatory steps a disciple must take (over the course of many incarnations) in order to gain true liberation and enlightenment.

Spiritual Initiation

It has been said that there are no shortcuts in cosmos. This is an idea based on the principle that spiritual development does not simply happen, but instead must be earned. Within Christian theology, there is the axiom that belief and acceptance of Christ will permit one entrance into heaven. This is a view requiring the use of faith as the means to find union and confidence in God's existence, as well as life after death. From the esoteric perspective, this idea has much value, but only for those who stand at a particular place in their spiritual development. Eventually, faith must give way to experience as the measure of one's relationship to the Divine.

Faith provides spiritual solace, void of the conviction that springs forth from one's own inner experience of divinity. Eventually, this inner experience will occur, though it does so rather late in the development of a human being. Through countless incarnations, faith in God, rather than the experience of God, is the dominating force in human consciousness. The experience of God, as something beyond mere faith, only emerges toward the later phases of the monad's sojourn through the human kingdom. Prior to this, the monad (via the soul) spends thousands of incarnations occupied with preparing the personality to

Faith eventually gives way to an experiential discovery of the soul deep within.

eventually register the experience of the indwelling soul. When the personality finally becomes conscious of this, the initiatory journey can commence.

It is interesting to note that in the Esoteric Tradition God is considered a relative term. Indeed, God is understood as any unit of life whose scope of consciousness is vaster than that of a human being. For example, the entity that ensouls our Earth (Planetary Logos) is an enormous being within cosmos. All units of life upon this planet are really cells within this greater cosmic entity. As such, it is correct to refer to our planetary deity as God. Yet such an entity is still a relative God, inasmuch as He too is only a cell within the more expansive entity whose physical body encompasses the entire solar system. Still, this entity (the Solar Logos) is itself only a unit of life within a grander cosmic being. On and on does this principle of expansive life continue. Every unit of consciousness is a substructure within a greater life entity, ad infinitum. Even our Milky Way galaxy, composed of countless millions of stars, is but an entity within a still grander and more expansive being. Herein is found another definition of *hylozoism*. Specifically, every unit of life is a cell within a vaster unit of life.

Because of hylozoism, a human being is a god, at least from the perspective of less developed categories of life. To an animal, for instance, humans are godlike. Comparatively speaking, humans demonstrate a deeper and more expansive state of consciousness than do animals. Humanity's understanding of life is far vaster than is found within any type of animal form. As such, and relatively speaking, human beings are equivalent to the godhead when considered from the animal domain. From this, we must again emphasize the principle that God is a relative term. Indeed, it is a fundamental principle in occultism and is applicable at any level of

The doctrine of hylozoism gives foundation to the idea that God is a relative term.

entification. Entification is a term that I am using to indicate an inner point of identity realized upon the descending ray of the One Life.

For a human being, the first conscious experience of God (as registered psychologically) is an encounter with the soul itself. Compared to the personality, the soul is the next higher state of consciousness to be touched. As such, the soul is a relative god in contrast to the temporal nature of the personality. When one first comes into *conscious* contact with the soul, the experience is often overwhelming and blissful. One feels united with God, as well as all of creation. Yet because of the newness of the experience and the expansive love that is felt, the individual will often surmise that God (in the ultimate sense) has made personal contact. Though erroneous in conclusion, this perception is nonetheless understandable. Initial contact with the soul is a powerful event. It is therefore not surprising that one would interpret such an experience as contact with the God of all things.

Ironically, out of this perception, the belief in a personal relationship with God emerges. In a sense, this perception is correct, inasmuch as the soul *is* a personal god, for the causal body is exclusive to the individual. Indeed, the soul is the center of one's individual divinity. Even so, the relativity of God is usually not understood, or even considered, when contact with the soul is first achieved in some particular incarnation. As incarnations continue and the experience of soulful contact becomes more regular, the relativity of God becomes more evident. In addition, the individual will slowly shifts from the belief in a personal relationship with God to seeing the Divine in more impersonal ways. However, the quality of personalness will still be evident, though it will now be understood as the experience of the soul itself, not the God of creation.

When first the soul is touched, it is believed to be the all-pervading God. This changes when the relativity of God is known.

Spiritual development is incremental by nature. Initiation is founded on this truth.

In the Esoteric Tradition, it is understood that every human being will eventually be subjected to a series of initiations, each of which is a milestone of spiritual development. These initiations indicate the changing nature of the soul-personality relationship. Over the course of thousands of incarnations, the soul is slowly developing. To some, it may be a surprise to consider that the soul evolves. Often, people hold the view that the soul is inherently divine and already fully developed. In truth, all things within the universe are in a constant state of evolution and change, and the soul is no exception. It is true that the soul is inherently perfect and pure, but only in potential. The purpose of its long sojourn through many incarnations is to slowly actualize the potential that it holds. It is to externalize its essential nature through the threefold personality, eventually with perfection. When the soul can *fully* do this, liberation prevails and the need to reincarnate is no more. To discuss initiation is to discuss the stages that lead to this objective.

Within spiritual circles, the term "enlightenment" is often used. Generally speaking, it is a word used to depict a state of liberated consciousness. This definition is certainly appropriate and valid. However, it is wise to view enlightenment as the gradual consequence of one's growing capacity to recognize light, both within oneself and in the outer world. Enlightenment is therefore best understood as incremental, and is a measure of one's capacity to identify with the light of the soul. Development in this direction always entails the purification of the mind, emotions and physical appetites so that the soul's light can shine through the personality with less and less encumberment. It is a rather paradoxical process when one seriously considers it. For we must *lighten* the darkened areas of our lower nature, and by so doing, experience the light of the soul with greater clarity. To lighten the lower self is to invite the light of the higher self into one's life. Such is the nature of spiritual enlightenment.

Initiatory status is measured by the degree of soulful light expressed through one's personality. Though the soul is always (while on the path) seeking to express itself through each of the personality vehicles (mental, emotional and physical), it is nonetheless focusing most of its influence through one of them. The vehicle through which it is working hardest to manifest is indication of which initiation it is working toward.

The Common Features of Initiation

Before entering into discussion about each of the initiations, it would be well to first examine the characteristics common to all of them. In addition, we must consider the principle of hierarchy, for initiation represents advancement within hierarchical structures of consciousness.

The hall of wisdom is entered through initiation's gate. Sublimation of the intellect is needed.

1. *Further Entrance into the Hall of Wisdom*
   The Hall of Wisdom is a category of consciousness where wisdom supersedes knowledge. As one takes initiation, he enters further into the Hall of Wisdom. As such, one is increasingly able to distinguish the Real from the unreal. This ever involves the ability to intuitively perceive truth apart from the reasoning faculty. However, this is not to say that knowledge and reason are not of value. Quite the contrary, they are crucial on the path. Wisdom does not emerge through rejection of intellect, but *upon* the intellect. The Hall of Wisdom simply indicates that one has learned to transcend the mind, thereby touching the source of sacred wisdom. This is achieved by riding

upon the shoulders of a reliable and well-stocked mind.

2. *Shift of Polarization*
Each initiation indicates that a person's soul has successfully shifted its polarization from one level of the personality to another. Over the course of many incarnations, the soul seeks to express itself primarily through one vehicle over the others. This is what is meant by the term polarization, at least in this context. Where one is polarized indicates where consciousness is preoccupied. Initiation testifies that the soul has developed relative success in working through a particular vehicle (mental, emotional or physical) and is now repolarizing itself toward another vehicle.

3. *Heightened Spiritual Understanding*
Initiation will always enhance an individual's ability to understand something previously not grasped. This is because at each initiation, the third eye opens a bit further. The *eye of vision* (as it is sometimes called) makes it possible for one to better discern and understand the hidden purpose within outer forms and events. Through it, life is seen as less random, and circumstance is recognized as being revelatory in nature. Each initiation heightens one's capacity in this regard.

4. *Secret of Good and Evil Revealed*
Initiation always conveys to the disciple a wiser understanding of the interplay between soul and form. As such, this always requires a deepened comprehension as to the nature of good and evil. At each initiation, evil is revealed in a new light, and its purpose becomes increasingly evident. While evil

Each initiation opens the single eye a bit further. The transcendent meaning of evil comes to light, and circumstance is understood as revelatory.

has historically been viewed as the antithesis to good, it comes to be perceived as its necessary companion. Goodness only has meaning when it is contrasted with evil. This revelation emerges incrementally according to the initiation involved.

5. *Change in Atomic Matter*
   As previously discussed, each vehicle of the personality is composed of living substance called elementals. These elementals are of differing densities, and are related to different experiences in consciousness, ranging from lofty to profane. Spiritual evolution involves altering the chemistry of one's vehicles so that its substance becomes less dense and of higher grade. This is done through the purification of the lower nature. Such change ultimately results in a healthier body, loftier emotions and a tendency toward elevated thought. The highest grade of substance (in any vehicle) is called atomic. Initiation is therefore an event indicating that one has purified the lower nature to such an extent that a given percentage of atomic substance is now present within each of the vehicles. This is consummated at the fourth initiation, thus indicating that the mental and emotional vehicles are now solely composed of atomic substance.

Purification and decentralization open the way to initiation. The first corrects the form, while the latter gives remedy to ahamkara's grip.

6. *Increased Decentralization*
   Each initiation is a confirmation that the disciple has gained a measure of decentralization in life. By this is meant that he is now less prone to the tendency to self-reference. Sometimes called *ahamkara*, this tendency slowly disappears as spiritual development moves forward. However, as the disciple evolves upon the path, ahamkara becomes increasingly subtle to detect, and is amazingly surreptitious. It

therefore requires that one be increasingly vigilant to detect it. Initiation is bestowed when a specific measure of decentralization has been established. Each initiation indicates that less and less ahamkara is operative within the one's consciousness.

7. *Sacrifice of the Heart*

Sacrificial crisis emerges as the gate of initiation nears. Pain and fear come forth, though fallacious are their roots.

In any initiation, there will always be a measure of sacrifice involved. Interestingly, it is the personality that experiences the loss that accompanies sacrifice, not the soul. The nature of this forfeiture will be different for each initiation. Nonetheless, what is relinquished will be something that the personality has intimately used to define itself. The pain the personality feels at such times is indicative of the deflation it experiences by such sacrifice. Yet beyond the pain, the personality senses that the soul shall give it new life and meaning through the process of letting go. Trust is therefore a needed ingredient when making such sacrifice. Indeed, the path is largely governed by the processes of death and resurrection. It is a death to previous definitions of self, and resurrection into a higher aspect of one's spiritual self, the soul. The pain of sacrifice comes from the fact that the death experience must ever precede the resurrection. Such is the sacrificial nature of spiritual transformation, and this as prerequisite to initiation.

8. *Emergence of Crisis*
Crisis is ever a precursor to initiation of any degree. This is because, immediately prior to initiation, the personality realizes that it must surrender an aspect of itself to the will of the soul. As such, the personality believes that yielding to the soul is a prescription for its own demise. This is a fallacy. In

truth, the soul is seeking the cooperation of the personality, not its destruction. Because of this fallacious belief, the personality will tend to rise in defiance. For long it has been in control, and has seemingly been effective in its independence. However, the soul now is pressuring it to yield. The experience of this defiant stance then gives birth to a crisis of some kind. Such a crisis may be physical, emotional or mental in character. It can be a single event, or it can be protracted over many years. In essence, it represents a test to determine if one is ready and worthy of further soul-infusion, and the added responsibility that such infusion entails. The burning ground must be walked, and the personality must do the walking.

Each initiation adds unique potency and responsibility in service to the Larger Life.

Beyond these common characteristics, each of the initiations is quite different. Each indicates a different aspect of the personality that has supplicated to the soul's will and intention. Each bestows upon the disciple a greater responsibility and service opportunity. Shortly, we shall examine the nature of the five major initiations, plus the probationary requirements that lead to them. Before doing so however, it is fitting to briefly discuss the nature of hierarchy. For it will be seen that initiation is essentially an indication of spiritual status and is therefore hierarchical.

The Principle of Hierarchy

Hierarchy is an idea that is rather offensive to many spiritually inclined people. Often, people recoil at the thought that spirituality is based upon gradation. Instead, there is clear bias in favor of spiritual equality and parity. This attitude is certainly understandable.

Historically, humanity has suffered greatly through the misuse of hierarchical structures within society. The suppression of the masses, wielded by the powerful and elite, has left humanity with a distaste of anything resembling hierarchy. Today's society yearns for equality and human respect—something that has been woefully lacking for most of human history. It is therefore not surprising that the notion of spiritual hierarchy is frequently rejected. Nonetheless, when rightly understood hierarchy is realized as a pervasive and inescapable feature of creation itself.

The Principle of Hierarchy is woven into the fabric of creation.

Hierarchy is actually a law governing evolution. As such, it is often referred to as the *Principle of Hierarchy*. It is abundantly apparent in nature, both terrestrial and beyond. For example, many animal types have social orders that are distinctly hierarchical. This can be readily seen in various mammalian forms, such as chimpanzee and gorilla species. From an astronomical perspective, a planet has central authority over the behavior of an orbiting satellite, such as the Earth's relationship to the moon. The sun has hierarchical authority over the many planets that orbit it. In turn, our sun is subjected to the authority and forces emanating from the galaxy of which it is a part, namely, the Milky Way. Such is the principle of hierarchy evident upon and beyond our earthly sphere.

Though the Principle of Hierarchy is universal, this does not negate the Principle of Equality, for it too is a fact woven into creation. It may be asked therefore, how can both hierarchy and equality be true, for they seem mutually exclusive? The answer to this must be sought in a twofold manner. That is, all living things must be considered from the perspective of life and from that of consciousness. When we examine this question from the *life perspective*, all things are utterly equal in cosmos. Whether we are pondering a human being, an insect or the entity that ensouls a star, all are equal in that they all are cells within the body of the One Life. As such, nothing has any more life value than any other category of life. This is a fact that has historically been overlooked by humanity. Indeed, it is this fact that is now being inculcated in contemporary society, as it should. Humanity's growing demand for social equality and our burgeoning concern for the protection of the environment both indicate this fact.

However, when we consider this question from the *consciousness perspective*, hierarchy is present and unavoidable. For example, though in essence a human being is equal to the life ensouling a blade of grass, a person is far more advanced in his consciousness when compared to that blade of grass. When we speak of spiritual evolution, we are really discussing the evolution of consciousness, not that of life. For life *is*, while consciousness must become.

Comparatively speaking, consciousness between units of life is simply not equal. This is clearly evident when we compare life existing between kingdoms in nature, but it is equally true when considering life within a kingdom. Just as some animals have developed consciousness further than other animals, some humans are further developed in their consciousness than are others. We need only examine the many people we have known throughout our lives to see the truth of this statement. Do we not know people who are extremely wise and profoundly developed, as well as others who demonstrate relatively primitive states of consciousness? I am not here making a statement of condescension, but simply one of fact.

When it comes to the development of consciousness, people are different, and for a variety of reasons. If we compare the consciousness of Jesus with that of Hitler, do we not know, somehow, that one of them is more

Equality is certain when considering the sacredness of life. Hierarchy is evidenced through the spectrum of consciousness.

spiritually developed than the other? It could be argued that such differences are based upon one's upbringing and cultural influences. Though there is certainly validity to this statement, it is only partially true. Esotericism holds that, beyond questions of childhood nurturing and environmental upbringing, there is inherent developmental distinction among people. Souls have differing incarnational histories. Over aeons of time, they have unfolded in different ways and at different rates. As such, and regardless of cultural influence, there are innate capacities and deficiencies to every soul, and it is this that is most influential in shaping one's consciousness. Wherever one stands, there will always be some people who are more developed, and others who are less developed. This is the basis of the so-called chain-of-life. It applies to life between kingdoms, as well as life within a particular kingdom. The importance of understanding this principle can not be overstated. As such, we will later examine hierarchy, but with our focus on the dangers associated with its inversion.

Having examined the commonalities of all the initiations, as well as the inescapable nature of hierarchy, let us now look at each initiation specifically. We begin at the point in time when the light of the soul is first recognized by the evolving human being.

The Probationary Path
The Path of Purification

Though initiation is a series of incremental steps leading to increased soul infusion, there are preliminary requisites that must be established before initiation is possible. When one is living life in preparation for entrance upon the path of discipleship, that individual is said to be on the *probationary path*. During the long

> *Humanity is hierarchical. Some are near the gate of liberation, while others find the path wide and new. Most stand betwixt the two.*

sojourn through time, there comes an incarnation when the personality has its first *conscious* glimpse of the soul within. Note the emphasis on the word conscious, for there has been an unconscious knowing of its existence all along. It is this unconscious force that has lead to the formation of religions around the world, and the yearning within humanity to understand the deeper meaning of life.

Also emerging from this "spiritual touch" is the belief in an eternal soul. As stated earlier, there comes a time when faith in the soul is superseded by its actual experience. The light of the soul flashes forth within oneself, and from that point forward, faith slowly, very slowly, gives way to a knowingness of the soul within. This event marks the point of entrance upon the probationary path. Though the length of time spent upon this leg of the journey varies widely, it does last for many incarnations, nonetheless.

When the aspirant experiences this initial flash from the soul, it is usually fleeting and short-lived. The soul makes its mark, then seemingly vanishes from the sight of the amazed individual. The aspirant now knows that the soul is real, but is bewildered by its rapid disappearance. This motivates him to try to recapture the experience once again. A seeker is thus born. The joy of seeing the soul, even for a moment, propels him to seek it again and again. It eventually becomes the main incentive of his life.

From the fundamentalist Christian perspective, this event has correlation to the so-called born-again experience. It signifies the moment when one becomes a conscious participant in his own spiritual development. Prior to the probationary stage, an individual will live life through the spiritual authority of others. Historically, the clergy has held responsibility for the spiritual development of its flock. Yet at this stage in

The soul irradiates the mind and heart, its light fleeting and true. The yearning to recapture its vanishing glow consumes the probationer's view.

development, and for the first time, the aspirant shifts this burden onto himself.

There are several characteristics indicative of the probationary path. In its early phases, the aspirant becomes immersed in a frenzied quest, and this in hopes of recapturing the soulful experience that has been lost. This search will normally be expressed in one of two ways. Either the individual will commit to a narrow dogmatic approach, or will choose a wide (though shallow) path. In the first case, an orthodox spiritual system is favored, and the aspirant will often become its fanatical exponent. The other possibility is that he will become a spiritual shopper, so to speak. Here the seeker will sample many spiritual systems in hopes of quickly finding that which will work. In actual fact, both ways are lacking. In the first case, orthodoxy prevents the aspirant from the wider vision of spiritual approaches, and it nurtures dogmatic and separative thought. In the second, he sees the many paths, but is unwilling to truly penetrate any of them with heartfelt commitment. In either case, the aspirant is taking his own spiritual development in hand, even though naïvely so, at least initially.

A preoccupation with vertical duality is the guiding paradigm of a probationer's life. By this is meant that he is keenly aware of his dual nature, soul and personality. His life is committed to recapturing his experience with the higher pole, the soul. Yet, there is also growing concern that perhaps the reason for the soul's rapid departure (seemingly) is that there is something repulsing it. Herein lies the core of the probationary crisis, for the aspirant realizes that his own impurities are the source of the problem. He therefore takes stock of these impurities and is determined to do something about them. This then becomes a foundational feature for living a spiritual life. The purification of the mind,

A fanatical quest often engages the seeker who is newly wakened. Orthodox code or shallow inquiry then capture his searching heart.

emotions and particularly the physical body take center stage, sometimes fanatically so. This is why the probationary journey is sometimes called the *path of purification*. It is to purify the personality instrument so that it can become a fit receptacle for the soul.

When treading the probationary path, disciplines are inculcated within the life, including attempts at restraint of animal appetite. Often diet and/or physical exercise become a preoccupation. The physical body is viewed as the major hindrance to the soul's downflow, and the purification of it is believed to be the remedy. As preparatory to the first initiation, the gestation of the *Christ within the Heart* is occurring, and this over many lifetimes. The nurturing of selfless love becomes important, and the probationer is now determined to become a fit receptacle for the Christ Principle. Much of this has to do with a growing capacity to introspect, and to gradually "know thyself." Such is truly the mantram for those who tread the spiritual path.

Discipline of the outer form guides the probationer's life. Purification and character building are his sought after aims. The love of Christ is thus seeded.

First Initiation

The Birth of the Christ within the Heart

The probationary path is a period that is preparatory to the first initiation. Much of the aspirant's effort has been directed toward the purification of the form nature (with emphasis on the physical), as well as the gradual awakening of selfless love. Both of these qualities serve as a foundation for eventually taking the first initiation. It has been said that the first initiation is as monumental as the time of individualization, an event that took place millions of years ago. Legend states that at that time humanity emerged from its animal root and became a kingdom unto itself. Then it was that the monad left the third kingdom (animal) and entered into the fourth, the human. On a higher level, it is at the first initiation that the monad (via the soul) begins its entrance into the fifth kingdom in nature, the kingdom of souls.

From this, we can understand the similarities between individualization and the first initiation. Both represent initial entrance into a new kingdom of nature. The first initiation is a beginning step into the *kingdom of the soul*, and subsequent initiations serve to further that entrance. This higher domain (fifth kingdom) represents the state of consciousness evident when the soul is fully flowered. All souls are already members of the fifth kingdom, though only in potential. In truth, the soul's evolution is based upon the gradual awakening of this potential. It must prove that it can express itself fully through form, and this without encumberment. Perhaps needless to say, this process takes many incarnations to consummate.

The evolution of the soul is to unfold its beauty, wisdom and love through its threefold vehicle (the personality). When this occurs in its completeness, the soul earns the right to fully enter into the fifth kingdom. Until then, the soul is best considered a provisional member. The first initiation therefore signifies that the soul has unfolded an aspect of its nature through the personality, and is therefore partially admitted into this fifth domain. Perhaps it would be more accurate to say that at this initiation the disciple enters into the aura of the fifth kingdom, the region where the Hierarchy of Masters is found.

> *The first initiation signifies that one has stepped into the aura of the fifth kingdom in nature.*

The first initiation has been called *The Birth of the Christ within the Heart*. It is an appropriate name, in that the Christ force becomes radiatory through one's heart center at this initiation. That is to say that the heart chakra is enormously vivified, thus making it possible for the love of the Christ to be transmitted through it. While the probationary path provides gestation to Christ-like love, this initiation triggers its birth. The previous work of character-building and purification has made possible the birth of the Christ within. In the Christian Tradition, this is metaphorically conveyed through the virgin birth motif. Occultly interpreted, it is out of virgin substance (purified form) that the Christ principle is born. It is therefore not surprising that the zodiacal sign of Virgo has close connection to the first initiation. It is the sign of the virgin, and relates to the harvesting of love.

It should be here noted that the word *Christ* is a multilevel term. Though Christianity has only used the word in reference to "the teacher alike of angels and of men," it has other applications as well. For example, the soul itself is an expression of Christ, for it is the center within one's spiritual constitution founded on the principle of selfless love. Herein lies a useful definition of Christ. From the larger perspective, there is also the cosmic Christ, representing the Christ Principle pervasively radiating throughout all of cosmos. When speaking of the Christ in relation to this initiation, it refers to the soul birthing forth through one's form nature. It is the birth of the *personal Christ* (soul), and it is recognized through the radiatory force expressed through the disciple's heart chakra. In short, it is the soul shining forth into outer expression, and this via the radiation of Christ-like love.

One of the important features of the first initiation is that it indicates the soul's triumph over the appetites of the flesh. The objective of the soul, at this stage of development, is to create relative mastery over the cravings of the physical body. The soul needs a physical body that is willing to follow its lead, but the body's unbridled appetites represent a hindrance in this regard. The body has a consciousness of its own, quite apart from the soul-consciousness seeking to work through it. This independent consciousness manifests as the

The birth initiation opens wide the disciple's heart, and Christ-like love then guides.

longings of the body. Normally, this includes those cravings for food that go beyond what is needed to sustain the form, as well as sexual yearnings that transcend the need to perpetuate the species. In addition, it also has much to do with how the individual uses the body in the physical world.

Prior to taking this initiation, an individual will have a strong attraction toward life circumstance that stimulates the physical body in some fashion. When this initiation occurs, these physical appetites are relegated to their rightful place. No longer does the body hold unnecessary demands upon the soul. Of course, this is not to say that all physical cravings have been transcended. Such a state of consciousness does not occur until the fourth initiation. However, this initiation does indicate that the weight of influence over the physical body is now within the soul's domain, and no longer governed by the personality's attraction to physical stimulation.

This initiation has much to do with one's sexual drive, and the transfer of energy from the sacral center to the throat. As such, the creative urge shifts from sexual cravings to the expression of creative ideas governed by the soul working through the throat center. Again, the sexual urge is not completely subdued at this juncture. Instead, much of the energy normally dedicated to it has been shifted upward, along the etheric spine, and is now used by the soul in the development of creative thought.

The transfer of energy from the sacral to the throat center can cause much sexual turmoil in one's life. Often, there is an oscillation that takes place between these two centers, and this can be quite distressing. In addition, at this stage, one is prone to the tendencies of sex magic.

The lower creative urge is lifted to the place where soul gives shape to innovative thought.

To understand sex magic and its emergence, it must be realized that at the first initiation a measure of detachment from sexual longing has been achieved. This is as intended, and is essential for continued development. Yet, this also means that a disciple of such status is able to wield sexual power while remaining the detached onlooker. This is one understanding of sexual magic. It is the ability to manipulate people and events through the deliberate utilization of sexual energy. Needless to say, sex magic represents a wrongful use of energy. Yet when nearing this initiation, and to some extent beyond it, this tendency may be operative. Vigilance is therefore well advised.

Staying with this theme for a moment, at the first initiation the disciple *begins* to realize the esoteric meaning of human sexuality. He intuits that sexuality is a lower expression of a larger principle evident within creation as a whole. This understanding is grounded in the notion that sexual intercourse is a reflection of the soul interacting with the personality. It is therefore seen as a horizontal rendition of the interplay occurring between spirit and matter, and as such, is part of the cosmic drama of duality and its synthesis. Through the embodiment of this sensed truth, the disciple then begins to readjust his relationship to sexuality so that its expression more closely reflects its spiritual intention.

A profound yearning to serve also manifests when the first initiation is taken. For the first time, the oneness of humanity is recognized, and this beyond theory. As such, first-degree disciples will commit themselves to living their lives in service to human betterment. The burden of the future is assumed, for the disciple knows that to serve the soul is to serve the evolutionary intention of the larger life. How such service will manifest varies widely from disciple to disciple. Variables, such as soul ray and karmic circumstance,

Human sexuality is a horizontal rendition of the vertical duality of spirit and matter.

will play heavily on the mode of service to be rendered. Nonetheless, the disciple's life will be far less selfish than it had been earlier, for the needs of the whole now outweigh the wants of the personal self.

It may be asked, who is it that officiates at these initiations, and where and when do they occur? We are given to understand that the Christ himself is the Initiator at the first and second initiations. Symbolically considered, in his hand is held the Rod of Initiation, so called. This rod is said to be a conduit through which our planetary god, *Sanat Kumara*, transmits the energy of divine will and purpose. In other words, through his disciple, the Christ, Sanat Kumara transmits his energetic will into the body of the Christ, and then to the waiting disciple.

Technically speaking, Sanat Kumara is the *One Initiator* on our planet. However, at the first two initiations the Christ acts as an intermediary. Through his body, this tremendous burst of energy is transformed and stepped down before it is conveyed to the disciple via the Rod of Initiation. This stepping down of God's energy is crucial, for without it the disciple's body could not bear the force. The Christ applies the Rod upon the causal body (and by extension, the etheric body) of the disciple, and the resultant charge is enormous. The disciple's system is henceforth heightened in its capacity to energetically effect the environment. This is why purification of the form nature is so important. When we purify our thoughts, feelings and physical body, we are altering them in such a way that they become better containers for higher energy.

Regarding the location and timing of initiation, it must ever be kept in mind that it is the soul that is initiated, not the personality. Initiation takes place within the causal body itself, located upon the plane of higher mind. For this reason, most people who have

The Christ himself officiates at this initiation and the next. With rod in hand, and loving heart profound, he applies the power of planetary life.

taken the first initiation have no recall of it. When there is remembrance, it is frequently through a symbolic dream experience or meditative vision. However, more often than not, there is no memory of the event.

The timing of an initiation varies widely. Most important are various astrological considerations, including the esoteric indications related to transits and progressions. There are also karmic considerations that define if and when a candidate can stand before the Initiator. As such, it must be understood that these major initiations are quite rare. This will become more evident as we further explore the nature of the initiatory journey.

Second Initiation

The Baptism

The time that transpires between the first and second initiation can be quite lengthy. Most often, it will take several incarnations before the second initiation can be taken. During that time, the soul must rise above the emotional vehicle (astral body), and thereby become its master. It is for this reason that many incarnations are required. The astral body has long governed the personality. Because of this, relative mastery over it is extremely difficult and painful. Generally speaking, the consciousness of humanity is largely directed by human emotion. Though humanity is fast developing its mental faculty, emotions still hold sway for most human people.

It would be well to truly examine the relationship between thinking and feeling, for it shall be seen that feeling states most often direct the trend and bias of thought. As unbiased as we believe ourselves to be, an undercurrent of subtle emotion will often color the nature and direction of our thoughts, elusively guiding the mind along certain lines. Indeed, the power of the emotional body to influence the personality is quite

Subtle are the emotions that give directional impulse to thought. At the second initiation, they are no longer granted this license.

subtle, and it is this that the disciple must learn to recognize and overcome as prerequisite to the second initiation.

At this initiation, one must demonstrate a measure of detachment from emotional experience. The astral body is governed by desire. As such, it is difficult to detach from it, for it contains the energy of personal longing and want. Therefore, it is not surprising that the second initiation always involves a major emotional crisis in one's life. This crisis may be acute, or protracted over many years.

Feeling states condition most of what people think and do. One's career, recreational interests and personal relationships are largely governed by emotions related to likes and dislikes. Sentiment has a tremendous power to shape every department of human life. Emotion can be so subtle and pervasive within our thought processes that it is difficult to recognize its influence. Its juxtaposition in everyday life is often too close to see. This is what the disciple must come to know and witness within himself. Indeed, it is this realization that triggers the initiatory crisis leading to the second initiation.

The achievement of the second initiation requires that a profound sense of introspection be applied to one's life, particularly as it pertains to the emotional body. One must study his emotional actions and reactions, and by so doing, learn how to untangle the threads of thought from the fluidic and elusive feelings associated with thought. Not surprisingly, such inner analysis requires the development of a discriminative mind.

The correct use of the mind is truly the antidote to the problem of astrality. To use the mind in its observing capacity necessitates remaining detached from what is being observed. This suggests that one must learn to

Emotional persuasion is remedied through detachment and discriminative thought.

observe emotional phenomena, while ever remaining disengaged from it. It is from this detached and objective perspective that the disciple gains understanding as to how emotions can serve or imprison him. I must say, this is a significant realization emerging upon the spiritual path. The emotional body is destined to be a servant on behalf of the soul. Yet because it is also associated with the desires of the personality, emotion has historically been the controlling agent. This must change. When evidence of such change has reached a certain point, the second initiation can then commence.

Between the first and second initiation, the disciple tends to develop a fuller understanding of his spiritual nature and purpose, and does so with fervency. This is all well and good. However, because the emotional body is not yet mastered, undue enthusiasm is being connected to the various spiritual principles held within the mind. This is particularly true as these principles pertain to fundamental aspects of life and the perceptions related to one's spiritual purpose.

In addition, at the second initiation the disciple must demonstrate that he is free from the "slavery of ideas." By this is meant that he must remain removed from the ideas held as profoundly true and meaningful in life. When undue emotions are added to an idea, such views become overly dominating within consciousness. They then begin to control the self, rather than the reverse. The curse of mental obsession then looms large, and the disciple is surely victimized by the dearness of his ideas. When the second gate is reached, the disciple must be free from any and all fanatical tendency. This is so even regarding one's relationship with a spiritual leader or guru. Such devotion, though at one time needed and useful, is now a nemesis that must be transcended.

He who passes the second gate is no longer the slave to his cherished ideals. Temperance gives him needed perspective.

The second initiation is sometimes called the *Baptism*. This idea has correlation to the baptism of the Master Jesus in the Jordan River. Water is ever the symbol of the emotional body, and immersion in it is the test. It is to be immersed in the waters of emotion, while remaining detached and aloof from them. Also relevant is the idea that the astral body must be filled with lofty emotion. While the disciple is learning how to dissociate from feeling states, he is also nurturing higher emotions within consciousness, such as feelings of compassion and intelligent aspiration.

A deeper calling to serve is also evident at this transition point. The disciple is now determined to enter into the field of world service with full and unwavering commitment. Emergent within the mind is a sense of the inner group. This is actually something realized at the first initiation. However, at the second gate the group begins to mean more to the disciple than himself. From this state of inner group dedication service is rendered to the outer world.

> *The call to serve is unwavering and profound. Support to the inner group becomes one's reason for being.*

Today, most disciples are developmentally found between the first and second initiations. For them, the opening of the heart has already occurred, and a measure of mastery over the physical body has also been achieved. The great challenge facing most of us now is to rise above the influence of our desires and longings, and thus learn to master our passional nature. Such is the baptismal demand.

Third Initiation

The Transfiguration

In many ways, the third initiation is the most pivotal. It represents the stage of development when the soul gains dominion over the whole of the personality. At this initiation, the soul has infused itself into the personality to such an extent that it now has authority over all the vehicles of the lower self (physical, emotional and mental). No longer is it possible for thought, feeling or physical sensation to hold the soul in thralldom.

The third initiation is called the *Transfiguration*. At this developmental milestone, the entire personality is transfigured in the effulgent light of the soul. Within Christian mythology, this is depicted for us in the story of the transfiguration of Jesus upon the mount. Accompanied by three disciples, Jesus was transfigured in the glory of God's radiant light. At his feet, his disciples prostrated themselves in reverence to this supernal radiance. This is symbolic of the soul as it irradiates the threefold lower nature. Each of these disciples symbolizes one of the personality vehicles yielding to the radiance of the soul. Biblically, Peter was called the rock, and corresponds to the physical body. James characterizes the deceptive nature of the emotional vehicle, while John relates to the mind, for his name means "the Lord hath spoken." In this wonderful biblical account, we see symbolized for us the supplication of the threefold personality, thus indicating that the third initiation has been surmounted.

At transfiguration, the lower three completely yield to the soul's glowing presence.

As we consider this initiation, it is not surprising that the zodiacal sign of Capricorn has relevance to it. Capricorn is the sign represented by a goat climbing a mountain. When the summit is reached, the goat is transformed into a sacred unicorn. The two-horned goat, symbolizing the duality of soul and personality, is thus changed into the unicorn with its single horn thrust toward heaven. This symbolism suggests that a facet of duality has been resolved, which is precisely what occurs at the transfiguration. The third initiation marks the time when the duality of soul and personality are fused into a profound singularity. The initiate of the third degree is the unicorn, and in biblical terms is called a *full grown man in Christ*. The inner Christ (soul) is now fully unfolded and infused into the personality.

At the transfiguration, the mind is mastered, at least relatively so. It indicates that the initiate is able to internally discern between a thought, the thinker and the process of thinking. As such, and for the first time, the mind is now the servant of the soul. No longer does it wander according to its own whim. The initiate knows himself, experientially, as something transcendent to thought and the mechanism of thinking. Through this realization, the Son of Mind emerges in full glory. The Son of Mind is an ancient title for the soul itself. The soul is essentially the son of divine ideation. That is to say that it represents the Mind of God within every human being. When fully flowered, the soul is able to manifest the purity and wisdom of God's thought.

At this initiation, the Law of Sacrifice dominates the life. Sacrifice is a foundational feature when on the path of initiation, particularly as one nears transfiguration. There emerges a willingness to "sacrifice all forever" in service to the larger whole (God). To be transfigured is to know that all is truly One. No longer does the heresy of separateness deceive the initiate. Union with the All (relatively speaking) has finally been achieved, and the initiate becomes conscious of his participation in the life of the Hierarchy. That is to say, an intimacy with his inner master is inwardly recognized. and his ashramic responsibility is known. All is then sacrificed in support of that responsibility.

To the initiate, the theme of service is further enhanced within the life. The world, as a whole, is viewed as the field of service, for all of humanity is now seen as one. It is therefore not surprising that the third degree initiate is occultly called the *world disciple*. However, it is important to understand precisely what is

> *The law of sacrifice governs the initiate's life. The lower three cannot deflect him from the demand sounded from above.*

meant by this title. It does not mean that, because someone is widely traveled and spiritually dedicated, he must be a third degree initiate. If such were the case, world disciples would be everywhere. Actually, there are very few initiates in incarnation today, though admittedly their numbers are growing. To be a world disciple means that the scope of the disciple's service will have global ramifications, either now or as a legacy to the future. And of course, such worldwide influence must be fundamentally uplifting to the human condition.

Also important is the fact that, at the third initiation, the antahkarana is fully constructed, or nearly so. This bridge within consciousness makes it possible for the soul to have dominion over the personality. Though the antahkarana is built over countless lifetimes, it is not *consciously* and fully erected until the transfiguration. Because of this, the soul is finally able to gain control over the independent proclivities of the personality. However, there are said to be two spans of the antahkarana. The first extension (lower span) is that which connects soul and personality. The higher span is what links the soul with the life of the monad. This higher extension, though not yet complete, is now able to profoundly influence the initiate's perception of reality.

Because the antahkarana (in both its spans) is now well developed, the third degree initiate is able to consciously sense the radiation and influence of the monad. The key word is *consciously*, in that prior to this initiation, the monad is operative, but unconsciously so. A genuine (and non-imaginative) glimpse of the monad is internally realized and witnessed for the first time by the astounded initiate who stands at the third gate. Monadic consciousness is far removed from what we typically understand consciousness to be. Yet at this monumental transition, something of this state of being

The antahkarana gives to the initiate a fleeting glimpse of monadic being. Identification is then understood, though faintly.

is sensed. In esoteric literature, the inadequate term used to describe this state is *identification*. It is the process of identifying with pure Being, a thing transcendent to consciousness as we understand that term. It is identification with the universal oneness of life, and to realize oneself to be both the part and the whole simultaneously. Though the full realization of this is not possible until the sixth initiation, it is first experientially glimpsed at the moment of transfigured glory.

Interestingly, the quality of aspiration is not evident at the third degree. In fact, aspiration must give way to conscious experience. This is a point often overlooked. Up to this stage, the disciple has aspired to become the full expression of his soul. At the third initiation, such a state is achieved, and aspiration is no longer of use, comparatively speaking. Indeed, the third degree initiate is fully living as soul, no longer needing to strive toward that objective.

Also indicative of initiate consciousness is the fact that the third eye becomes creatively effective. Because the initiate has mastered the mind, his capacity to create evolutionary thoughtforms is tremendously enhanced. The white magician is truly born, and it is the opened third eye that ensures successful creative endeavor. The third eye has sometimes been called the *eye of vision*. Magically considered, this eye makes it possible for the initiate to maintain full control of the thoughtform-building process. The elemental lives, contained within his thoughtform, have supplicated to the will of the soul, and it is the power of the third eye that forces this allegiance. This is an important subject, and is presented in this text when later discussing the magical work of this spiritual eye. Suffice it to say that the fully opened third eye gives the initiate the power of inner sight,

> *The eye of the soul opens wide to the transfigured one. The creative work can then proceed, untainted.*

wisdom and authority. Through it, he is able to create forms that truly support the plan of evolution.

At the transfiguration, the Christ no longer acts as the initiator of the Rite, but instead it is Sanat Kumara himself. Unlike the first and second initiations, the third requires that the Christ step aside, thus allowing the force wielded by the Lord of the World (Sanat Kumara) to make direct contact with the disciple's etheric system. It is no wonder that the requirements are so high in order to partake of this rite of passage. The disciple's etheric vehicle must be purified to such an extent that it can withstand this tremendous influx of energy, direct and unmitigated.

In conclusion, it should be stated that, from a certain perspective, the third initiation can be considered the first. This is because it represents the first time that the soul has proven its mastery over the full personality. When considered in this light, the first two initiations are called *initiations on the threshold*. They are on the threshold leading to transfiguration.

At the moment of transfiguration, it is He, to whom the Christ bows low, who applies the needed charge.

Fourth Initiation

The Renunciation

After the transfiguration, there is a comparatively rapid accumulation of spiritual knowledge. This is due to the fact that as one approaches the fourth initiation, the content of the causal body is being synthesized into the buddhic sheath. The buddhic sheath is really the intuitive vehicle used by the initiate. Though this sheath is being formed over many lifetimes, as one nears the fourth initiation it is rapidly coordinated. Because of this, two events occur. The first is that the storehouse of wisdom contained within the causal body is being drawn into the buddhic sheath. Secondly, because the buddhic vehicle dominates the initiate's consciousness, a profound realization as to the deeper mystery of existence begins to dawn within his consciousness.

The buddhic plane (plane of intuition) is the region of consciousness where the wisdom of divinity is found. In ancient lore, it was called the "raincloud of knowable things." Interestingly, the consciousness of a fourth degree initiate is polarized in this raincloud. This plane is the field of consciousness wherein are found the archetypes seeking to be manifested into the outer world. As such, the arhat (fourth degree initiate) finds his *resting consciousness* centered in the same locality as these divine archetypes. This makes such an initiate an amazingly effective magician. Because the buddhic sheath is being speedily coordinated (in preparation for the fourth initiation), the initiate is experiencing an amazingly rapid accumulation of divine knowledge and wisdom.

The most notable characteristic of this initiation is that it involves the destruction of the causal body. As you know, the causal body is the container of one's higher consciousness, the soul itself. It is made up of intelligent substance of a very high order, and acts as the repository of positive attributes acquired over countless incarnations. This is why the causal body has sometimes been referred to as the treasury. It contains within it the experiences (recorded as vibration) pertaining to one's personal spiritual journey, and is the thing that one strives to become. Yet at this initiation, the causal body must be destroyed, for it no longer is useful to onward development.

This may seem a distressing thought, and to the one about to pass through this initiation, it certainly is that. For long the disciple has believed that the soul is eternal. More accurately, the consciousness of the soul (which represents the experiences and wisdom stored within the causal body) were believed to be everlasting. Yet at the

> *The consciousness of a fourth degree initiate rests within the buddhic plane, the place wherein the archetypes reside.*

fourth gate, the initiate realizes that what he believed was his eternal consciousness is not really eternal. You may recall that the monad is the being that is eternal, not the consciousness within the causal body, which we call the soul. As such, there comes a time when the causal body is recognized as an obstacle to further evolution. This time marks the fourth initiation, and demands that the causal body be disintegrated, thus freeing the indwelling self to rise toward the monad. It is for this reason that the fourth initiation is the most distressing of them all. One must forfeit that which has, for ages, been viewed as the sacred and eternal part of oneself.

At the fourth gate, the causal body itself is renounced.

In the East, this initiation is called the *Renunciation*. It is to renounce all previously cherished views of one's spiritual identity. This renunciation reflects itself in the initiate's outer life as well. Often, such a person must forfeit all that is humanly valued and cherished. Friends, money, character and reputation are all renounced, and painfully so. From the Western perspective, this initiation is called the *Crucifixion*. Two thousand years ago, the master Jesus took this initiation and demonstrated to the world the profound measure of sacrifice required at such a stage of development. However, to understand this initiation, it must be kept in mind that it is the causal body that is crucified.

The destruction of the causal body is distressing, to be sure. Compounding this is the fact that, at the time of initiation, the disciple is left bereft of anything to rely upon. From the third initiation onward, the vision of the monad has been held. However, at the fourth gate, the light of the monad is blocked from view. He therefore finds no solace above to give reassurance. Outer human living also seems void and without meaning. As such, he stands detached from that which is above and that which is below. A feeling of utter aloneness thus envelops the initiate, and yet there is still an inner knowingness that *the vehicle* for soul consciousness must be discarded. This is revealed to us in the story of Jesus upon the cross, when he called out, "My God, why has thou forsaken me?" The Esoteric Tradition teaches that the monad represents the Father Principle within the human system. As such, it is the monad that *seemingly* forsakes the one who faces this crisis. Such is the great dilemma that confronts the initiate at the renunciation. It requires complete reliance on one's own inner wisdom and conviction, void of any crutch to give support. The initiate must prove that no sense of dependency or fear remains as a liability upon the upward path.

Personal karma is now fully released, and the demand for earthly return is no more.

This initiation indicates that all personal karma has been released, and reincarnation is no longer mandated. When completely passed, the light of the monad once again emerges, and now with far greater radiance and splendor. An arhat is thus born. The renunciation truly represents triumph over death. Nothing remains within his consciousness that gives support to the illusion of finite existence. There is now the knowledge that death is merely a self-imposed limitation created out of naiveté and ignorance. The initiate moves now with utter assurance of immortal beingness. Communication with the master occurs with ease, as well as contact with the Bodhisattva (the Christ) should the need arise.

Fifth Initiation

The Revelation

Within the realm of human development, the fifth initiation represents the point of consummation. Though there are several initiations beyond this, they are of an entirely different category, for they take one to states of consciousness beyond the realms of earthly evolution. The fifth initiation is therefore crucial, in that it represents a transition point between one regime of development and another. When one reaches this lofty state, the title of master is fittingly bestowed. It represents a refinement of the qualities demonstrated at the fourth initiation, the renunciation.

At this stage, the initiate is truly perfected and liberated, and is called either a Lord of Compassion or Master of Wisdom. The distinction between the two is based upon whether the individual has primarily traveled along the heart or mind path of development. In both cases, these beings epitomize true spiritual freedom. The capacity to manipulate devic substance is now at a highly perfected state, thus making it possible for the *adept* (fifth degree initiate) to wield his will to create forms that uphold and support the evolution of our planet. The master is one who is intimately connected to the Will of God, and has a profound responsibility to be a conduit for its expression.

Often, a master will take the position as hierophant of an *ashram*. Such a being is therefore responsible to carry forward some aspect of the Plan (of God). In addition, an adept holds the responsibility to assist those who are evolving within his ashram. An ashram is a hierarchy of souls responsible for the development and expression of some aspect of God's evolutionary agenda. From the perspective of the soul, every human being is affiliated with an ashram, either directly or peripherally. The degree of participation in an ashram is largely defined by one's evolutionary status. It is at the third initiation that intimacy with the master is consciously felt, and ashramic responsibility is correctly realized.

The work of the master is extremely broad and influential to the world. Invariably, such labor will have far reaching effects upon the consciousness of humanity as a whole. The master must implement a new project that will have both esoteric and exoteric implications to

At the fifth, the title of Master is rightly conferred, for perfection has been achieved.

life. Whatever the project may be, it will always carry the saving force of love within it. For the work of the master ever relates to the salvation of life on Earth, human or otherwise. In short, through the very nature of his being, a master must demonstrate his *masterpiece*. It is a masterpiece that has the power to uplift the human condition through the power of divine love and wisdom.

The fifth initiation is sometimes called the *Revelation*. This title makes reference to the fact that, at this initiation, the revelation of the Higher Way of Evolution opens up before the eyes of the adept. The *Higher Way of Evolution* is an occult reference to the fact that evolution continues beyond the fifth initiation, and there are seven paths available to follow. These ways out of our earthly system represent the next regime of spiritual development. At the fifth initiation, these pathways become evident. They are, as it were, a revelation. However, the choice of which higher path to follow does not occur until the sixth initiation, an initiation entitled The Decision. Nonetheless, insight of further opportunity is granted at the fifth initiation. Also revealed at this time is the nature of planetary purpose. With such insight, the adept can rightly apply his force in the creation of his magnum opus.

This overview has been an attempt to broadly examine the nature and requirements of initiation. They are, as it were, milestones of development. Each initiation indicates a degree of mastery over the form nature. Knowing where one stands in his evolutionary development is crucial, and this for two reasons. The place where one stands determines the scope of service that may be rendered. Each initiation adds potency to the radiation of the disciple. This heightened vibration will then translate itself into acts of service. The higher the vibration, the broader will be its uplifting effect

The Master is the greatest of white magicians, for he knows of planetary purpose, and the masterpiece he must create.

upon the environment. Secondly, where one is stationed on the path defines his developmental challenge, for it indicates the nature and character of the burning ground (tests and crises) across which he must learn to walk.

Initially, when people try to determine their place upon the ladder of evolution, their assessment usually tends toward an inflated view. Indeed, inflation is not only possible, but even probable. The imposter of the soul is initially involved in this assessment, and will amplify the truth as a function of its own self worth. Later, we will discuss the imposter in much detail. For now, simply understand that the imposter represents an aspect of the personality that believes itself to be the soul. As such, it will create images and thoughts within the mind that seem to support higher status than is truly the case. The imposter has a vested interest in viewing itself as spiritually elevated, particularly as compared to others.

Frequently, inflation will be based upon a similarity that exists between certain initiations. For example, the first and third initiations resemble each other in certain respects. As such, it is common for a first degree initiate to believe that the third initiation has been taken. The first and third initiations are sometimes referred to as *solar initiations*. By this is meant that the realization of the soul (solar) is the centerpiece of the initiatory experience. In the case of the first degree, the disciple's personality is flooded by the light of the soul, while at the third initiation the light of the soul intensifies so as to take dominion over the entire personality. Herein lies the root of the confusion, for they both seem to indicate the soul's victory. Yet in the case of the first degree, the personality is only partially *solarized*.

There is similar confusion when comparing the second and fourth initiations. These are sometimes call *lunar initiations*. Central to them both is a crisis related

Knowing where one stands on the path of evolution is important, though inflation is often woven into the conclusion.

to the forfeiture of some cherished form (lunar nature). In the case of the second initiation, it is a crisis related to prized feelings. Such states must be surrendered, even though they hold much appeal. With the fourth initiation, it is the relinquishment of the causal body that stages the crisis. Both are therefore centered on the repudiation of attractive forms. Both are extremely painful, at least as compared to the first and third initiations. The discomfort stems from the pain of relinquishing a form (emotional or causal) that the disciple has relied upon as confirmation of his spiritual identity and value. The point to be made here is that, due to these similarities, people will often gauge themselves wrongly. Humility, and a vigilant eye to detect the imposter, is the best antidote against the tendency to overestimate one's place.

Looking in two directions at once will neutralize the inflated view. The disciple then can know where he truly stands.

There is a paradoxical aspect to be considered when trying to determine one's place. Throughout the esoteric teaching, the injunction to take the eyes off oneself is sounded forth. Behind this idea is the notion that when one "revolves upon the pedestal," attention is placed on serving others. There is a definite tendency for spiritually committed people to become overly preoccupied with their own development. This is a form of spiritual selfishness, and is rampantly found. It is therefore sound advice to direct one's attention to the needs of others. Yet, paradoxically, to know where you personally stand is an occult platitude of importance as well. Herein lies the paradox.

At first glance, these two axioms may appear contradictory and mutually exclusive. Yet when they are properly understood, both are recognized as true and need to be experienced simultaneously. The key to solving this mystery can only be discovered through inner experience. Nonetheless, a clue can be given in considering the words *decentralized introspection*. The disciple must learn to condition the act of introspection with an enveloping thoughtform that is decentralizing. Implicit in this is the ability of the disciple to look honestly at himself, while simultaneously knowing that he is but a cell within a larger life. Indeed, it is to move consciousness in two directions at the same time. As always, the resolution of a duality holds the key to transformation.

In closing this subject, it is well to remember that the spiritual path is incremental by nature. The effort toward enlightenment can therefore be viewed as a step-by-step process, and the initiations are the steps themselves. Importantly, initiation is ever something that is earned. It is not something that one simply stumbles upon. Each initiation is inherently laborious, and pain is ever its companion. For initiation always entails the death of something deeply cherished within. One does not take initiation in an attempt to expand consciousness. Rather, initiation indicates that such expansion has already been achieved. A person is therefore initiate before being initiated. Initiation is a rite of passage only bestowed to those who have demonstrated that they have already arrived.

Initiation is not an invitation, but an acknowledgement of status earned.

The Third Eye

Returning now to the overarching subject—magic upon the mental plane—we consider the third eye. It would not be an overstatement to say that successful magic is governed by the use of this *eye of vision*, as it is sometimes called. The third eye is an etheric organ of perception that directs the magical process along intended lines. Through it, the soul sees outwardly into the realms of form. By so doing, it is able to navigate the creative process in accordance with the archetype that the soul seeks to outwardly manifest. It therefore would serve greatly our considerations if we examine the third eye, its nature and role.

To begin, it must be understood that the third eye is an organ of discernment existing primarily in etheric substance. Though it has been equated with the ajna chakra (center between the eyebrows), this is only partially true. When we want to consider the third eye as it relates to the seven major etheric chakras, it is useful and appropriate to associate it with the ajna center. More fundamentally true, the third eye is something that emerges through the interaction of two chakras, and later a third. The two chakras are the ajna and crown centers. It is within the energetic interplay occurring between these two centers that the third eye emerges.

During one's spiritual development, this eye of the soul gradually opens through the increased free flow of energy moving between these two centers. However, as one nears the stage of transfiguration, the alta major center also becomes awakened and operative, and a triangular interplay between the three then appears. This center is found near the base of the skull, approximately where the head and neck join. Technically speaking, the third eye becomes *fully* opened through the interplay of these three centers. When this occurs, the third eye emerges precisely in the same place as is found the cave within the head. From one perspective, the third eye (when fully developed and opened) and the cave are identical structures within the head's etheric field.

When considering the third eye, we must examine the unique contribution it offers to the magical work of the soul. The eye of the soul facilitates the creative process in three ways, and an understanding of these functions is crucial as the would-be creator gradually learns how to regulate his creative urge.

> *The third eye slowly opens over time. When wide, it rests within the etheric cave.*

*The third eye sees the soul
hidden within outer forms.*

The third eye makes it possible for the magician to see the soul hidden within all things. No matter how diverse and distinct the outer forms may be, there is the sense that something of the divine is working within and through all forms. Forms represent an aspect of divinity encased within a shell of substance. As such, this material shell (mentally, emotionally or physically considered) is merely the out-picturing of the divine spark of life hidden deep within it. However, it must be remembered that the manifesting shell (form) is never as pure as the divine light found at its core. Instead, it is always distorted to some extent. When the third eye is at least partially open, the magician is then able to see through the distortions of a particular form, and thereby detect the spiritual essence attempting to express itself through that form.

The capacity to witness the soul within all things varies greatly from person to person, and is a measure of one's standing upon the path. The wider the opening of this *eye of vision*, the greater is one's capacity to see through the distortion. When the eye is fully opened, the magician is able to see the sacred fire hidden behind all forms, even those considered gross and despicable by ordinary standards of judgment.

With such vision, the magician also recognizes that underlying the multiplicity of surrounding forms is a hidden unity undetected by the five senses. Because of this, he is able to ascertain the divine purpose seeking to be expressed through such forms. The fundamental goal of magic is to uplift the environment. Therefore, sensing the spiritual love and purpose seeking expression through environmental forms (mental, emotional and physical) is an obvious prerequisite to any magical

Hidden within every form and circumstance is a unitive field, and when the eye is open, soulful unity is truly revealed.

endeavor. Upliftment of a larger whole facilitates the evolutionary intention of the unitive life animating that larger whole. From this understanding comes a useful definition of service. That is, service represents any action rooted in the vision of the soul lying behind form or circumstance, and a yearning to give assistance to its outer expression.

The third eye is the director of the magical process.

> *The single eye provides the directional cue. Right placement and timing are known through its view.*

The second role played by the third eye is that it acts as directing agent for the magical process. Spiritual teachings have long proclaimed the occult axiom that "energy follows thought." Such an idea is essentially true, for the act of attending to an idea is to dedicate living energy toward it. Yet, what is often overlooked is the concluding phrase of this ancient aphorism. In its entirety, it states that *"energy follows thought, and the eye directs the energy."* By this is meant that when we speak of the magic of the soul, it is the third eye that guides the entire creative process. This capacity makes it possible for the soul to correctly aim the thoughtform. In addition, the eye not only provides placement insight, but also discerns the correct timing for such placement. If wise timing does not accompany the magician's creative work, then all his efforts become impotent. However, when the third eye is fully functioning, an accurate assessment of timing is assured.

The personality, in its attempts to ascertain right timing, will usually gauge it incorrectly. Most often, the sense of timing possessed by the personality will be conditioned more by convenience to itself, rather than the needs of the environment. In truth, this is a litmus test of great value when creating in the outer world. To what extent is creative timing governed by personality convenience, as opposed to actions impulsed by the deeper rhythms sensed within circumstance? This is the question that we must ask ourselves at each and every creative moment. We will examine this process in greater detail when discussing the final stages of the magical process. For now, let it simply be said that the third eye sees this deeper rhythm, and will direct the magical process according to this vision.

The third eye acts as a destroying agent on behalf of the soul.

Lastly, the third eye acts as a great destroying agent for the magician. To understand this role, we must first review the nature of thought and the composition of the mental plane. It must be remembered that thoughts are living things. A thought is an assemblage of a myriad of minute lives of mental substance called elementals. Every thought is a construction of these elementals configured in such a way so as to depict an intended idea. As such, a soul-inspired thought is a living form that *represents* a formless intuition.

You will also recall that elementals are the living particles that, in their totality, compose each of the planes of consciousness. For example, the mental plane is really a field of mental elementals. Each particle of this living substance is a single elemental life. When these elementals assemble into a form, a thought is then realized within the thinker's mind. These elementals have, inherent within them, a measure of rudimentary intelligence. A thoughtform is therefore understood as the sumtotal of the rudimentary intelligence contained within the many elementals that go into its assembly. Actually, a thoughtform is more than this, for through its assembly, synergy emerges.

A soul-inspired thoughtform gives representation to a formless intuition, and is composed of living particles of substance.

Interestingly, elementals are not free agents. Instead, they are the living cells within a much vaster devic (angelic) entity. Devas are beings of wide and profound intelligence. In their totality, they are intelligence itself, and exist as part of the Mother Principle within creation. Each deva is composed of a myriad of elemental lives. Elementals are therefore the intelligence found at the cellular level of a devic being. Devas could therefore be regarded as intelligences, each composed of uncounted granulations of living substance.

When we consider the plane of mind, mental elementals are the living cells within the devic entity that ensouls the entire plane. This is an important idea to remember. In the Eastern tradition, this great angelic entity is called Lord Agni. These elementals have an ancient loyalty toward this overshadowing deva, and are therefore subservient to it. The magician must find the means to force these elementals (contained within the thoughtform) to transfer their allegiance to the soul, and away from this overshadowing angelic entity. This is however no easy task. Only the soul is capable of creating this abdication, and this via the utilization of the third eye. This is what is meant when we say that the third eye is a destroyer. It destroys the bonds of loyalty held by mental elementals toward the deva of the mental plane.

We need only examine the nature of our thought life to see the power of the elementals in their faithfulness to the larger devic life. During the process of concentrated thought, if the mind strays from an intended idea, this indicates that the elementals composing the idea have departed back to their mother deva, and have not yet yielded to the soul's authority. Such elementals are still loyal to the larger devic life ensouling the mental plane. While the thinker is focused upon the thought, these aggregated elementals will gradually (or abruptly) be

Strong are the bonds of loyalty that the elementals have toward their mother deva lord.

pulled away from the thinker by their deva superior. As such, the thinker (soul) has not yet won the allegiance of these elementals.

To truly do spiritual work, the soul must gain the loyalty of the elementals it utilizes, for magic demands that the will of the soul ever be the controlling agent. The soul must therefore gain directive mastery over the thoughts it constructs. The awakened third eye gradually makes such capacity possible. When the third eye is opened and operative, it has the power to force these elementals to forfeit their allegiance to Agni, and yield to the soul's dictates. This is done through the destructive power wielded through the third eye. When this power is transmitted via the eye, the bonds that tie these elementals to Agni are destroyed. The soul is then victorious, for it has forced the constructed thoughtform to bow to its reign. No longer is the thought capable of being pulled from the control and regulation of the purposeful thinker.

The wielding of this destructive power is a capacity possible only when the disciple nears the third initiation, the transfiguration. It marks a point when the third eye is almost fully open. This power becomes emergent when the two previously discussed capabilities of the third eye are already well developed. The magician's ability to see the unity underlying diversity and to sense correct direction of the magical process are both essential prerequisites before the third eye, in its destructive role, can be used safely.

At first glance, it would seem that a battle is here suggested between the thinker and the angelic entity (deva lord) that overshadows the mental plane, the prize of which is the elemental lives themselves. Such a view, though seemingly natural to conclude, is nonetheless erroneous. It is not that the soul must commit theft against Lord Agni. Rather, the soul must demonstrate

> *When the eye opens wide, the elementals yield to the soul's creative will. A deva lord they no longer seek.*

that it has earned the right to gain control of the mental elementals it is using to construct its thoughtforms. It is an occult fact that devas seek to give to the evolving human soul precisely what it needs to achieve its creative aim. However, this gift is not one that is freely given. Instead, the soul must demonstrate that it has developed a rightful relationship with the intelligence inherent in the elementals it seeks to possess. We must therefore determine what is meant when considering right relationship between devic life and the human soul, for it is fundamental to the magical process.

Devas give to the soul the elementals it needs, though conditional the gift will always be.

As already mentioned, the deva kingdom represents the livingness of substance itself, and is the sacred expression of the Cosmic Mother. However, occultly considered, substance is far more than simply the physical substance with which we are all accustomed. All planes of consciousness are planes of living substance stratified according to its essential nature and density. Certainly it is not difficult to consider the possibility that substance within the physical plane is living, particularly when considering the nature of the cellular life that composes one's physical body. In point of fact, all physical substance is living, not simply that which science has labeled as organic. Inorganic matter is as much a representation of life as organic substance. It is only humanity's limited perception and understanding of life that prevents us from recognizing the life inherent in all physical substance. Most important to our current considerations is the notion that feelings and thoughts are categories of living substance as well, and they too are living.

Every emotion or thought we experience is really an assemblage of minute lives of substance of a grade far subtler than the substance of the physical plane. When experiencing a thought within the mind, we are really experiencing a thoughtform. This thoughtform is the product of countless particles of living mental substance assembled in such a way so as to reveal an idea within the mind. Indeed, the grade of devic substance used to build a thoughtform defines the nature of the idea that has been constructed. In simple terms, a thoughtform constructed with mental substance of high grade will be experienced in the mind as a lofty and progressive idea. Naturally, the converse of this is also true.

The geometric patterning of a thoughtform is what determines its content and character. We are told that God is the great Geometrician, and the out-picturing of His work is creation itself. By analogy, this is true of the white magician as he seeks to manifest forms within the outer world. The geometry of a creative thought is revealed in the fundamental principles that it reveals. Sacred principle is at the core of all creative ideas. These ideas come forth from the buddhic plane, the plane of geometric archetypes. When the geometry that substands (underlies) a thought is correctly embedded within it, beauty emerges as a feature of the thought itself. In truth, this is a gauge of creative expression coming from the soul. When of a spiritual source, a thoughtform (and its effects in the world) is recognized by its inherent beauty. This is because, at its most essential level, beauty and truth are synonymous terms. The beauty inherent in divine geometry takes form as sacred ideation. This is an occult axiom of monumental import.

The geometry of a soul-inspired idea is revealed through the sacred (though hidden) principle that it embodies.

To experience an emotion is to experience an emotional form within one's astral body. Just as with thought, an emotion is a thing, and because it is, we become conscious of it. In truth, consciousness cannot exist without the perception of an object, either within or without. This principle is obviously true when we consider physical experiences as well. We can't internally register anything in the outer world unless the physical environment presents itself to us as a form(s). To see, touch, taste, hear and smell is to become conscious of physical form in some fashion.

Right Relations with the Devas

Having reviewed the role of substance and its relationship to thinking, we shall now consider our topic under discussion. That is, that the goal of evolution and magical work is to establish right relationship with the substance used in the construction of thought. As earlier stated, the soul does not simply take dominion (via the third eye) of the elementals that it uses. It must also earn the right to possess these particles of assembled thought. The question is, what constitutes such a right? Within the magical process, what must the disciple demonstrate for the soul to take control of these mental elementals? What does it mean when we say that right relationship with devic life must be established?

The answer to these questions is twofold. First, there is the right relationship that must exist between the thinker and the thoughtform he has constructed. This relationship must be based upon detachment. It is crucial that the sense of identity (self) not be associated with the thoughtform that the magician has built. This type of detachment may seem easy, but such is not the case. Until the third initiation, the self will have the tendency to define itself by the thoughtforms it has constructed. There is an automatic proclivity of the psyche to believe itself to be the thoughts that it is having.

To illustrate this, let us say that a doctor believes himself to be a brilliant surgeon because his mind easily conceives of new and progressive medical techniques. In short, he tends to define himself based upon the mental experiences he is having. Yet these are just

Right relationship occurs when the thinker avoids identifying with the productions of the mind.

labels that define identity, and are not identity itself. Beingness (a word for true identity) transcends all thoughts, feelings and physical experiences. Until the third initiation (transfiguration), an individual will have the tendency to misidentify himself in this way. As we have stated, right relationship must be established before the Mother (representing herself as a devic entity) will release the elementals that an individual uses in his thoughtform constructions. He must show that he can create thoughtforms, but do so while remaining disidentified from them. When such is the case, right relationship is achieved, and the soul thereby earns the right to take dominion of the elementals involved. Prior to this, the overshadowing deva will not permit their departure.

The second type of right relationship that must be established deals with inter-elemental relations. It must be remembered that each elemental life represents a spark of living divine intelligence. Needless to say, this intelligence is amazingly small and rudimentary. Yet, it is in the assemblage of these fiery particles that a synthesis of intelligence occurs, and a thought then manifests within the mind. The better and purer the construction, the loftier and more profound will be the thought. To earn the right to dominate these elementals requires that the thoughtform be built in such a way that the highest truth possible is produced.

As simple analogy, let us examine the construction of a home. Using the same materials (analogous to elementals), an individual can assemble a home in many ways. Yet, there is a pattern of construction that, if sensed and followed, will result in the erection of the best home possible given the quantity and quality of the materials available. It is to get the absolute premium performance out of the materials used. So it is with thoughtform construction. Each elemental has inherent

"Assemble my intelligence into forms that yield wisdom true." So say the angels.

intelligence within it. When constructing thought, the disciple must assemble these elementals so that they yield the highest truth possible. This requires that the thoughtform be built efficiently, and without waste. The ability to do this is not possible unless the soul, rather than the personality, remains the guiding force in the magical effort.

This explains why the third aspect, the Divine Mother (intelligent substance), wields the cosmic *Law of Economy*. This law simply states that evolution is perpetuated when thoughtform construction is done in an efficient manner. It mandates that the elementals (used in the construction of an idea) be configured in a manner that will reveal the highest truth possible through their assembly. This suggests therefore that when economy of thoughtform construction is evident, right relationship between the elementals has been established. The resulting thought is then geometrically beautiful, and is able to convey the greatest wisdom possible (given the evolutionary status of its constituent parts—elementals) to the mind of the thinker. When this relationship is achieved, the soul wins the loyalty of these elementals. Devas seek to serve the will of the human soul, but only when the thinker can establish right relationship with the elementals they (devas of the mental plane) have donated to his cause.

The Law of Economy is wielded by the lords of devic life.

Condensation Next Ensues

- Magic on the Astral Plane -

We now consider a most interesting and important phase of spiritual creativity having to do with the role of emotion. Often in occultism, there is discussion about the negative aspects of emotion. We have been told that the emotional body is colored by desire, and is therefore antithetical to spiritual development. This is, of course, quite correct. Desire is a major obstacle to be overcome on the road to enlightenment. This we shall soon discuss in great detail. Nonetheless, it must be stated that emotion is also a great asset when used correctly in the magical process. After a thoughtform has been constructed, it descends into the magician's emotional body where needed warmth is added to it. This descent represents a movement of the thought or idea toward its externalization into the outer world. We must therefore consider the importance of emotion as it contributes to the creative process.

Though emotion must one day be transcended, it is still used to create magical effects.

The Attributes of Emotion

Emotion adds two attributes to the creative process. That is to say that emotion serves to qualify the creative process with two essential characteristics. They are:

- Astral vitality
- Magnetic appeal

As a thoughtform descends into the emotional body, a sheath of astral (emotional) substance begins to encase it. This sheath is essentially fluid in nature in that the astral plane corresponds to the element of water. Metaphorically, the waters of emotion condense upon the thoughtform. This moist layer adds a feeling quality to the soul-inspired idea held within the mind. At this point in the process, the magician is not only thinking a creative thought, but also is experiencing a feeling about it. This is what is meant when stating that a sheath of *astral vitality* has been added to the thoughtform. It simply suggests that the individual has now associated an emotion with his creative idea. This added layer is crucial to the magical work in that it gives vitality to the thoughtform. Because of it, an individual is able to experience a measure of enthusiasm for his idea, which is an essential factor in its externalization.

Vitality and attraction are added when a layer of emotion enwraps an idea.

This notion should be no surprise to us, for we are all too familiar with this principle in our day-to-day lives. Are we not best able to manifest those things toward which we *feel* conviction? This is the great gift that emotion can bring to the creative process, for it adds conviction and zeal to our ideas. By so doing, a new vitalness becomes operative in the magician's inner experience. With this added vitality, there comes a sense of propulsion, and it is this that drives the thoughtform outward toward full externalization.

The second attribute that emotion gives is the power of *magnetic appeal*. When a thoughtform takes to itself an emotional sheath, it then becomes attractive. In the highest sense, the emotional body is a vehicle governed by the Law of Love. When emotions are used correctly, the descending thoughtform becomes attractive and appealing. Warmth and magnetism are added to the thoughtform, both of which are essential to the soul's creative effort. Soulful magic is ever conditioned by love, and should be appealing to others. The emotional sheath gives humanness to the thing being created. It is often the feeling aspect of an idea that is first recognized by those whom the magician is trying to reach and uplift. Most often, the service he renders relates to the upliftment of others in some way, and the means is through interpersonal warmth and caring. In other words, the majority of people (but not all) will tend to distrust the ideas of another if there is not a sense of warmth connected to the person and the idea being advocated. This quality of magnetic appeal is therefore essential in the work of white magic. It is the force that personalizes an idea as a prerequisite to its acceptance.

The Problem of Desire

As we have discussed, emotion plays a vital role in the magical process. Yet, the world of emotion is filled with peril as well. Given this fact, the magician must learn of these dangers in order to steer clear of their perilous consequences. There are two broad categories of challenges related to one's emotional body. They are the *problem of desire* and the *problem of inversion,* both of which need to be addressed. Due to its desirous nature, the emotional body is extremely powerful. In addition, this vehicle has had historical dominance over the affairs of the personality. That is to say that one's emotional and desirous tendencies have been the central force leading the personality to act and react to life circumstance. As such, it is not surprising that disciples find their emotional experiences to be most challenging.

Though subtle to detect, desire is at the root of most of the personality's actions and reactions in life, with rationalization lending its support. Desire tends to give impulse to thoughts in support of itself. This is the great challenge related to the personality as it (rather than the soul) initiates thought. When the personality gives impulse to thinking, it will often do so in conformity with its desires. This is why the emotional body is

The desires of the personality are the greatest obstacles to disciplic life and magical work.

considered a great impediment to spiritual development. More precisely, it is the desire nature inherent within the emotional body that the disciple must learn to transcend or redirect.

The personality is essentially one's consciousness as defined by form and desire. Yet, the spiritual journey requires that one disidentify with the personality, and thereby discover the true eternal self (soul) within. In the magical work, one must therefore realize the subtle power of the emotional vehicle, and be vigilant to detect its actions. For those upon the path, this tendency can be difficult to detect, for it is often surreptitious. It is very easy for an individual, if not watchful, to color his thoughtforms with personal desire, rather than the magnetic quality of love and warmth.

Desire and love are similar in both vibration and experience. In fact, desire can be understood as a lower expression of love. This reduced expression is also magnetic, for implicit in desire is the notion of attraction to something. As noted earlier, the emotional vehicle is destined to conform to the Law of Love. It is this law that leads the disciple to create forms that are divinely magnetic rather than desirous. Fundamentally, this is done through the transfer of energy within one's chakra system. Magnetic desire is transformed into divine love, and corresponds to the lifting of the solar plexus energy to the heart chakra. By so doing, the magnetism rooted in personality yearning is converted into the attractive power of unconditional love.

For rightful white magic to be performed, the heart, not the solar plexus, should be the source of magnetic appeal. Unlike the solar plexus, the magnetic appeal of the heart is not based upon a need to possess. Instead, it is rooted in the realization that all things are truly one, and therefore there is nothing outside oneself to possess. The solar plexus vibration, though also a generator of

Desire is a lower rendition of love. Both are attractive, though one self-servingly so.

magnetic appeal, has individualized that appeal. As such, its magnetism is limited and is rooted in the urge toward self gratification. Indeed, desire gives impulse to form's yearning to possess other forms.

Spiritual evolution is in an inverse relationship to desire. For what is evolution, but the gradual process of detaching from all forms that have the capacity to attract? This is true whether speaking of desires as they manifest within the physical body, or those that are rooted in emotional craving or mental yearning. All are forms of desire, and all must eventually be mastered for true spiritual liberation to be had. Every human being must eventually learn to face his desires and find the means to overcome their attractive pull. We must therefore deeply examine the origin and nature of desire in order to eventually overcome its persuasive power.

Out of Oneness flashes forth the Sons of Necessity. A choice they have not.

Sons of Necessity

To truly appreciate the nature of desire, we must first consider it from a cosmic perspective. Essentially, desire is a force that pervasively exists within the entirety of cosmos. That is to say that desire is the energy that drives all things into manifestation. It is a yearning inherent within all units of life. This is true whether we are referring to an atom, a human being or the life that ensouls an entire galaxy. All entifications (grades of realized identity) are inherently conditioned by the need to express themselves within and through substance, and this for the purpose of self-discovery and creative expression. It is to *shine forth* into form. From the human perspective, this is the soul's magical decree. Occultly speaking, all forms of manifested life are therefore referred to as *Sons of Necessity*. Out of cosmic necessity, all units of life must leave the unitive condition of the One Life and enter into the field of form and multiplicity.

No matter what magnitude of life we may consider, desire is foundational to it, for it represents the search for Identity within the confines of form encasement. Desire is, in essence, the force of involution within the entire universe. Wherever desire exists, life also is found in a form-bound condition. From the universal perspective, desire is the *divine will to manifest*. It is an inescapable necessity governing all categories of life, and is inherent in creation itself.

Though desire is responsible for outer human existence, it also is a major hindrance to spiritual evolution. It is therefore a paradoxical force within creation. From the highest perspective, desire is the impulse that causes all to incarnate for the purpose of self-discovery. Yet when life finally evolves into the human kingdom, desire becomes the nemesis to that discovery. Desire directs the soul to incarnate for the purpose of growth and development, while at the same time it is responsible for the glamours and illusions that inevitably arrest such development. Hence, there is a great dilemma and mystery that surrounds desire and the means to overcome it.

The reason for the paradox is, in point of fact, not the fault of desire, *per se*. Rather, it is our inability to properly relate to the force of desire that makes it an obstacle upon the path. Here is where the problem can be found. Desire thrusts the soul into incarnation, but paradoxically leads one to misidentify with that which is being desired. For example, when desire leads the soul to experience itself in mental substance, the soul then tends to confuse itself with the mental forms in which it is immersed. Desire to possess then emerges, and the indwelling entity (soul) assigns self-value to that which it desires. In short, desire has been converted from a

> *Desire is a paradoxical force. It gives birth to life, though also imprisons it.*

vertical energy (which is what perpetuates incarnational existence) into a horizontal force (resulting in the tendency to misidentify with form).

For the purpose of clarity, we shall henceforth refer to desire as a horizontal misapplication of the vertical energy evident in all of creation. With this definition, we will consider desire strictly by its negative effects, divorced from using the word to depict the urge to manifest inherent in the One Life itself. Actually, this is an important notion in that it does give added clarity to the evasive relation existing between will and desire. In occultism, these two forces are viewed as mysteriously connected, though their link has been difficult to fathom. From the distinction just made, we can see that will is the desire to manifest, as it is impulsed from the One Life (or the human monad), while desire (in its typical usage) represents the horizontal conversion of this will, and the consequent distortion that inevitably arises due to such a conversion.

Will and desire seem similar, and yet they are not. The first moves vertically, while the latter favors the horizontal.

The Root of Ahamkara

Desire is what gives birth to *ahamkara*. When operative, it causes people to perceive themselves as existing within a condition of lack, and it is from such perception that a preoccupation with "I-ness" emerges. The tendency to self-reference (ahamkara) is based upon the notion that one is separate from the larger whole, and as such, is deprived of the qualities inherent within that larger whole. Desire therefore creates within consciousness the need to acquire things outside oneself, and this under the false belief that a deeper sense of inner wholeness will be achieved through its satisfaction. Here we see that desire is being misapplied. It is being used as an agent in support of building self-awareness, when in fact the opposite is really happening. Identity, which is the sacred root of self, is transcendent to form, not dependent upon it. The higher purpose of desire is to provide the impetus to establish right relationship with the outer world, rather than identify with it. Self-discovery comes not from being possessed by form, but by realizing oneself as the possessor of form.

Interestingly, though we have suggested that desire will lead human beings to misidentify with form, it is also true that evolution necessitates this illusion. Misunderstanding oneself is a precursor to true self-knowing. Therefore, it is true to say that, up to a certain point, desire serves a necessary function in the development of the soul. Essentially, the human soul loses itself within substance, only to later rediscover itself. This rediscovery involves detachment from the forms previously desired. Misidentification with form therefore serves the evolutionary needs of the soul. It teaches the soul what it is not.

When considering desire and the psychological variables that relate to it, fear is obviously involved. Fear is ever the companion of desire, for if desire is based on the perception of lack, then fear will inevitably emerge as a reaction to that perception. Fear has no footing when one experiences a genuine condition of psychological wholeness. When fear is absent and wholeness is experienced, there is no sense of want. Considered in this manner, we can see why mastery over desire is a prerequisite to enlightenment.

Spiritual development is truly the process of coming into greater and greater states of wholeness and self-realization. Desire and fear are therefore antithetical forces arrayed against the soul's evolutionary intention. These two forces are paradoxically both friend and foe to the soul. They are enemies to the soul from the perspective that they prevent one from further spiritual

When fear and desire unite, want is confused for need.

ascent. Yet they are friends when viewed as way-showers, revealing that which is next to be redeemed within oneself. Where fear is found, so too is found one's imprisoning shackles. The nemesis to spiritual development is found where desire holds sway. Through the recognition of one's fears and desires, an individual learns what next to overcome. This is the blessing ever hidden within the curse of desire.

How then does one manage to overcome desire? Before exploring this question, it should be noted that the conquering of desire is truly a relative event, and not absolute. That is to say that when viewing desire as a fundamental force propelling the evolution of cosmos, desire is something inescapable. Viewed in this manner, every unit of life within creation is confined by desire. As has been said, this is true whether speaking of the life within an atom of substance, or the entity that ensouls a solar system (Solar Logos). However, if we limit our consideration of desire to the three worlds of human evolution (mental, emotional and physical), it is then possible to speak of freedom from desire. In point of fact, those beings who are often called the Masters of Wisdom have demonstrated that the overcoming of desire is not only possible, but is a prerequisite to final release from life within the human kingdom. Down the ages, these great sages have demonstrated this release. By their example, we are given insight into the nature of our own struggle toward liberation and freedom.

Mastery over human desire is possible and must eventually be. The way has been shown.

Desire and Karma

There is a direct relationship between the measure of desire operating in one's life and the calibration of his karma. Karma is created through the misunderstanding and misapplication of desire as that desire expresses itself over many incarnations. All human karma needing redemption is rooted in one's misuse of desire. As such, desire has been operative through countless lives.

This idea is foundational to the teaching given to us by Gautama Buddha twenty-five hundred years ago. He wisely conveyed the esoteric precept that desire is the source of all human suffering. Within consciousness is found the tendency to grasp or possess. This impulse is fundamental to human woe, for it is the force within each of us that ultimately separates us from each other. It is this *heresy of separation* that inevitably brings pain. Desire gives birth to this heresy. It persuades us that by possessing what we desire, we shall then feel more complete. We desire to possess something simply because, in our yearning, we unconsciously believe that we will gain a sense of wholeness from it.

The heresy of separateness is an illusion created by man's desirous nature.

This unconscious assumption is not given only to material attractions, but is related to the subjective impulse to possess as well. For example, our yearning for personal love is also based on desire, and if over-emphasized, is detrimental to spiritual advancement. Invariably, the object (or subjective feeling) that is desired never seems to make us feel as whole as we had thought it would. The positive feeling associated with the purchase of a new automobile, for example, wears thin after a short time. When first purchased, the feeling is quite good, and unconsciously we feel better about ourselves because we feel good about what we now possess. However, as already mentioned, this good feeling is relatively fleeting and eventually leaves us in a condition of wanting once again.

The same is true when desire for another person is experienced. When acted upon, we assume (usually unconsciously) that he or she will offer us a deeper sense of self-realization and satisfaction. This is based on the notion that the feeling of happiness is a barometer indicating movement toward self-realization. Yet such an assumption is an illusion, for to find oneself through another is not possible.

In truth, desire always involves outward movement, while the search for the self is ever based on an inward and upward motion. We all must eventually learn that wanting is a force far greater that having. For aeons, we have been seeking to find ourselves through that which we desire. The attraction toward form must eventually give way to the realization that the outward tendency to grasp is essentially ephemeral in its results, and only deflects one from the eternal within.

Overcoming Desire

How then does one overcome the persuasive pull of desire? To answer this question, it must first be recalled that the emotional body is the personality vehicle having the greatest affinity with desire. From the occult perspective, emotion is desire after being personalized. That is to say that to a human being, desire is experienced as a personal feeling state. It is a yearning that prompts one to outwardly move on behalf of self-satisfaction. Desire is therefore any feeling experience that results in self-validation. Anything that is self-satisfying is self-validating.

One's emotional nature is therefore the instrument that is prompted by the dictates of desire. When we desire something, we experience a feeling of attraction toward it. Indeed, when we experience repulsion toward something, this too is the product of emotionally impulsed desire, though in a reverse manner. For when rejecting something, we are experiencing the desire to be what it is not. In short, emotion (as well as desire) is always dualistic and is self-defining through either attraction or repulsion.

Desire governs our attraction to form or our repulsion from it.

When considering how one overcomes the seemingly inescapable power of desire, it must be remembered that no problem is ever solved on its own level. Simply stated, desire cannot be overcome through its own agency. Instead, the solution is only possible when one observes the nature of the desire body (emotional vehicle), but does so upon a higher perch within consciousness. The higher perch noted here is that of the mind itself.

The mental vehicle is made up of substance of a higher grade than that of the emotional instrument. As such, when it is rightfully (and soulfully) used, the mind is considered a superior vehicle through which the soul functions. In point of fact, it is on the mental plane that the soul itself, the causal body, is found. Therefore, when the mind is well developed and spiritually oriented, it has the capacity to help one to defeat the covetous tendencies of the emotional body. It does this through the power of discrimination—an attribute of the mind essential for spiritual progress. The discriminating mind has the ability to provide one with the capacity to discern the subtleties of his desirous yearnings.

Desire is so pervasive within the average individual that detection of it, as a force separate from the object of desire, is nearly impossible. Due to its juxtaposition, desire goes unchecked by most people. It is so much a part of one's reactive nature that we tend to view it as inseparable from the object of our yearning. Yet through the use of clear discerning thought, an individual can begin to observe his emotional responses to life and circumstance. An understanding of the conditions that trigger desire can then slowly be recognized. From this emerging insight follows a cognitive consideration as to how to master desirous impulses. The mind first learns to understand the desire body, then slowly discovers the means to gain dominion over it. It is the discriminative

The problem of desire is always solved on a higher perch deep within.

nature of the well-exercised mind that makes such a victory possible. This is because the discriminative mind can discern the difference between desire and the object of desire. It is also the mental faculty that helps the self to know itself as something separate from that which it desires.

At this juncture, it is important to state that mastery of the emotional body is not achieved through hardened restraint of one's astrality. Too often, people willfully put their emotions into a state of repression, believing that through an enforced subjugation, mastery is achieved. This view is based upon a misunderstanding of emotion and the role it plays in service to the soul. When the mind is used to hold emotion in a condition of repression, it is not transforming emotion, but rather denying its value or even its existence. The soul seeks not to deny the desire body, but rather to transmute its independent tendencies so that it becomes a cooperative instrument in service to the soul. In order for the soul to be creatively effective, it needs a reliable emotional instrument to relate to the outer world. The goal of personality transformation is not the elimination of emotion, but the surrender of the emotional body to the soul's creative agenda.

Repression is detrimental to one's psychological health and the magical intention of the soul. Most often, it represents an inner defense emerging in response to a fear of emotion. This fear is rooted in a mistrust of emotional experiences. As you know, the discriminative mind is essential to spiritual progress. Yet due to this fear, the mind can wrongly restrain emotion via repression or denial. Such defense does not eliminate the energy behind feeling states. Instead, it imprisons it within the recesses of the unconscious, only for it to eventually find an outlet that is pathological to healthy personality expression. Needless to say, psychologists

> *Repression of emotion is not advised. Instead, its independence must give way.*

→ Bach flower

have long understood that neurotic tendencies are symptomatic of this phenomenon. The psychoanalytic model of the human mind is essentially correct in this regard, though wayward in its corrective measures.

From the esoteric perspective, it is the mind, as guided by the soul, which is used to transform the emotional body, thus making it a willing servant. The mind must be astute to the subtleties that give rise to desire within the emotional body, while simultaneously honoring and loving the thing it is discerning. The soulful mind ensures that divine love accompanies the discriminative process, thus preventing the tendency to repress. Lovingly, the mind must keenly discern the impulse of desire. When an emotion or desire is found to be unwholesome (via the distinctions made with the discriminative mind), the soul then bathes the baneful form with transformative love. In short, it is the mind that can detect the desirous enemy in need of transformation, and it is the soul that applies the corrective measure. Such is the way of evolution.

The discriminative mind gives remedy to the problem of desire.

The Problem of Inversion

We shall now consider a most challenging feature when living a spiritual life. It has to do with what can be called the *problem of inversion*. When speaking of this, we must first realize that life within the three worlds of form (mental, emotional and physical) has an inherently distorting effect on the soul's capacity to express itself. The self (soul) seeks to redeem and transform the three vehicles of the personality so that they become pure and unfettered reflectors of its purpose and creative intention. When this has been fully achieved, it indicates that the soul has developed mastery over all the lower cravings that have long governed the personality. This is a notable achievement, and one that every spiritually oriented person is destined to accomplish in some incarnation. Prior to the soul's liberation from the independent tendencies of the personality, there is found a wide range of distorting effects that occur within consciousness. The sum total of these effects represent the *great illusion*, a collective distortion rooted in our tendency to perceive reality in an inverted manner.

All of humanity, including those who are living a spiritual life, are conditioned by the great illusion, though at varying degrees. Such a claim can be made simply because there are few who have as yet won liberation from the distortions of form life. We do however have the testimony of the Great Ones, those liberated souls who have shown humanity the way, and have proven that freedom from the illusions of form is possible. In point of fact, it is inevitable, though the time factor varies according to the discipline and readiness of the individual in question. Because of this, it behooves us to consider the nature of these distortions, for we will then be better prepared to win freedom from them.

Occultly considered, there are three categories of distortions, each corresponding to the three vehicles of the personality. *Maya* is the category of distortion caused by the physical body's tendency to act independently of the soul's agenda. *Glamour* is the term used to describe the misperceptions created by the ungoverned passions of one's emotional vehicle. *Illusion* is the term related to the misapprehension of truth formed within the human mind. However, the purpose of this discussion is to present these distortions in a slightly different manner. We will not examine here these categories of distorted perception, but rather focus on the subtle distinction existing between divine truth and personality distortions in general. The premise is that there are misapprehensions occurring within consciousness that are very similar to divine truth.

Humanity is imprisoned by the Great Illusion, a distortion created by consciousness and its tendency to invert.

Sometimes these are referred to as the *near enemies* of truth. They represent divine principles that have been inverted as a result of the impure forms through which they are seeking to work. They are up-ended perceptions of truth, therefore very similar to the truth itself. The need to discern the difference between a divine principle and its near-enemy is therefore quite important.

An example of this inversion is related to the quality of compassion or empathy. Compassion is a feature inherent in soul consciousness itself. To care about another's welfare, from the vantage of soul-centered realization, is to experience genuine empathy. Empathy gives evidence that the soul is conditioning one's perceptions. It is rooted in the capacity to sense the soul within another person. This type of perception is only possible when the third eye is at least partially open. The soul then has a means to reach deep within the other, and to thereby sense the soul behind the veiling forms.

When one subjectively experiences empathy for the suffering of another, it means that his soul is (at that moment) in a communal relation with the soul of the one in pain. As such, empathy emerges as a reflection of an established inner unity. Because of their subjective union, the pain witnessed by the perceiver is felt as if it were his own. Such is the nature of a genuine empathetic experience. Yet, we must realize that the near-enemy to empathy is sympathy.

Sympathy is easily confused for empathy, for it has similar features to it. They both represent responses to the pain of others. Both are experienced as feeling states of discomfort, and both give the appearance of soulful compassion. However, sympathy is the near-enemy to empathy because it contains within it the element of separation. Sympathy is an emotional response to the pain of others, but not due to identification with their pain, but instead through mere recognition of it. Always

The inversions of consciousness give birth to the near-enemies of truth.

with sympathy there is hidden a sense of gratitude that one is not the person experiencing such pain. Sympathy is therefore based on the emotional discomfort one has when witnessing the pain of others, coupled with a hidden appreciation that the other person's predicament is not one's own.

Empathy, on the other hand, is always experienced as an embodiment and identification with the pain of another simply because the soul recognizes itself in the other. This does not mean however that empathy results in the forfeiture of the observer. The "director on the stool" is still internally held. The sensed unity is still experienced, but is realized at the level of higher consciousness, and not on the emotional level, as is the case with sympathy. It can be seen therefore that sympathy is an inversion of the soul's natural capacity to be empathetic.

Sympathy is the near-enemy of empathy.

The above example is just one of many inversions that we experience. Through the distinctions made between them (spiritual qualities and their inversions), progress upon the upward way is possible. The reason for such inversions is interesting. It is a phenomenon largely due to the deflecting power of substance itself. As the truth and quality of the soul radiates into the substance of the personality, it is distorted by that substance. This mutation of the original energy is due to the impurities found within the personality. Prior to the Transfiguration (third initiation), the personality still has a measure of independence. This independent aspect has not yet been purified enough so that it can supplicate to the will of the soul. Even so, it is still being energetically irradiated by it. As such, it takes the soul's radiation and twists it ever so slightly to meet its own ends. The personality does this by personalizing the radiation it is receiving. Always at the heart of any near-enemy will be found a measure of self-reference, as well as the tendency toward separative perception.

To understand these inversions, it may be useful to examine them as phenomena emerging out of astral substance. In the lower three worlds, the emotional plane is most prone to invert truth coming from the intuitive realms of the soul. As you know, emotion corresponds to the element of water, while intuition (buddhi) is most related to air. For purposes of analogy, let us consider these two elements in their physical relation to each other in the outer world. The sky (air) is above both land and sea, just as the intuitional plane hovers over the lower planes of consciousness. Considering this, imagine sitting on a hill overlooking a pristine lake. On a calm day, the blue sky and clouds are reflected in the water below. When the water is perfectly still, this reflection will likewise be perfect, but with one major exception. That is, it will always be an upside-down reflection. Herein lies a useful metaphor regarding the nature of astral substance within consciousness. As in this metaphor, the watery plane of emotion tends to invert the vibrations descending from the intuitive (air) realm of the soul. The resulting forms seem to be truth, but they are in fact inversions of truth, having been distorted by personal desire. This is the root source of the near-enemies we are discussing here. Spiritual evolution therefore requires a vigilant eye toward these psychological inversions. Sometimes, the gap between truth and distorted truth is nearly imperceptible.

Viewed from a still deeper perspective, the culprit of this inverting tendency is more than simply one's emotional body. The substantial life composing the threefold personality (as a whole) is also responsible. To understand this, it must be remembered that the substance contained within the mental, emotional and physical vehicles is living. Sometimes called elemental

Truth and its inversion can be quite difficult to differentiate. Their similarity is the source of this difficulty.

lives, these minute living particles have an ancient loyalty to the demands of a much vaster angelic entity. This entity is the Deva Lord that gives life and animation to the substance of an entire plane of consciousness. For example, though the emotional plane is teeming with astral elemental life, the sum total of these elementals represents the consciousness of a vaster overseeing Deva Lord. These elemental lives have a historical loyalty to this overseeing deva. Yet when a person has established a measure of soul-infusion into the substance of the personality, that substance is understood to have abdicated its allegiance in favor of the soul. As such, the soul, and no longer the Deva Lord, has sovereignty over these elementals. When this occurs, the energy and truth transmitted to these elementals will be rightly registered. When the substance is not yet soul-infused, that substance is still devoted to its devic superior. The energy received (from the soul) by these elementals is then distorted because of this misaligned allegiance. Such distortions are the near-enemies of the soul's radiation and truth. Discussed below are a few other inversions worthy of note.

Inversion is rooted in the loyalty that elementals have toward a vaster angelic entity, a Deva Lord.

The Inversion of Love

As is well known to anyone seeking to live a more spiritual life, love is an essential characteristic of the soul itself. Love governs the power of the individual to recognize the unity that underlies the multiplicity so apparent in our world. Yet in most cases, love has been misunderstood, even by many well-meaning spiritual people. More often than not, what people call love is really a feeling state based primarily on an unconscious need to be loved and wanted. As such, love is typically viewed in the context of self-reference. It is viewed as a prized feeling that, when experienced, is largely self-gratifying. In short, the inversion of love is desire.

From the deeper and more soul-inspired levels, love is experienced as something void of self-reference. To the soul, love represents the magnetic principle woven into the fabric of creation. It is the force that unites all things, and this for the purpose of demonstrating that all is one. Esoterically, love is not an expression of need. Instead, it is the magnetic power inherent in divinity to draw all things into right relationship so as to reestablish the memory of the Original Condition. Love is a thing unto itself, and it needs nothing for itself. By this it can be seen that the personality's usual relationship to love is conditional. Therefore, it is an inversion, for genuine spiritual love is unconditional, and is never governed by desire or need. The near-enemy to divine love is therefore desire, and to internally recognize this distinction is crucial to spiritual development.

The near-enemy of love is desire. Authentic love wants not for itself.

The Inversion of Intuition

This type of inversion is commonly experienced by many people, particularly those of spiritual inclination. What is often thought to be an intuition is actually the reflection of intuition within the emotional body. As a result, this reflection is usually associated with a feeling state. However, true intuition has little relationship to emotion.

In its pristine state, intuition is actually formless realization. When registered in consciousness as a thing (a form), it is frequently noted as an emotional form. However, this is really a psychic experience, not an intuitive realization. When an intuition is primarily registered as an emotion, the likelihood of distortion is great. Indeed, most (but not all) psychic experiences are inversions of intuition and are colored by personality emotion. As such, reliable intuitive impression should not be evaluated based upon its feeling quality, but rather upon the wisdom it conveys. When impressed by an intuition, it is the higher mind that is the rightful recipient, while its emotional reflection is best viewed as secondary. The abstract mind is the layer of consciousness that is immediately below the intuitional plane, and it is there that correct registration of intuition is most likely to occur.

Though psychic experience is usually an inverted reflection of intuition, its real power comes forth from the instinctual mind. That is to say that the foundation of psychic phenomenon is in our animal nature, not our divine nature. Esoterically understood, instinct is a lower reflection of intuition, but is not intuition itself. Before the monad began its development in the human kingdom, it spent aeons of time evolving instinctual consciousness within the animal kingdom. Instinctual mind is still with us, as it should be. It provides human beings with the capacity to broadly sense outer circumstance in such a way that a reflexive response is made possible when needed. However, when the gift of instinct is coupled with emotion or desire, we experience an elaboration of it beyond its natural usefulness. This elaboration is what is most often referred to as a psychic experience. Fundamentally, psychism is an inversion of intuition due to emotional embellishment of instinct.

Psychism is rooted in the instinctual mind, and was developed when living life in animal form.

It can be quite difficult to distinguish between psychic impression and a genuine intuition, at least at first glance. Both intuition and psychism represent the capacity to sense something beyond normal perception. In addition, they are revelatory in that they both reveal something seemingly important or even prophetic. Yet, the litmus test has to do with the nature of the impressions received. Psychic impressions are normally clear cut and well defined, while real intuition is comparatively vague and difficult to touch and hold. Psychism will have an obvious feeling component to it, and it is therefore related to the solar plexus. Hence, one may say, "I have a gut feeling about something." On the other hand, true intuition is far less related to feeling states (though it does connect to the heart center). Intuition is felt in the heart and registered in the mind. Lastly, psychic phenomenon is far more personal and self-referencing than is divine intuition. Listed below are a series of contrasts between intuition and psychism that may be useful to consider.

Table 1: Intuition Versus Psychism

Intuition	Psychism
Rooted in the nature of the soul	Rooted in the instinctual nature (animal soul)
Governed by upward inclusiveness tending toward synthesis	Governed by separative tendency
Requires a well-developed abstract mind to interpret impression	Requires a sensitive emotional body, and the negation of the discriminative mind
Inclusive of psychic powers	Not inclusive of intuition, but is a forerunner to it
Willfully utilized and controlled by the thinker	Not controlled by the thinker, but instead it simply happens
Realized through mental illumination	Realized through feelings of aspiration

Table 1: Intuition Versus Psychism (Continued)

Intuition	Psychism
Relates to group consciousness, and is guided by ashramic purpose	Relates to herd consciousness, and is guided by personality desire
Reaction (by others) results in contemplative thought leading to mental understanding	Reaction (by others) is emotional, often giving comfort or inflaming pre-existing biases

The Inversion of Group Consciousness

As we enter into the Aquarian Age, the theme of group life becomes increasingly important. Aquarius is the sign of group activity and service. As a result of its energetic influence, humanity is destined to gradually evolve toward collective activities that promote human amalgamations and humanitarian initiatives. This philanthropic tendency will emerge as a result of humankind's growing capacity to see its unity. Such vision will be dependent upon our ability to recognize ourselves as servants working on behalf of a larger life, which is the single livingness of humanity itself. Group mind can be understood as service-consciousness based upon an inner sense of spiritual unity.

It must be stated here that true group consciousness is related to unity experienced on the level of the soul, and not based upon personality sentiment. It is governed by an interior recognition of our spiritual commonality. This is group consciousness as it is understood in the higher sense. Yet, the inversion to group consciousness clearly exists. Commonly referred to as mass consciousness, this inversion holds much of humanity in its grip.

Humanity is still largely governed by its collective opinion. By and large, most of society unconsciously tends to conform to the view held by the masses. This form of mass consciousness, though representing a necessary step on the ladder of evolution, must eventually give way to true individual thought and initiative. We must each learn to rise above mass persuasion to become independent free thinkers. Yet, this too is only a step that will eventually lead to group consciousness. True group consciousness is unitive by nature, yet simultaneously honors and supports the gifts of individualism. Mass consciousness, on the other hand, is an inverted reflection of group consciousness. It tends to negate individual reason in support of emotionally generated unity. From the occult point of view, the evolution of the human species is a movement from mass consciousness to group consciousness, via individual reason and intellect.

To see the hold mass consciousness has upon humanity, one need only examine the power of propaganda in our society. Its capacity to move the masses is phenomenal, and largely governs societal opinion. The distinction between group consciousness and its near-enemy, mass consciousness, has to do with several factors. First, true group consciousness requires that individuals possess a mind that is independent and free from mass persuasion. Secondly, a spiritual group is governed by an inner sense of unity, and does not necessarily require that they outwardly assemble. Group consciousness suggests that one is sensitive to an inner unity of purpose, and that this purpose is being touched by a world group. It therefore has no relationship to physical location of group members, or even having interpersonal acquaintance with them. In addition, each

Human evolution moves from mass consciousness to inner group awareness, but does so via the freedom of intellect.

member of a truly spiritual group will act upon the sensed inner purpose in unique and creative ways.

Conversely, the masses will define their unity based upon physical or emotional elements of commonality. Nationalism is an example of this force within society. It is largely based on mass acceptance, and when strong enough leads to isolationism and sometimes war. This is a frequent characteristic of mass consciousness. It tends to isolate itself by polarizing its view in opposition to another view.

Fundamentally, mass consciousness is rooted in the herding instinct developed when living life within the animal kingdom. This herding tendency still largely governs the behaviors of much of humanity today. For many people around the world, the urge to reside in large metropolitan areas can be traced to the fear of being separated from the herd. Clearly, it is an instinct that serves the animal kingdom well in that it provides power and safety in numbers. An animal is completely identified with its physical form. As such, its physical survival looms large, and from this emerges the herding instinct. The same tendency is still rooted in human beings, even though the destiny of humanity is to rise above misidentification with the physical body. As such, mass consciousness is essentially governed by fear related to survival issues. This is however not the case with group consciousness. Instead, to respond to an inner group calling results in a yearning to help humanity in its evolution toward spiritual liberation from form, and away from fear.

Mass consciousness is a derivative of the herding instinct and is governed by fear and survival concerns.

Unanimity and its Inversion

In contemporary society, the theme of unanimity is widely promoted. This can be seen in the many and varied group initiatives operative in the world today. However, upon close examination, it will be seen that what is often considered unanimity is actually an expression of its near-enemy, uniformity. Though thought to be synonymous, these two terms are actually defined quite differently. The distinction can be found in the construction of the words themselves. Unanimity relates to the unity inherent in *anima*, the soul. Conversely, uniformity reflects the establishment of unity via the regimentation of *form*. One relates to the inner unitive field where all souls know themselves as one, while the latter is suggestive of outer compliance through the obedience of form.

Sacred and wise is the principle of unanimity, though its outer reflection, uniformity, will often lurk nearby.

Unanimity is a sacred principle governing the soul itself. It does not demand the forfeiture of individual free will. In truth, it is based upon the commonality of soul quality, and the unity of spiritual purpose inwardly sensed. As such, groups that really function as centers of unanimity do so without any forced conformity in the outer world. All members are completely free to express this united purpose in individual and unique ways. This is not so when groups give way to uniformity, for it does not provide for individual expression. Uniformity is therefore the inversion of unanimity.

Hierarchy and its Inversion

In the ancient esoteric teaching, the Principle of Hierarchy is fundamental. It is the notion that all units of life exist at different stages of development. All things evolve, but their place upon the evolutionary ladder of life will differ widely. We can speak of this principle as it plays out within any particular kingdom in nature, as well as compare the stages of advancement between kingdoms. We must remember that *essentially* all units of life in creation are equal, for they are all sparks of light emitted by the one great light, the One Life itself. The life unit that ensouls a tree is absolutely equal to that which animates a human being or even a superhuman entity. When it comes to examining pure spirit, all is utterly equal. Yet, there are differences when it comes to the *degree of consciousness* that has been developed, and this is the basis of all expressions of hierarchy existing within creation.

All units of life (monads) are gradually seeking to develop the capacity to be fully conscious, and are evolving through kingdoms in nature to acquire such capacity. As such, there is clear developmental distinction within creation. For example, a human being has developed his consciousness further than the monad living within a flower or animal. Humans have the capacity to be self-conscious—a thing not yet possible within the animal or plant domains. However, if we compare a person to the entity that ensouls a planet (planetary logos), we also see an enormous contrast, but in a reverse direction. A person is far less developed than a being of such magnitude. This is essentially the nature of hierarchy. In truth, hierarchical structures of life are found in all dimensions of creation and are therefore inescapable.

Even from the cosmic perspective, this principle is operative. The Solar Logos is developmentally superior to all planetary logoi contained within His body of manifestation. When comparing the development of different planets, some planetary logoi are further evolved than others. For example, the entity ensouling Venus is far more developed than our planetary logos, and ours has developed its consciousness farther than has the Lord of Mars. From this we see that even when

Hierarchy is a principle inherent within creation, and manifests as gradations of consciousness.

comparing equal categories of life (in this example, planetary logoi), there is differential development. Within the human kingdom, this is true as well. Some people are further along the path toward enlightenment than others. There is therefore a hierarchy of spiritual development within the human kingdom itself. The key point to grasp is that hierarchy is pervasively evident throughout all of cosmos. We see it in nature itself, as well as in the differing spiritual capacities that people have gradually acquired over countless incarnations.

The Principle of Hierarchy and that of Equality, are not mutually exclusive.

Interestingly, as we enter into the Aquarian Age, there is emerging a resistance to the Principle of Hierarchy. Many spiritually minded people choose to deny hierarchy because it seemingly negates equality. Yet as I have mentioned earlier, equality is the most fundamental truth present within all aspects of creation. Occultly considered, equality and hierarchy both stand as foundational spiritual truths. It is therefore crucial to accommodate both these truths within one's perspective.

The reason for the resistance to hierarchy is twofold. First, it is an immature reaction to the Aquarian energy slowly coming into manifestation at this time in history. Though Aquarius provides humanity with the stimulus to see the unity of life, its adolescent effect tends to create an initial denial of hierarchy. It is through this rejection that Aquarian unity will be sensed. In the early phases of the Aquarian era, this is to be expected. Yet, such reactionary shifts must eventually find a point of equilibrium again. If not, humanity (as we now know it) will surely collapse into chaos and decay. For if hierarchical distinction between genius and ignorance is not acknowledged, evolution itself shall surely be arrested. The future of humanity rests on the eventual recognition that hierarchy and equality are both spiritually true. Indeed, they are inescapable laws woven into the very fabric of existence itself.

The second reason today's spiritual community tends to reject hierarchy is actually more important to consider. It has to do with the historical misuse of this principle within the human kingdom. For centuries, humanity has suffered under the oppressive force of hierarchical structures within society. Historically, people who have risen to positions of power and control have tended to misuse such power through the exploitation of those they lead. Naturally, I am speaking in wide generalities. Nonetheless, within contemporary society and throughout history, ambition and greed have usually been companions in the exercise of power. Regrettably, it is the mass of humanity that has suffered as a result of this deadly combination. The wrongful use of hierarchical structures by humanity is the near-enemy to the Principle of Hierarchy.

In occult literature, it is common to refer to the Masters of Wisdom as the Hierarchy. These beings have risen to heights of spiritual accomplishment far beyond humanity's developmental status. They represent the acme of our earthly evolution, and have selflessly chosen to commit themselves to the upliftment of our world in some way. They are hierarchically superior to us in consciousness, and are guides that can and do lead the way. However, the Hierarchy is not operating through greed and oppression of the masses. Rather, these masters demonstrate profound selflessness and wield no power that creates wrongful effects. From the spiritual perspective, this is how the Principle of Hierarchy is rightly to be expressed.

This has been an overview and discussion of a few of the many inversions of truth that occur within human consciousness. Following are additional inversions that frequently manifest as well. A watchful eye toward these distortions is well advised.

The near-enemy to the Principle of Hierarchy emerges through the misuse of authority.

Divine Principle	Inversion of Principle
The Soul	Imposter of the Soul
Spiritual Power	Ambition
Integrity	Separateness
Wise Caution	Fear
Self Respect	Pride
Discrimination	Criticism
Interdependence	Codependence

Solution to the inversions of the mind lies in our ability to look beyond what we abhor in order to sense the sacred truth that it veils.

The solution to the problem of inversion necessitates that we begin to examine those aspects of our world that we most abhor, then probe deeper into them to determine what divine principle(s) they are distorting. Instead of discarding what we think is wrong, let us seek the spiritual truth hidden within it. Too often, spiritually minded people overlook the fact that humanity's expression of divine principles (such as hierarchy) are inherently convoluted and distorted. Out of frustration, we tend to discard the principle, believing it to be erroneous, rather than seeing it as a malformation of something sacred. From the esoteric perspective, this approach to interpreting reality is essential.

The Emerging Mist

Returning to our discussion, it must be realized that moving a soul-inspired idea into the emotional plane is intrinsically difficult. This is due to the fact that it involves the interaction of relatively incapable elements. When we speak of the mind, we are really discussing a state of consciousness related to fire. The "fire of the mind" is the producer of thought. Yet, the emotional body is related to the element of water. We therefore see an inherent challenge. To bring a thoughtform into the emotional body is to bring fire into water. Whenever these two elements are joined, steam is the consequence. A foggy mist emerges. This characterizes well the magical process at this juncture. Often, the disciple will begin to add an emotional feel to his thoughtform, and the resulting fog can lead to internal bewilderment. Regrettably, this misty condition is often not recognized by the creator. Herein lies the problem.

When we have a good idea, there follows an emotional surge. This surge is that which ultimately generates commitment toward the idea. Yet as this happens, a measure of uncertainty emerges as well. This uncertainly centers upon the question of how to direct the thoughtform into the outer world. Questions as to method and timing also come to the mind, and answers to these questions seem elusive and unclear. In short, the emotional energy that generates a sense of enthusiasm and conviction also creates a veil that blocks one's perception of the *correct* next step.

Paradoxically, with this obscurity of vision, there is also an impulsivity that is simultaneously felt. The enthusiasm (now built into the idea) causes the individual to passionately jump forward to further manifest his thoughtform. However, this step is often done too quickly, particularly when the inner state of blurred vision still exists. It is akin to standing in open space on a foggy day. The fog is spotty and undulating, thus at one moment distant vision is possible, followed by a loss of such sight due to the shifting mist. When traveling through such countryside, it is well to take added time before moving on, and this in order to be certain that the perceived direction is actually the correct one. The fog must be lifted so that the traveler can ascertain the correct heading to travel.

Metaphorically, this is precisely the dilemma the magician faces when building emotion into his thoughtform. There is a measure of uncertainty as to

When the fires of thought meet the watery sphere, mist and fog billow and swell. Vision is then impaired.

what the correct next step should be, and when it should be advanced. A pause is therefore well advised. This pause facilitates the sharpening of the magician's vision. It allows time for the disciple to establish an inner balance between thought and feeling, and to gain clearer vision in the process.

When facing this phase of uncertainty, the utilization of intuition is crucial, for it is a trusted compass used by the magician at such times. The stillness of intuition gives the disciple a sense of the larger whole once again, and affirms how and when the thoughtform should move forward. Such a pause is also a test of sorts. As already noted, the emotionally charged thoughtform will tend to trigger an impulsive urge to move forward. When acted upon, as it often is, the magician has failed the test, at least for the moment. It indicates that the emotional body is not under his control. Instead, it is controlling him. It gives clear evidence that the form led the thinker, rather than the reverse. Many progressive thoughtforms, inspired by the souls of well-meaning people, have been prematurely moved forward in this way. This is why today we witness a tremendous amount of distorted truth evident within the spiritual community. Many of the activities of the so-called New Age Movement are examples of this distortion.

An impulsive urge toward activity is strong when water bathes the form, yet clear direction suffers. A pause is therefore well-advised. Intuition then serves as compass true.

Meeting the Left-Hand Path

The dangers of magic on the astral plane are often not recognized. When this is the case, the resultant forms can become grotesque disfigurements of what was intended by the soul. In the more extreme cases, this has caused well-meaning people to unknowingly step upon the left-hand path, the path of selfish magic. Perhaps needless to say, the term "left-hand" in no way references people who favor their left hand over their right. It is nothing more than a very old convention used in occult literature to identify spiritual waywardness. In point of fact, many of the most advanced disciples in today's world favor their left over their right hand. Please keep this in mind as these terms are used.

In the esoteric literature, we are given to understand that a disciple cannot be fully trusted (by the Hierarchy of Masters) until he has demonstrated relative mastery over his emotional body and its desirous tendencies. No one is truly a white magician until such mastery is achieved and proven. Until then, the level of service the disciple can render will have limited scope, though certainly useful nonetheless. When the emotional body has been reigned in by the soul, then the magician is given the opportunity to more broadly serve the human race. He is now trusted, and the commensurate level of responsibility is bestowed upon him. Such expansive and inclusive opportunity is most often revealed within the context of the initiate's life circumstance.

Until a disciple is "trusted," the left-hand path poses a danger to him. As such, it would be useful to discuss this perilous path, for it is upon the astral plane that its enticement is first encountered. Fundamentally, the left-hand path is the way of the so called black magician. Essentially, this path is the route that supports selfish gain. Creative processes that are largely self-serving are given to this left-handed approach to life's travels. In short, it is personality magic.

Interestingly, there are very few (if any) real black magicians operating in the world today. However, many people, including most spiritually committed people, would best be described as grey magicians. This is because aspirants usually create with mixed motive. Altruistic intentions are frequently interwoven with selfish motives. Through honest self appraisal, most of us are forced to acknowledge that we often walk two

The wayward path must be walked beyond before one is occultly trusted.

paths simultaneously, and therefore are neither white nor black magicians. Instead, gray appears to be the shade of choice. This is not a criticism, but simply a statement of fact. In truth, one's place upon the spiritual path can be gauged on this truism. It is the ratio of soulful magic versus personality magic, demonstrated within the crucible of life, which gives evidence of one's spiritual status. The mixture of soul versus personality magic simply reflects the measure of soul-infusion within the personality.

One of the most deceptive aspects of spiritual living is the fact that the left-hand path often looks like the right-hand path in the beginning. Frequently, an individual will have a soul-inspired idea and will desire to share it with the outer world. Yet when emotion is added to the idea, there is often a misperception as to the correct path to outwardly direct it. There is frequently a lack of clear directional discernment. Usually, there are several options that the disciple will see, and all look attractive and spiritually useful. Even so, there is one path of expression most favored by the soul.

The left-hand path looks much like the right when first it is encountered.

The discernment between directional options is crucial. Without it, the magician may follow a line of activity that looks spiritually uplifting, but is not, or is only marginally so. More often, good intentions mask hidden motives. Importantly, these are the motives that give subtle impulse to the choices made. Herein lies the challenge. This is additional reason why the magician should pause from action at this point in the creative process. Such an interlude will give him the time needed to internally assess the motives behind his interest in pursuing one path over another. Again, it is not always the obvious motive that is important to recognize. Instead, it is the hidden motives that one must vigilantly examine. In truth, it is the motive lying behind the *apparent* motive that is most threatening to successful magical work.

With an added pause, the disciple will have the needed time to sort out the correct option, and this based upon the litmus test of selfless intention. Motive is always measured by the degree of ahamkara existing at the time. Ahamkara is defined as the tendency to self-reference. It is the personality in its many guises that is prone to ahamkara, not the soul. Not only does this pause give time for assessing true motive, but it also counters the impulsive need to act which naturally arises when one charges an idea with feeling. Therefore, it can be seen that pausing at this stage in the magical process is the solution to two forces that work against the magician. They are the force of hidden motive and the unbridled urge toward action.

The Imposter of the Soul

Because of the dangers associated with left-hand magic, it is well to discuss the imposter of the soul. To begin, we must understand the nature of the self and its role in the magical process. The self is a construct used to define oneself. It is actually a working hypothesis of identity and is governed by the *vertical axis of being*. By this is meant that the self changes as one inwardly evolves to higher states of consciousness. When loftier states are realized *and held*, the self is also vertically uplifted and changed accordingly. At any given moment, one's sense of self is polarized at some point upon this vertical axis of being.

Where a person is polarized (on the vertical axis of being) reveals his current level of development. It also reveals the breadth and scope of his capacity to serve the outer world. The higher one's consciousness (therefore self-construct), the deeper and broader is his capacity to

The self is a construct within consciousness, and is found upon the vertical axis of being.

work with finer grades of mental and emotional substance. In turn, this reflects itself in the magician's capacity to outwardly influence and uplift, for the power to do so is defined by the grade of substance one is able to manipulate. This is a fundamental principle in all magical work.

Though the process of assessing one's point of development is crucial, there is an inherent danger to be avoided while doing so. The glamours that easily creep into one's self-perception are what create the challenge. These glamours are distortions of the self, and are best understood as self-referencing inflations. In truth, they are over-estimations of one's developmental position, scope of responsibility and spiritual authority. For aspirants and disciples, these inflations have their root in the personality. However, it is not the entire personality that is the culprit, but only an aspect of it. That aspect is here referred to as the *imposter*.

The imposter represents an aspect of the personality that wrongly believes itself to be the soul. It is the spiritually attentive aspect of the personality, and is soul-like in its appearance. Upon the spiritual path, the emergence of the imposter is a certainty. The challenge is to discern it from the soul itself. Without such internal discrimination, an individual can become prey to traveling a wayward path, while falsely believing that he walks the right-hand path, the path of soulful magic.

To understand the emergence of the imposter, we must first discuss the nature of soul-infusion. Occultism teaches that the soul seeks to infuse its nature and guidance into the personality. When this is achieved, the individual is said to be fully soul-infused, a point of development reserved for initiates of the third degree. However, the expression "soul-infused" must also be understood as relative, as are so many of the descriptives used in this teaching. Technically speaking,

The imposter is the part of the personality that falsely believes itself to be the soul.

soul-infusion means that a part of the personality has yielded to the authority of the soul. In truth, a person's initiatory status is simply a measure of how much soul-infusion has thus far been achieved *and held*. Therefore, spiritual evolution is really based upon gradational development. It is a gradation rooted in the ratio existing between the soul-infused portion of the personality, and the part of it that is still unwilling to yield to the soul's authority. The gradual infusion of the soul into the personality is graphically depicted in *Figure 7, Soul-Infused Personality*.

Spiritual development is gradational, and is based upon soul-infusion and its measure.

Soul-Infused Personality
(partial)

Figure 7

The soul-infused portion of the personality is that aspect of the lower self that has been redeemed. It is the part of the personality that has supplicated itself to the soul's regime, no longer wanting for itself. This is the part of the personality through which the soul can work. Importantly, the soul needs a cooperative personality to provide upliftment and service to the outer world. Hence, the degree of soul-infusion evidenced in an individual defines how effective will be his soul-inspired service in the world.

As the soul infuses the personality, there is a non-infused aspect of the personality that benefits from the radiation of the soul, but is not yet infused by it. From this portion of the personality emerges the imposter of the soul *(see Figure 8, The Emerging Imposter)*.

The imposter is that part of the personality next to be infused.

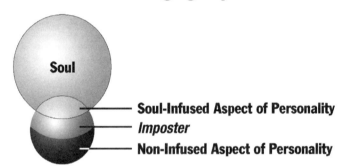

Figure 8

Fundamentally, the imposter is that part of the personality that is aware of the soul's radiation (due to its proximity to it), but is not yet subservient to its regime. It is that aspect of the personality that is on the threshold of soul-infusion. The imposter learns what it means to be soul-oriented, but is not yet required to yield to the soul's superior influence. Instead, it poses as the soul, and therefore portrays itself as the spiritual part of the self, when it is actuality a clever impersonator.

Discerning the Imposter

All upon the spiritual path must eventually find and confront their internal imposter. To do this, an individual must develop a discerning eye. For spiritual liberation cannot be achieved while the imposter still exists and has influence. There are several characteristics of the imposter that are important to note. By being watchful of these imposter traits, aspirants and disciples can begin to recognize their own imposter, and then do what is necessary to counteract it. The characteristics of the imposter, in contrast to the soul, are given here for your consideration.

1. *The imposter falsely believes itself to be the soul.*

Its main method of influence is to disguise itself in altruistic attire, even though it is still oriented toward selfish gain. It must be understood that the imposter gives impulse toward altruistic action, but does so with a sense of planned deliberateness. On the other hand, the soul does not act with near the same level of planning or premeditated consideration. The soul is altruistic by its very nature, and will spontaneously (though wisely) demonstrate this quality.

2. *The imposter is driven toward actions that contain within them the element of self-reference.*

The imposter is a feature of the personality. As such, it is governed by the laws foundational to the personality's existence. Namely, it is an expression of the *third aspect* in creation. That is to say that the personality (and therefore the imposter) is a synthetic point of selfhood rooted in matter. Therefore, the imposter's existence is based upon identification with one's mental, emotional and physical experiences.

Most important to this discussion is the fact that any aspect of the self that is misidentified with matter will tend toward actions that are self-referencing and self-serving. This is a natural and expected feature of the non-infused personality. The reason the imposter will always self-reference is that, by so doing, it reinforces the notion that it is the soul.

This self-validating tendency, though often subtle to detect, is clear evidence of the imposter's presence. Fundamentally, it is an act of self-deception.

3. *The imposter will always have a necessity of seeing the fruits of its labor.*

Validation of the self is determined by the observable effects we create—so says the imposter. The soul, on the other hand, is never in need of such reassurance. This need of the imposter is based on the perception of its finite relationship to time. That is to say that the personality is essentially a finite structure, and as such, its actions are based upon a sense of time gauged within the context of a single incarnation. Because of this, the imposter wants to see the fruits of its labor. However, the soul has a multi-incarnational perspective. It sees over the span of many lifetimes and knows that seeds planted today may not flower within this particular lifetime, but instead during a subsequent incarnation. In addition, the soul is energetically related to the Plan of evolution, while the imposter is not. This Plan, as sent forth by the Masters of Wisdom, covers a vast period of time, and not simply the minute time scale of a single incarnation.

4. *The imposter knows separation, but projects the image that all is one.*

Essentially, the soul sees itself in others, while the imposter doesn't. The soul sees the oneness that underlies the multiplicity of everyone and everything in the outer world. In short, through the opening of the third eye, the soul is able to witness the spiritual dimension of all things, and knows that what it sees is *essentially* itself. However, the imposter cannot see in this manner. Instead, its instinct is to observe the outer world with an eye to the separation that exists between itself and another. It is not able to consciously recognize the underlying unitive field, as is the soul.

When the soul observes another, it knows the other as itself *in essence*, while the imposter has a vested interest in seeing itself as quite distinct from the other. The soul therefore works through the power to resolve duality, while the imposter is incapable of such resolution. Even so, the imposter knows that to be spiritual implies that a unitive vision must be operative. Because of this, it will manufacture (within consciousness) the belief in unity and the conviction that it exists, even though it cannot really perceive it. It will construct a false perception of oneness through the utilization of the lower mind and emotions. In truth, it is an act of self-deception unparalleled.

5. *The imposter sees the trends evident in outer events, then adjusts its altruistic pattern so as to gain from such trends.*

The soul envisions the trend of events as well. However, it sees them as outward manifestations of unfolding spiritual essence as that essence works through circumstance. Conversely, the imposter sees the trends evident in outer forms, but is incapable of sensing the spiritual purpose working behind them. Also important to remember is that the imposter is always self-gratifying. Yet to be effective as an impersonator of the soul, it must create the illusion that there is no personal gain at stake. As such, and with practice, the imposter will eventually become quite adept at disguising personal gain so that it is almost unrecognizable. One of its strategies for doing this is to structure circumstance so that it provides indirect benefit.

6. *The imposter will interact with circumstance to reveal its spiritual prowess.*

The imposter recognizes that by taking advantage of circumstance, it can further its desire to prove its legitimacy and spiritual authority. It therefore looks at circumstance opportunistically. The soul, on the other hand, has no need to demonstrate the proof of its legitimacy, nor does it exploit circumstance in such a manner. It simply expresses what it is. Most importantly, the soul seeks to reveal itself *through* circumstance. When aligned with the higher-self, an individual realizes that every circumstance reveals the soul and its purpose in some way. Stating this idea in a different way, the imposter exploits circumstance while the soul reveals itself through the wholeness of circumstance.

7. *As compared to the soul or soul-infused personality, the imposter will more rapidly rise to levels of spiritual responsibility.*

Governed by the third aspect (form), the imposter's ability to navigate through the outer world with speed and effectiveness is enhanced. This is because the social, economic and political structures that define success are largely based on third aspect principles. Hence, the game played by the imposter is governed by the same rules that society uses. For example, in our Western society, uniqueness is prized, and implicit in this is the notion that sameness is of less value. This is essentially a social paradigm rooted in the third aspect, which tends to support individuality through the negation of unity.

Also evident is that power and influence are usually equated with money and resources, which is another expression of the third aspect manifesting within human consciousness. Uniqueness and power are the fundamental motives at the root of the imposter's actions. It seeks to express its unique spiritual authority and, by so doing, demonstrate power and influence over others. However, as noted earlier, it does so under the guise of equality and false humility. Conversely, the soul always works from the perspective of unitive vision and sees diversity as only a temporal expression of a more fundamental oneness. As such, the soul is ever the representative of the *second aspect* of creation, which espouses unity and the love that underlies outer diversity.

8. *The Imposter is prone to the glamour of destiny.*

The imposter considers its actions to be an expression of its divine right and destiny. The soul too is conditioned by destiny. However, when the soul is operative in the consciousness of the individual, spiritual destiny is not viewed as a divine right, but rather as an inevitable result of soul consciousness. To the imposter, destiny is understood as a preordained right to act along a certain line, while for the soul it is simply understood as a natural outgrowth of being what it is. From the soul's perspective, spiritual destiny does not emerge as a function of *doing*, but rather as a by-product of *being*.

9. *The imposter is oriented around measures of quantity, while the soul attends to quality.*

The imposter evaluates its actions using quantitative measures as the gauge. The magnitude of its effect upon the environment, the number of people it can influence and the volume of spiritual knowledge it has are all considered essential measures of authority and success to the imposter. For the soul, qualitative considerations are fundamental to its actions. When an individual is being guided by the soul, the subjective quality of outer events and circumstance is primary. The soul makes it possible for the disciple to sense the underlying quality seeking to express itself through form. The energy of love, beauty and knowledge are just a few examples of such qualities. The soul understands that quantity is merely a by-product of hidden quality. To the soul, largeness is not a measure of spiritual greatness, while to the imposter, it is.

10. *The imposter seeks opportunities for spiritual expression, while the soul understands that every circumstance offers such opportunity.*

The imposter is selective in its assessment of expressive opportunity. It wants to assert its spiritual insights only under those conditions that seem favorable to its success. Yet when an individual is prompted by the soul, every moment is an opportunity to radiate love and light. Importantly, the readiness of the environment is a consideration to both the soul and the imposter, but in quite different ways. To the soul, an environmental circumstance does not define whether or not to express itself. Instead, the soul assesses the degree of environmental receptivity, then expresses its love and light commensurate to that level. However, to the imposter, the decision to express is comparatively black and white in this regard. Either the environment is able to receive what it can offer, or it isn't. The imposter resists modifying its expression in accordance with environmental need, while the soul has the wisdom and fluidity to make such adjustments.

11. *The imposter holds the view that what is spiritually significant to itself is precisely what others need.*

However, to the soul, what is meaningful to the whole is what it must lovingly give. Here again we see that the imposter is self-referencing. The imposter asserts that what is good for itself must be good for others. When inspired by the soul however, the individual will realize that while there are fundamental principles of spiritual growth that are universally applicable, there are a myriad of developmental factors that vary with each individual or circumstance.

12. *Generally speaking, the revelations offered by the imposter, as compared to those impulsed by the soul, are realized more rapidly.*

Intuitive impressions (coming forth from the soul) are comparatively vague, having little structure to them, at least initially. They are nebulous impressions transmitted from the formless regions of consciousness, the intuitional plane (buddhi). As such, they need time to take shape and develop into clearly defined thoughts and images. In addition, because of their nebulous nature, such impressions will tend to be more difficult to recall. The imposter, on the other hand, hasn't the capacity to access the buddhic plane. Therefore, the images it projects into the mind are not characterized by this initial vagueness, but are instead well formed (comparatively), thus permitting more rapid registration within the mind.

The Surreptitious Imposter

When examining the nature of the imposter, it is crucial to understand that its power and influence become increasingly subtle as one progresses upon the spiritual path. As soul-infusion increases in one's life, the imposter becomes ever more surreptitious within consciousness. Its ability to evade detection increases because, over time, it develops competence at its own self-deception. Perhaps it would be fitting to say that the imposter slowly becomes comfortable with the disguise it is wearing. This results from the fact that it increasingly resembles the soul-infused portion of the personality. In itself, this is both a blessing and a curse. It is a blessing from the standpoint that the imposter is, in one sense, even more ready for soul-infusion, and this due to its familiarity with what is required to be soul-infused. Yet, it is a curse from the perspective that, though the imposter is more ready for infusion, it is harder to distinguish from the soul-infused personality. The disciple must learn to make this distinction.

As the imposter matures, its surreptitious skills will likewise increase. Vigilance is well-advised.

A prerequisite to further soul-infusion, at any stage of a disciple's development, is that the part of the imposter that is next to be infused must first be recognized as inauthentic. One needs to first recognize his deceptive demon before it can be transformed into a cooperative agent of the soul. Because of this, it becomes evident that we must be increasingly vigilant toward this agent of stealth within.

On the next page *(see Figure 9, The Imposter)* is found a symbolic depiction of the surreptitious nature of the imposter. It illustrates that, as soul-infusion increases, detection of the imposter becomes more difficult. This is depicted by the shading in each stage of development. Each level of maturation sees the imposter becoming more soul-like, but not yet infused by the

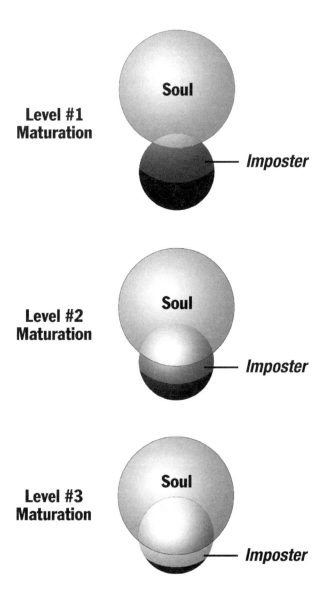

Figure 9

soul. This is what makes discrimination between the soul and the imposter increasingly difficult. At the final stage, we see that the magnitude of the imposter (depicted by its width in the diagram) is greatly decreased, and its shade has lightened considerably, thus making it almost indistinguishable from the soul. We therefore see, in symbolic form, that as one spiritually evolves, detection of the imposter becomes more and more difficult.

It might be asked, when is it that the imposter is eliminated? To answer this question, it is important to realize that the imposter will exist as long as there are aspects of one's lower nature that are not spiritually redeemed. That is to say that as long as there are impurities of any kind within one's physical, emotional or mental vehicles, the imposter still has a stronghold. Indeed, such impurities are the source of its influence and power.

As was discussed earlier, the fourth initiation (the Renunciation) represents the stage of development where one is freed from all impurity and the karma that accompanies it. At this initiation, the individual has been liberated from any distorted tendencies rooted within his form nature. Therefore, at this stage the imposter is completely negated. Much, though not all, of the imposter is actually eliminated by the time the third initiation (the Transfiguration) is reached.

When impurity vanishes, so too does the imposter. Liberation and enlightenment are then due reward.

The Two Types of Imposters

It should be noted at this point that there are two types (or expressions) of the imposter, either of which can be operative within one's consciousness. First, there is the *strategic imposter*. It is this type that has been primarily discussed thus far. The strategic imposter is cunning in its motives, and moves toward influencing one's thoughts with deliberateness and forethought. It is therefore strategic in its actions, for it intentionally positions itself so as to increase its influence by way of stealth. It resolutely believes itself to be the soul, and maintains this conviction.

The other type is the *innocent imposter*. This type of impersonator also believes that it is the soul, but does so out of naiveté, rather than for strategic advantage. Unlike the strategic imposter, this type does not really know that it is misconstruing its identity. It simply concludes that, because it sees itself as good, its identity must be that of the soul.

The imposter, whether of the strategic or innocent type, is essentially a center of temporal self-reference. It knows (consciously or unconsciously) that its existence is finite and can only be maintained for the duration of a single incarnation. Fear of its own mortality stages the imposter's emergence into one's consciousness. It is a kind of existential defense mechanism. When effectively employed, it will shift the imposter's assessment of itself from an identity doomed to future annihilation to one having eternal existence. This defensive shift relieves its existential fear, and must be maintained in order for it to avoid re-experiencing that fear. From this, we can see the deeper reason for the imposter's increasing deceptiveness. Fundamentally, its elusive nature is a safeguard from the perception of its own mortality and the fear that accompanies such perception.

It may be asked, how is the soul-infused personality able to overcome this existential fear? The answer is that this part of the personality is redeemed in that it willingly yields to the soul. As such, it has learned that it is merely a tool of the soul, and not an independent agent. In other words, the soul-infused personality

> *The imposter, whether strategic or innocent, will emerge in response to existential fear.*

knows itself to be the *soul-in-extension,* while the imposter does not have this realization.

The real issue is not based on the termination of individual identity, as the imposter falsely believes. Rather, it is discovered at the time of infusion that the essence of the personality is the soul, and that for the personality to yield means only that it is now willing to establish relationship with its eternal root. What makes the soul-infused portion of the personality different than the imposter is that it no longer misconstrues itself as something independent of the soul. Instead, it knows itself to be merely the soul's appendage. The soul-infused personality knows through experience that that which seems like death is merely a veiled resurrection in waiting. The imposter does not yet know this.

As one progresses upon the upward way, it becomes increasingly important to look for the imposter. History is filled with examples of people guided by their imposter while believing they were led by the inspirations of the soul. One need only look at the many Christian evangelists demonstrating their selfish motive while clothed in altruistic attire. Whether in religious, political or economic circles, everywhere are found wolves disguised as sheep. For those in positions of power, most often it is the strategic imposter that has taken them prisoner. For the masses of well-intended people, the innocent imposter is more to be found. Because of the elusive nature of the imposter, it is not surprising that such misguided actions are common. Everyone is victim to it while treading the path. No one is immune to the imposter's naive or manipulative ploy. As such, vigilance must eventually come into being as a guiding principle of self-examination. Fundamentally, it is ever a question of motives and the discernment of those motives.

The personality is merely the soul in extension, yet the imposter knows this not.

The Imposter as Friend

When learning about the imposter, there is always the risk that the reader may become overly doubtful about his spiritual experiences for fear that the imposter is at work. From this author's perspective, this would be regrettable. The purpose of our discussion has been to reveal the self-deceptive tendencies existing when we attempt to consciously live a spiritual life. Though the tone has, thus far, been critical of the imposter and its motives, it is equally true to call the imposter a friend.

There are two reasons for viewing the imposter as friend and companion upon the path. First, the esoteric philosophy has long advocated the "act as if" technique, seeing it as a valuable tool for spiritual development. This is most certainly true, and it is the imposter that rightly utilizes this technique. To *act as if* builds faculty for eventually embodying the spiritual quality that one is mimicking. As such, imitation is a necessary prerequisite to further evolutionary development. It can therefore be seen that the imposter serves an important and necessary function in one's spiritual growth. What is most important is that this technique be used only when we are fully conscious that we are employing it. Too often, people will wear the mask of the imposter, only to later forget that they are wearing it. Herein lies the danger and why alertness to the imposter must ever be present.

Secondly, the existence of the imposter forces people to develop the power of mental discrimination. That is to say that the imposter creates the conditions needed for the disciple to discern that which is spiritual from that which only seems to be so. It forces one to make the necessary discernment between truth and pseudo-truth. It demands that before an expansion of consciousness can occur, one must learn to distinguish

> *The imposter is a friend upon the upward way of life, for through its rehearsal, infusion comes to be.*

between his spiritual and material natures, and this with unfettered clarity. In truth, it is the imposter that makes this possible, for it creates the subtle illusions needed to test one's discriminative faculty.

It should not be surprising therefore that the fifth ray of divinity (the ray of discriminative thought) is an essential feature to spiritual development. The use of this sacred ray ensures that one is eventually granted entrance into the fifth kingdom in nature (the kingdom of souls), a numerological correlation of enormous import. Learning of the imposter and how to avoid being its victim ensures that the soul will eventually *shine forth*, and this without encumberment. One of the many keys to spiritual evolution has to do with our ability to discriminate a genuine impulse coming from the soul versus one generated by the imposter. *(For a tabulation of soul and imposter distinctions, see Table 2, Soul Versus Imposter, page 242.)*

By recognizing the imposter within oneself, the sword of discrimination is sharpened.

Self Evaluation

- In Search of the Imposter -

Listed below are various questions one would do well to ask. They are specifically designed to help an individual recognize the imposter and counteract its influence.

1. *Do I believe that there is an imposter operative within me?*

    The most obvious weapon used to combat the imposter is the knowledge of its existence. The imposter's greatest strength is in its secrecy. Most often, it is something not recognized by the individual, and therefore not guarded against. The acceptance of an imposter within, even though not immediately recognized, is wise. It demonstrates a willingness to acknowledge that there is a deceptive element within one's personality, and a determination to do something about it.

2. *Am I willing to acknowledge that, because there is an imposter operative within me, I may tend to over-estimate my spiritual status?*

    Because the imposter is an aspect of the personality, it is essentially self-referencing. When operative within consciousness, there is a tendency to over-estimate one's spiritual status and point of development. This inflation is not surprising when we remember that the personality is essentially separative by nature. Because of this, the imposter will always see its developmental status in relationship to others. Stated differently, because of the imposter's separative nature, it will seek to rise in spiritual stature through comparison and competition.
    The inflation tendencies of the imposter are often quite subtle. For when the imposter is well developed, it is aware that spiritual competition is contrary to the nature of the soul, which is what it is seeking to mimic. As a consequence, this competitive urge is usually well disguised in garments of thought that are seemingly soul-like in

appearance. One would be wise therefore to assume that an inflation of status has probably occurred in his self-assessment. This *technique of assumed overestimation*, when truthfully done, can temper the influence of the imposter, thus diminishing its power.

It should be noted that the reverse occasionally occurs. There are times when the imposter will cause a person to evaluate his spiritual position below what it truly is. However, in such cases it is most often an expression of false humility. It is therefore inflation presented in the form of modesty. Again, this is usually a subtle perceptual experience, but an honest appraisal of one's motives can reveal this to the disciple. Admittedly, there are times when someone underestimates their developmental status without duplicitous motive, but such cases are an indication of low personality esteem, therefore lack of personality integration. In such cases, the imposter is not involved.

3. *Do my spiritual actions emerge spontaneously?*

It is important to get into the habit of discerning spiritual motives in terms of their degree of spontaneity. The question is, to what extent does one's spiritual actions emerge automatically. Do altruistic and loving impulses emerge without effort, or are they instead experienced as labored expressions? This is an important consideration. A genuine soul-inspired action is normally experienced spontaneously. The soul only knows how to be what it is, and therefore is inclined toward spontaneous service, regardless of the particular circumstance. In short, the soul does not hesitate to express. Its only gauging tendency is related to the level of expression required in order to meet the needs of the environment it seeks to uplift.

On the other hand, the imposter (particularly the strategic type) will always assert its spiritual agenda in a planned manner, and without a willingness to adjust to environmental need. In addition, it will invariably have the element of contrivance as a feature shaping its impulse to act.

4. *To what extent do I desire to see the fruits of my spiritual labors?*

An examination of one's relationship to time is a valuable means of detecting the imposter. Because the imposter is dependent on form for its existence, it is temporal in nature. As an independent agency, it will only survive the duration of one incarnation, and on some level knows this to be the case. As a result, it will initiate spiritual action, but always with an underlying need to see the fruits of that action. Indeed, its relationship to time is quite limited. The imposter yearns to see the results of its work. This need is essential to the imposter's existence, for it is through this process that it validates itself as the soul.

Conversely, the soul is not governed in this way. Instead, it has a much longer view of its labor and the resulting fruits. Though production of outer results is important to the soul, it measures its effectiveness over longer periods of time. Often, the soul's greatest work will not bear fruit during the incarnation in which the seeds were planted. As such, it has the benefit of a multiple incarnational perspective. Therefore, an assessment of how one views his labor, as it matures over time, is crucial. To what extent are we able to see ourselves as seed planters, rather than harvesters? Such a consideration is important as we try to identify the moments in life when the imposter may hold sway.

5. *How able am I to see the soul hidden within all things?*

A key distinguishing factor is found when one examines his relationship to the outside world. The soul has the capacity to perceive the likeness of itself within others, as well as within circumstance. The soul's capacity to do this is contingent upon the opening of the third eye, which is its organ of spiritual vision. Comparatively considered, the imposter doesn't have this capacity. It is not able to truly utilize the penetrative vision of the third eye, as can the soul. Because of this, the imposter is incapable of seeing the soul in another. Yet on some level, it is aware of this fact. As such, the imposter will tend to guide the individual into believing that he has this capacity, and is currently acting upon it. In other words, because the imposter knows that the soul has such vision, it must profess that it too can see behind the scenes, metaphorically understood.

Because of this, it is wise for the individual to assess his capacity to see the soul within others, as well as within circumstance. When inclined to spiritually act, we must honestly determine if we are truly seeing in this way. If not, then it is reasonable to assume that the imposter is having an influence (fully or partially) on our perceptions, at least at that moment.

6. *To what extent is my desire to spiritually express colored by a need to be conspicuous?*

The measure of *desired* overtness, as it relates to one's spiritual service, is an important consideration. Unlike the soul, the imposter considers overt expression (and the subsequent recognition it will engender) to be very important. It must be remembered that the imposter maintains its charlatan stance through the recognition, admiration and praise that it receives from the environment. Therefore, it will tend to navigate its expression into arenas of heightened visibility. Yet the soul needs no such recognition, nor requires overtness in its mode of service. To the soul, it is an irrelevant point. Instead, it simply serves, regardless of how noticeable that service may be to others.

In truth, many advanced disciples committed to soul-inspired service work behind the scenes. A self-assessment as to the degree one desires visibility in their spiritual service can often be a means of detecting the imposter. Naturally, a person must first acknowledge that he probably has an imposter within him, and that he is willing to put energy and time into its detection. Without such a commitment, we run the risk that it is the imposter that is being employed as the detective.

7. *How do I view circumstance as it influences my spiritual life?*

The role of circumstance is an area ripe for soul/imposter discernment. Do we see circumstance as random, or is intentionality recognized within it? For the personality, and therefore the imposter, circumstance is considered random. Yet to the soul, within any circumstance is found a deeper purpose seeking to express itself. As such, the soul's vision makes it possible to perceive outer events as purposeful, even if the personality sees it otherwise. Therefore, it is a good practice to assess how we really look at the circumstances playing out in our lives, for it may hold indication of the imposter's presence.

8. *Am I preoccupied with my spiritual destiny, and how do I see that destiny?*

The issue of destiny is truly a two-edged sword. On the one hand, it is true that the soul has a destiny toward which it is moving. Yet to the imposter, destiny is an idea that looms excessively large in its assessment of itself and its motives to act. The Ageless Wisdom speaks of the *glamour of destiny*, and it is the imposter who is prone to it. This glamour is based upon an inflation of self-importance, and is clearly a hindrance to genuine spiritual expression.

As mentioned, the soul has a destiny it is seeking to fulfill. Yet, its destiny centers on the need for it to outwardly express its nature, and this with eventual perfection. In truth, the destiny of the soul is far less related to some specific concrete activity in the world, as compared to the imposter. Rather, the soul's destiny is more associated with expressing what it is in its fullness. On the other hand, the imposter sees its destiny in more concrete and practical terms. It believes that specific influential acts reveal its destiny, while to the soul, the essence behind activity is what is relevant to its destiny. Herein lies an area of discriminative inquiry. The providence of the soul is founded on the expression of its inherent quality, and the outer activity that emerges from that quality is simply a by-product. What the imposter considers its spiritual destiny, the soul sees as merely an effect.

9. *How quickly and clearly do I perceive spiritual revelation or impression?*

The soul's influence is essentially revelatory in nature. By way of its downward gaze, it seeks to influence the personality. This it does by shedding divine light and promoting ordained creative action. Yet, how is such revelatory impression experienced? When comparing the imposter with the soul-infused personality, revelatory impressions are experienced differently. Most often, revelation offered by the imposter is experienced quickly, and is easier to recall. Generally speaking, the revelations offered by the soul are more difficult to grasp and retain in memory. They are initially experienced as vague, inchoate forms having little clear structure. Structure (clear delineated form) is what is needed for immediate recognition and recall to occur. Because soul-impulsed impressions are initially nebulous, added time is needed to allow them to properly germinate within the mind. This makes it possible for cognitive structures to form around the impression, giving it useful and memorable form. Indeed, this is a foundational premise in the science of white magic. This fact can therefore be a discerning variable when in search of the imposter.

Table 2: Soul Versus Imposter

Soul	Imposter
Altruism is innate, and is therefore spontaneous and automatic	Altruism is deliberate, and viewed as strategic
Focus is upon the larger life system, and is not self-referencing	Self-reference (though often subtle) colors thought and action
Identity is vertically defined	Identity is horizontally defined
Is innately whole, and has no need to reinforce itself	Needs reinforcement to feel whole; reinforcement is often sought indirectly
Sees itself in others	Is alert to how it is different from others
Sees quality give birth to form	Sees form give birth to quality
Views every situation as an opportunity for spiritual expression	Sees only certain situations where spiritual expression is advantageous
Knows oneness, and seeks to project it within the diversity of forms	Sees only separateness, but projects the image that all is one
Sees circumstance as meaningful and spiritually revealing	Views circumstance as random, though strategically useful
Increase in spiritual responsibility proportional to the degree of infusion achieved	Demonstrates rapid rise in spiritual influence and responsibility
Not immediately attentive to effects due to its multi-incarnational perspective	Needs to see the fruits of labor, due to its single incarnational view
Destiny is based upon the soul's ability to manifest its nature through the personality, and is qualitatively defined	Destiny is viewed egocentrically, and is focused upon activity and quantitative measures
Revelation is (most often) gradual, nebulous and difficult to recall	Revelation comes quickly, is well-formed and easy to recall

The Measure of Emotion

Emotion plays an enormous role in the magical process, for it adds a needed vitality and magnetism to a soul-inspired thoughtform. Paradoxically, we have seen that the bathing of a thoughtform with emotion can also have perilous consequences if not done skillfully. We therefore need to examine the correct means of building emotion into the thoughts we seek to express. Much of this process has to do with gauging the amount of astrality to give to an idea. The amount of feeling added to one's thought will result in three possible outcomes. They are:

1. Too much emotion, resulting in the exaggeration of an idea

2. Too little emotion, resulting in devitalized thought

3. Judiciously applied emotion, resulting in rightly animated thought

When emotion inundates a soul-inspired idea, drowning is its fate.

Too Much Emotion

This is the most common occurrence for the magician in training. Because the astral body has long dominated human consciousness, it is not surprising that there would be a tendency to add too much emotion to an idea. One need only recall those times in life when an idea took hold within the mind, and upon its heels an emotional charge is felt. We think a thought, and assuming it is meaningful or insightful, we quickly begin to experience a growing feeling about it. Most often, this happens automatically, usually resulting in a form of overstimulation. For when we add emotion to an idea, it becomes charged with added vitality. This vitality is experienced as a good feeling, and easily leads to enthusiastic fervor, sometimes with detrimental consequences.

Enthusiasm, in its own right, is a welcome addition to the magical work. However, it must be measured, or distortion of the idea will surely occur. Unbridled enthusiasm will result in an exaggerated belief in the importance of one's creative idea. To use an old adage, it tends to make a mountain out of a molehill. When the thought descends into an ungoverned emotional body, there is a tendency to magnify the idea beyond its true value and usefulness. It is common to become too enthusiastic about the idea, only to have it come to nothing in the end. Metaphorically, when too much water is added, the thought will frequently die of drowning. If it does survive and become externalized into something tangible in the outer world, it will be a gross distortion of what the soul had intended.

A soul-inspired idea dies of thirst when the waters of emotion are lacking.

Too Little Emotion

Not contributing enough emotion toward an idea can curtail its further advancement. It must be remembered that the magical use of emotion is to give to an idea vitality and magnetic appeal. These two attributes are essential if a thoughtform is to be externalized, and as such, have an uplifting effect upon the environment. However, emotional deficiency will usually arrest a thoughtform. Without it, the idea will lack the impetus to move further toward externalization. Indeed, the magician's emotional vehicle gives the descending thoughtform the needed force to propel it outward into the world of tangible effects. Undoubtedly, we have all had such occurrences in life. Have we not experienced an idea at times, yet failed to do something with it, and this because we imbued it with little or no conviction. Many soul-inspired thoughts come to naught for this very reason. When such is the case, the thoughtform is said to die of thirst.

Judiciously Applied Emotion

In the magical process, success is largely based upon how well the magician utilizes his emotional body in the creative process. Augmenting a thoughtform with emotion is essential, but it must be a measured contribution. As we have stated, too much emotion results in distortion, while not enough renders the thoughtform impotent. It is therefore crucial that we wisely gauge how much emotion to add to an idea. Such a process requires that one be observant of the emotional body, and possess the capacity to monitor its use. It is to know how much feeling to give to an idea, while also sensing the limit of such giving.

Using the discerning mind is crucial in this process. The mind offers the magician the ability to distinguish the line that divides too much from too little. This must be clearly determined to ensure rightful vitalization of the thoughtform. Learning to judiciously gauge the process comes with experience, to be sure. Mistaken application of emotion can be a great teacher. By observing ourselves, we slowly learn the circumstances (internal and external) that trigger wrong application of feeling.

Eventually, there will come a realization that effective use of emotion is proportional to the degree of one's detachment from it. Stated differently, one cannot rightly manage the application of emotion until he is able to remain separated from it. For most people, this is a tall order. The personality has long identified itself with feeling states, and therefore the *habit of being feeling* is well ingrained within us. This is particularly true when we consider positive feelings states, such as

Soulful magic requires that emotion be wisely measured and used. Detached application is its guarantee.

conviction, happiness or enthusiasm. Nonetheless, when the magician is able to rightly master the emotional body in this way, its correct utilization is ensured. The soul can then use the personality with confidence, knowing that emotion can now be judiciously applied to the descending thoughtform, and thus avoiding its distorting effects.

Astral Duality and the Middle Way

Duality is a feature evident in all dimensions of existence, but it is particularly potent within the emotional plane. For every feeling that we have, there is an opposite feeling that the mind entertains as a potential. The feeling of happiness cannot truly be experienced if we are not already familiar with sadness. These two feeling states contrast each other. It is through such contrast that meaning is derived from the emotional experiences we have.

From this perspective, an understanding of duality is important, particularly as it pertains to the shaping of our personality consciousness. We must learn to gradually rise above the many dualities experienced within the emotional body. There is the tendency within all of us to be attracted to positive emotions while repelling the negative feelings that contrast them. However, to the esotericist, both positive and negative emotions are considered states of imbalance when we relate to one at the expense of the other.

By swinging between various dualistic feelings, a person cannot transcend the emotional body, which is a necessary process in the evolution of consciousness. The seeking of happiness is as much a condition of off-centeredness as it is to repulse emotional sadness and discomfort. Both are indications that the individual is

Emotional duality must eventually be transcended.

overly invested in the emotional experience he is having. Most often, we seek to identify (therefore define) ourselves with positive feeling states. Indeed, the personality wants to experience itself *as* good feeling.

Identification with feeling states is the root of much illusion. To really know oneself is to rise above all phenomenal experiences, such as feelings, and this whether they be positive or negative. In so doing, the individual gradually comes to realize that the self is something transcendent to emotion. Resolution of emotional duality requires that the disciple rise to a higher perch within consciousness. From this loftier point of view, these dualities merge into a condition of realized oneness. By this is meant that the distinction between emotional pleasure and pain begins to fade away, for it becomes apparent that they represent two sides of the same coin.

As a prerequisite to expanding one's consciousness, pleasurable and painful feelings need to be viewed with equality. However, the very nature of the personality causes it to deny their equality. Instead, the personality will be preferential and biased. It will tend to favor that which gives pleasure, while repulsing painful emotional experiences. When such a polarity is transcended, this ensures that the correct dose of emotion will be given to the thoughtform. The magician is then able to maintain the objective view. No other principle is more pertinent to the magical process. Soul inspired creativity is always governed from an inner point of synthesis and detached objectivity. Metaphorically, the magician must direct the creative drama, while resisting the urge to identify with any of its actors. When this is the case, the soul (and its creative intention) can then *shine forth* in splendor.

The middle path is the needed place whereon one's feet are set. Preference for the poles of emotion then vanish.

The Garment That Uplifts

- *Magic on the Etheric-Physical Plane* -

The final stage in the magical process is to bring the now emotionally vitalized thoughtform into the physical plane. By giving it tangibility, it will have the power to uplift people, place and circumstance. As such, it is to the etheric-physical plane that we shall direct this portion of our inquiry.

As is well known in spiritual circles, the physical plane is divided into two broad categories: the etheric and dense. An understanding of the creative process, as it pertains to the etheric division of the physical plane, is of the utmost importance. The etheric plane (composed of four subplanes) is not densely tangible. Instead, it is best understood as an energetic field that underlies and supports the dense physical forms in the outer world. As this relates to a human being, everyone has an etheric body that lays beneath their physical form, providing that form with life and vitality.

The etheric body is composed of millions of interlacing threads of vital etheric substance called *nadis*. Amazingly, they underlie every nerve within the human body, thus providing energetic influence to them. Places where many nadis intersect are focal points of energy and force. Not surprisingly, the major focal points are the seven chakra centers spoken of in the Hindu tradition. These chakras represent points of intense energy reception and transmission. They are formed within the etheric body at the place where massive numbers of these threads intersect. In addition, there are twenty-one secondary centers, and forty-nine

Underlying the physical form is a field of energy that supports it. This is the etheric body, and its chakra centers of force.

that are considered subsidiary, all of which are understood as lesser chakra centers of force.

Through the etheric vehicle, all energies must pass, including the energies of thought and emotion. As such, the etheric sheath is responsible for translating all forms of subtle energy into something realized within consciousness or tangibly manifest in the outer world. An individual cannot experience an intuition, thought or feeling without the etheric vehicle acting as an intermediary capable of impressing such vibration upon the brain and nervous system, as well as the endocrine system. Through it, energy is converted into force, the effect of which is the registration of something within brain consciousness and/or the body itself.

In addition, the health and well-being of the physical body is largely defined by the condition of the etheric web that enshrouds it. This is why spiritual healing practices largely focus on the etheric vehicle. Such efforts are grounded in an understanding that by promoting the free flow of etheric energy, the physical body can be renewed.

The etheric body also acts as a conduit for the reception of the vital energy emitted from the sun, the source of divine life itself. In the East, this sacred energy is called *prana*, and is the spiritual force that sustains all life within the entire solar system. Prana is the breath of God's essential life, and the etheric body is the agency of reception for this sacred breath. It can therefore be seen that the etheric body plays an enormous role in the manifestation of all outer forms, human or otherwise. Everything densely physical has etheric substance underlying it and providing energetic support for its manifested existence. Outer forms cannot exist without this foundation of etheric substance. Dense physical forms are merely the concrete expression of

Nothing is experienced in consciousness without the etheric body acting as an intermediary.

etheric energy. As such, the human body is simply the densification of the etheric energy that underlies it.

The Building of the Etheric Sheath

From this brief discussion, it becomes clear why the etheric web has relevance to white magic. Up to this point, the disciple has constructed a soul-inspired thoughtform, and has imbued it with conviction via its newly formed astral sheath. The final phase of the process is to now construct a third layer of encasing substance, an etheric sheath. If all outer forms have etheric substance supporting them, then the same is true when trying to give tangibility to an idea. Essentially, the etheric web that one gives to a descending thoughtform emerges out of the etheric body of the thinker. Stated differently, the etheric sheath that will encase the magician's idea will be birthed from the vital energy of his own etheric vehicle.

Prior to expressing a thought into the outer world, the magician must consciously engage his own etheric body, and by so doing relate it to the thoughtform held within his mind. For example, the heart chakra needs to be consciously engaged. This then activates the etheric substance related to love. That substance will then affix itself to the soul-inspired thoughtform being patiently held.

You will recall that the magical triangle found within the etheric body relates to three chakra centers the heart, throat and head (inclusive of merged crown and ajna). These three are central to the magical process, and are pivotal to correctly constructing an etheric layer around the descending thoughtform. Each of these chakras provides etheric substance that is characteristic of its nature. As mentioned, the heart chakra will give to the thoughtform a type of etheric substance that

All that is outwardly created must first be given an etheric sheath. The magician's vital body is used in this offering.

promotes the transference of love when the idea is finally expressed. The throat chakra provides substance designed to effectively carry creative wisdom into outer expression. Finally, through the substance activated by the merged head center, a sense of purpose and direction will be imbued into the expressed thoughtform.

Through the deliberate activation of these three etheric centers, the magician becomes much more effective at manifesting thoughtforms. It is an ability that demands that he consciously utilize his etheric body as a tool in the creative effort. Though the etheric bodies of all people perform in this way, it is largely done unconsciously. Yet for the magician, the threefold personality must not be engaged through unconscious tendency. Magic requires that one learn to use the personality instrument, rather than be used by it. When any vehicle is unconsciously operative, the lower self is then governing the creative work. Creative expression based upon personality ambition is then operative. However, discipleship is based upon one's ability to reverse this tendency. It is to slowly take conscious control of the threefold personality and its innate tendency to create on its own behalf. Spiritual evolution moves forward when the soul can take increased dominion over this innate tendency, and to therefore guide the personality to create on behalf of its (soul's) agenda.

Through skillful use of the magical triangle, rightly proportioned energy is imbued into the creator's thoughtform.

The Etheric Field

Not only does the etheric body transmit energy, it is also a keen receiver of vibration coming from the etheric field that underlies the environment. This it does via the seven major chakras laced into it. Through them, the magician is able to sense the readiness (or lack of it) of the environment (etheric field) in its ability to rightly receive the wisdom he seeks to convey. The capacity to *etherically* sense the environment is therefore crucial. The chakras act as sensors that the magician must use prior to birthing forth a soul-inspired thoughtform.

When about to express an idea, the question must be asked, what is the condition of the etheric field and its measure of receptivity? This assessment takes place in an instant, as well as being operative over time. Admittedly, it isn't difficult to see how the etheric vehicle operates in this manner. It is common for a person to walk into some circumstance and sense the presence of an energetic undercurrent. Even if nothing is said among those who are present, the chakra system will register the concealed vibration. In truth, this happens to everyone, whether disciple or savage. All human beings register vibration coming forth from their immediate environmental field. The difference is that when one enters upon the path of discipleship, this etheric faculty is utilized with more conscious intention and understanding.

To the less evolved, environmental influences are not viewed as impressions of energy. Instead, they are simply considered reactions to physical events. To the magician, on the other hand, all physical circumstance is perceived as energy taking form. These currents of etheric energy reveal to the magician the condition of the environment, and its level of readiness for the words he is about to speak. It is this capacity that the magician must use increasingly well.

From this it may be asked, what is the medium through which this environmental vibration travels? Not only a human being, but also the physical environment, has an etheric web underlying its form. This larger etheric web represents the energetic life within the environment itself. Essentially, it is the condition of this

The creator's chakra system is deliberately used to measure the etheric field and its readiness.

environmental web that the human chakra system is designed to register.

Every physical environment we find ourselves in is a place bathed in a sea of etheric energy. The condition of this etheric field gives indication as to the current relationships existing between the physical objects (or people) within that field. Sometimes, harmony is detected in this etheric current, while at other times dissonance is sensed. At times, the etheric field is vitalized, yet on other occasions it is depleted and weak. Indeed, such determinations are crucial.

The environmental web reveals the condition of the etheric field at any given time.

With subtle attention, the magician learns to read the etheric web lacing through the environment. In fact, its condition determines the timing of the magical effort. When the magician speaks his divine truth, the measure of receptivity to it is determined by the status of the environmental web at any given moment. The objective is to create a positive and uplifting effect within the surrounding field. More accurately, the goal is to create a transformational effect within the environing web that the magician is placed within. When such is the case, and through the power of the words spoken, those contained within the etheric field will be potentially transformed because of it. This is the challenge and the opportunity facing the creator at this stage of the process.

Magic as Sexual Intercourse

It is well to view the etheric field as a place for the gestation of divine truth. Symbolically, the magician must learn to see this field as a womb of substance, and the soul-inspired thoughtform as a divine seed needing to be planted within that womb. For what is spiritual creativity, but the art of impregnating an environment with progressive thoughtforms? From the esoteric perspective, all acts of creativity are based upon the principles of sexual intercourse, metaphorically understood. This is true whether considering the creative efforts of an animal, a human being or of a god. All creativity is sexual, inasmuch as it always involves the interaction of two forces that give birth to something new. In the case of the magician, the seed of divine truth and the environmental field engage in energetic intercourse, and the consequence is the birth of a child. However, this offspring is not the emergence of a biological child, but rather, a psychological newborn. It is the birth of divine ideas that the white magician is destined to create.

In truth, sexuality governs the manifestation of all that is. Even from the cosmic perspective this is true, and is foundational to the One Life itself. For after the One Life (Universal God) divides into two (becoming the Cosmic Father and Mother), these two forces interact at all levels of creation, and the child of such intercourse is consciousness itself.

Considering this subject and its relationship to physical plane magic, the field shall either be receptive to the seed of truth, or it shall turn from it. Much of the magical art has to do with properly conditioning the womb so that the seed will be rightly received. As with biological reproduction, spiritual creativity requires that the womb be healthy and in a state of readiness. To move an environment (let us say a group of people) to accept a spiritually progressive idea, there must be authentic interest by those within that field. It is they that the magician seeks to uplift. As such, they must be brought to a position of foundational understanding. In this way, it is possible for them to receive the highest idea (seed) the magician is inwardly called to send forth.

Preparing the field (womb) is therefore crucial to magical success. It requires that the magician intuit

Sexual intercourse is at the root of all creative endeavor, metaphorically understood.

whatever supportive ideas need to be expressed to lay a proper foundation for the planting of his seed. To prepare the womb requires that the minds of the listeners be mentally engaged in such a way that they can be led to a condition of readiness for the seed. Such are the undertones of sexuality within esotericism.

A Question of Timing

The importance of right timing in the creative process cannot be understated. A soul-inspired thought may be very well formed and carry the potency needed to initiate positive change in the outer world. Yet if its delivery is poorly timed, it shall surely come to nothing. All of us have experienced this at one time or another. A great idea falls upon deaf ears not because there is resistance to it, but because the delivery was inappropriate to the moment. Usually, it is through hindsight that we realize our mistake. In such a case, the thoughtform can be considered stillborn, for it dies at the moment of its birth.

When the delivery of a thoughtform is poorly timed, a stillborn creation is often the result.

Disciples therefore have a responsibility to develop sensitivity to this question of timing. Importantly, it is a question deeply related to the condition of the etheric field. The degree of vitality evident within this field is the defining ingredient in this regard. It has been said that nothing is stronger than an idea whose time has finally come. This is most certainly a statement of truth. Though it is a notion normally associated with vast units of time (such as generational periods), it is also valid when considering a particular instant or circumstance.

A magician's thoughtform will create the strongest effect when the right moment is discerned and utilized in a given situation. Such recognized moments are crucial, for they represent gateways of creative success.

Through these temporal windows of opportunity, the power to transform can be effectively expressed. One's intuitive sense is an essential tool to be used in this regard. To read the condition of the etheric web requires a perceptual process beyond mere reason. As such, the third eye is the agent of the intuition, for it reveals the etheric currents underlying circumstance.

To understand this axiom, we must recall that everything within cosmos is living, and is governed by the *Law of Periodicity*. This universal law states that all things demonstrate an ebb and flow tendency. That is to say that everything in manifestation exists in cyclic expression. There is a pulsation to all things, large or small. For example, if we look at human beings we can see this operative on many levels. There is the great rhythm of incarnated existence representing the movement from birth to death, followed by rebirth once again. Within this incarnational cycle, many lesser cycles also exist. There is the cycle of wakefulness followed by sleep, thus constituting a daily rhythm. There is the rhythm of the heartbeat, and that of breathing, as well as the brain-wave cycles occurring during any twenty-four hour period. During the day, there are times when we feel mentally alert, while at other times we feel sluggish and less inclined toward activity. In truth, this ebb and flow phenomenon is present within all expressions of life, whether human, subhuman or superhuman.

The Law of Periodicity also governs all planes of consciousness, and it is in this context that we shall direct our attention. In particular, we are interested in the ebb and flow of the etheric field (plane), and its relationship to the magical process. This field pulsates, and the result is reflected in the condition of the forms that it animates. We need only consider those moments in life when we enter a room where there is much

Right timing is governed by the Law of Periodicity.

The environmental web has reciprocal relationship to the etheric vehicles contained within it.

activity. In such instances, do we not find ourselves also becoming increasingly vital? Generally speaking, the vitality (whether high or low) of any environment contributes to an individual's level of personal vitality. The cause of this can be traced to the condition of the etheric web within the field itself. More specifically, it is related to the interactions occurring between the environmental web and a person's individual etheric body.

When the field is etherically vital, its vibration is felt by those contained within its circumference. Of course, the same is true in reverse. When the web lacks energy, it is a devitalizing experience for those enshrouded by it. Again, this is only a generalization, for people do at times resist the energetic forces coming from their surroundings. Nonetheless, as a generalized truth, it is a notion of great importance. For magic has much to do with taking advantage of this etheric ebb and flow.

In actuality, the interrelationship between the environmental web and an individual's etheric body is reciprocal. Even though the environing web conditions the individual etheric bodies within its field of influence, it is also conditioned by them. This is because the environmental web is created by the collective relationship of etheric forms within it. For example, let us say that several people are gathered in a room and are interacting. As such, and over time, they are slowly building or modifying the environmental etheric web. Threads of etheric substance are extended to each and all within the room, and through this process the environmental web is built. Every thread of this environing net is made of substance extended from the etheric bodies of those who compose it. The word *compose* is quite useful here, for the environmental web is composed of extended threads of etheric force. It is, as it were, a composition of sorts.

These threads are projections of etheric substance contained within the etheric bodies of all forms present within the field, human or otherwise. Even the characteristics of the room itself, where people have gathered, will contribute to the etheric field, thus affecting those who are present within it. Such things as lighting, color and the position of objects within a room all contribute to the conditioning of the etheric field. From a certain perspective, the ancient teachings of Feng Shui artfully address this in its attempt at organizing living space so that harmony of form emerges.

As we have noted, there is a pulsating ebb and flow to the etheric field, as well as the etheric bodies of those within that field. When the etheric body of a human being is in a condition of vitality, that person will be particularly alert and animated. He will feel physically invigorated and will seem to have a reserve of energy. This is indication that his etheric body is in a condition of heightened activity. However, when the etheric body is in the lower part of its cycle, it is considered devitalized. When such has occurred, a person will feel exhausted and relatively non-productive. In terms of the magical work, these cycles are crucial to understand and detect. They are operative not only within the magician's etheric body, but also within the etheric field.

Both webs pulsate. They ebb and flow. This must be sensed by the creator.

Words of Power

The words used to express a truth have inherent power within them. The strength of an idea, as it is articulated in word form, can change the world. Magic has much to do with an acknowledgment of this fact. Nothing within our society would exist, but for the expression of ideas conveyed through language and the symbolism of art. Civilization and culture is nothing more than the effect of centuries of human thought expressed in word, deed and artistic form. When such ideas support the evolution of life, they are considered a product of soulful magic. Words have power, and when they are truly under the direction of the soul, the potency of upliftment is inherent within them. Yet, such words are impotent when the midway point is disregarded.

When the structure of language is designed by the soul, the sentences expressed are occultly called *words of power*. Their power is essentially vibrational in nature. When sounded forth, their potency is established by several variables of communication. Such things as word choice, intonation, syntax and cadence are all attributes of communication that condition the effectiveness of the message. When combined correctly, they have tremendous power to alter the thoughts and perceptions of others. One need only examine the methods demonstrated by an effective public speaker to see how words, skillfully employed, can influence the minds of others, and this for good or ill. In short, we shape our world through the shaping of our language. In the truest sense, this is magic.

The sacred nature of word and language can be readily detected in the Christian view that the creative power of God is in the *Word*. The same idea is also found in the East when we learn that Brahman sang the universe into existence. Such mythologies hearken to the same notion. That is, the creative process is founded upon the principle of outwardly expressed sound. In the context of our topic of study, it is through the vibrational nature of sound that the magician learns to transform and uplift an environment.

As one enunciates a soul-inspired thoughtform, its vibration will have an effect upon the surrounding etheric field. If done with intuitive skill, the effect will

When shaped by the soul, words have the power to uplift the world.

alter the energetic condition of that field; it will impregnate the environmental web with a loftier vibration. When planted with precision, this vibrational seed will begin to germinate, and eventually give birth to a newer and higher vibration within the etheric field itself. In other words, the environmental etheric web will gradually adjust itself to the higher note that is germinating within it.

For those people present within the field, this etheric birth is consciously experienced as a new insight regarding their life and/or service in the world. It can also provide an important revelation that can facilitate their next step in evolution. This is why the condition of the etheric field is so crucial when preparing for the magical moment; it will often define whether or not germination will occur. Essentially, there are two variables related to the impregnation and germination of the etheric field. They are:

- Distribution
- Penetration

Distribution and penetration define the effect that vibration has upon the etheric field.

The term *distribution* refers to the dispersing of a new and higher vibration throughout the etheric field. This lofty vibration is innate within the thoughtform to be expressed. It represents the vibration given to it when the thoughtform was first impulsed by the soul at the beginning of the magical process. When expressed well, it should energetically touch and influence as many people as possible within the environment. The most effective thoughtforms are those that have positive and uplifting effect upon all who are present within the etheric field. This is of course an ideal outcome, but it serves to convey the magical potential within a given circumstance.

Full-spectrum magic is truly transformational, but can only take place when the enlistment is fourfold.

The second variable is *penetration*. By penetration, we are referring to the depth of influence that the new vibration will have upon those individuals who are touched by it. When penetration is deep, the vehicles (mental, emotional and physical) of the listener are stimulated by the new and higher vibration. This again represents an ideal effect.

For some, the new idea (vibration) will influence them mentally, but will have little if any effect upon them emotionally or physically. Other people may emotionally feel the truth of what is said, even if they do not mentally grasp it. Still others will blindly react to the vibration, leading them to take physical action in response to it, but without real understanding. Each of these cases represents only partial penetrations, for the new vibration has not touched the full spectrum of the listener's personality vehicles. Yet, the most effective and transformational influence is when the thoughtform can stimulate all three aspects of the listener's personality. When such is the case, that person will experience the greatest measure of transformation from the thoughtform presented.

It should be noted here that to correctly touch all three fields of the listener's personality requires that penetration be deep enough to reach to the soul within the listener. When the words of power, as sent forth by the magician, have enlisted the listener's soul, that soul becomes a collaborative agent on behalf of the magical effort. This constitutes real magic, for with this aid real transformation is possible. As such, when considering the enlistment of the listener's soul, full-spectrum magic can be considered as fourfold. In a sense, this also sheds new light on the term *co-creation*.

The Midway Point

The midway point within the etheric cycle (human and environmental) is the key to successful creative work. In truth, this middle point of vitality is where the magical moment is found. Admittedly, this may be surprising to some. The natural assumption is that an environment will be most receptive when the etheric web is at its high point of vitality. Yet, such is rarely the case. Instead, it is when the etheric field is at its moderate level of vitality that receptivity to the magical message is most opportune. This is simply another of the many aspects of "walking the noble middle path." Always, evolution proceeds when extremes are reconciled and harmonized into a balanced condition. Such is the case when considering the etheric web and the disciple's effort at utilizing it in the creative process.

Because of the importance of the two variables we have been discussing (distribution and penetration), the magician must be alert to the condition of the etheric field in which he is working. When this web is overly excited, the environment will be unable to rightly absorb the wisdom conveyed. The key to the magical process is to allow the words spoken to be that which will gradually build the arousal of the etheric web along intended lines, rather than the arousal being built via other causes. This is why the magician begins this stimulation process at the midway point. When the etheric field is moderately vital, it is in a state of equilibrium, which is the ideal condition. At this time the magical work can be done most effectively.

If the field has been previously stimulated via outside influences, this indicates that the web has already been aroused. As such, this may or may not be helpful to the magician. To some extent, it depends upon the nature of the previous stimulation and the degree of

Within the etheric ebb and flow, the midway point must be sought.

When the web is overly excited, penetration lacks, though distribution remains. When under-aroused, both then suffer.

consistency it has with the new vibration that the magician seeks to germinate within the field. In most cases, previous stimulation of the ethers will have a negative effect, even when there is a measure of consistency. This is simply because the field is already aroused beyond its optimum level of receptivity. Therefore, though distribution may be well facilitated, penetration will likely suffer. Ideally, it is best if the magician brings the environmental ethers to the midway point independently, without outside influence.

Not surprisingly, if the etheric field is under-vitalized, distribution and penetration will both be inhibited. In such a scenario, the etheric web is inherently incapable of being receptive to impression. The experience of this, from the magician's point of view, is that the wisdom he conveys will fall upon deaf ears. A depleted etheric field does not have the vitality needed to adequately distribute the new vibration. From this we can see that the midway point represents the optimal starting place when beginning to speak magical words of power. It is for this reason that such a point of equilibrium is occultly viewed as the sacred place for the wielding of magical influence.

As can be seen, an understanding of the midway point in the etheric field is essential. Interestingly, within any etheric cycle there are actually two points of equilibrium *(see Figure 10, The Two Midway Points within the Etheric Vitalization Cycle, page 265)*. These two points have correspondence to the out-breath and the in-breath phases of consciousness. The out-breath phase occurs when the etheric web is gradually moving from its low point of vitality toward its apex of arousal. This occurs because, at such a time, the souls of those who are present within the field are becoming outwardly focused. This is, of course, a generalization. At that time, *most* of the people within the field are becoming increasingly alert because their inner beingness is slowly externalizing its focus. The result of this is a general vitalization of the etheric field as a whole. On the other hand, the in-breath phase refers to the withdrawal of consciousness from the field. This manifests as a sluggish awareness experienced by those within the field.

The Two Midpoints within the Etheric Vitalization Cycle

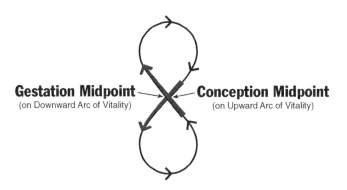

Figure 10

The two midpoints are the same when arousal is the measure, though different in the motions of mind they display.

Perhaps the use of an everyday example would be helpful. When a person is falling asleep, this indicates that the self (soul) is extracting itself from the physical body. It is an in-breath, so to speak, resulting in a movement of life energy from the outer world to the inner realms. This drawing of itself away from the physical form causes the body to become further devitalized, that is, beyond its naturally fatigued condition experienced at the end of the day. This leads one to withdraw into a condition of sleep. However, when we are awakening from a night's slumber, this is indication that the soul is beginning to out-breathe itself, the result of which is the vitalization of the etheric/physical body. We then awaken feeling physically refreshed, vitalized and outwardly focused for the day.

Let us now think about this in the context of the magical process, for it is the same principle at work. The magician must learn to be alert to the direction of breathing occurring within the environment, etherically understood. It is to sense whether the collective breath is moving toward form or away from it. Stated differently, the magician must intuit when the environmental forms (including the mental, emotional and etheric/physical bodies of those within the field) will be moving toward a heightened state of vitality or in the opposite direction. From this realization, he can then predict when the optimum moment approaches. This is always related to the midpoint on the upward arc of etheric arousal. This midway point is referred to as the *conception midpoint*.

At the conception midpoint, the creator should express the most profound truths into the environment. It represents a time when the field is at its optimal stage of receptivity. As such, it is a moment in time (or a duration) when a person's thoughtforms will be most influentially effective. When these periods occur, it indicates that both distribution and penetration are at their optimum. Therefore, it is important that words of power be conveyed when the etheric field is at (or near) its conception midpoint. Again, this occurs when the field is moving upon the upward arc of vitalization, and a balanced stage of etheric arousal has been reached.

It is important to remember here that magic is the process of seeding the etheric field with a higher vibration. Ideally, the seed is planted at the conception midpoint so that it can stimulate the etheric field to heightened arousal and insight. When planted well, its vibration then becomes the defining agent for further arousal of the field. This then facilitates the growth of

The conception midpoint is the place where the creative seed is planted.

the thoughtform planted. In short, the magician needs to learn to ride the wave upon the upward arc so that the thoughtform presented will successfully impregnate, then stimulate the etheric field along intended lines. It therefore requires that the magician keenly intuit when this midpoint has been reached.

As we have mentioned, the second midpoint relates to the devitalizing phase of the etheric cycle. When the field is moving from its high point of stimulation toward its lower point, it will eventually reach the midway point once again. This is the in-breath phase of the cycle in that the energy that is animating the field is drawing inward, resulting in a devitalization of the outer forms within the field. This devitalizing place of equilibrium is called the *gestation midpoint*. It indicates an opportune time for the previously planted seed of wisdom and insight to gestate through contemplative withdrawal.

From one perspective, each of these midway points will seem the same, and yet they are not. There is a tremendous difference that occurs, and this depending upon whether or not the etheric web is moving toward greater or lesser arousal. When the web is on the devitalizing arc, thoughtforms inserted at that time will have little or no chance of creating etheric arousal. Instead, they will tend to die, for the web is moving toward depletion, and is therefore incapable of holding a new vibration being transmitted through it. Magically considered, it is not a condition that supports the introduction of new ideas, but rather the pondering and integration of those already planted.

As stated earlier, the in-breath phase of the cycle indicates that the indwelling life is abstracting itself from the physical plane. If the thoughtform was well planted during the conception phase, the gestation period will serve to deepen the recipient's relationship to it. The downward arc is a period of contemplative

The gestation midpoint facilitates a contemplative withdrawal.

withdrawal. When consciousness withdraws from the etheric/physical body, it does so for the purpose of synthesizing the impressions it received during its previous phase of outer focus.

To illustrate, let us again use the analogy of sleep. One of the reasons for sleep is that it assists the soul in integrating the *essence* of the day's experiences. It is therefore an inward movement of consciousness that is quite purposeful. This is also the case during the gestation phase of the magical process. Those who were energetically part of the etheric field are now in a phase where deep integrative inner work is beginning. In truth, it is a phase of incubation within the etheric field, and by extension, for those who are present within that field. For the magician, it is a time to either reinforce what was already planted at the conception midpoint, or to be skillfully silent.

For successful magic to occur, it is crucial to detect the ebb and flow of etheric cycles. However, it is also important to consider the fact that there are greater and lesser cycles occurring within the etheric field. As a practical example, the morning is most evident as an out-breath phase, for there is usually more vitality in people during that part of the day. One need only be a public speaker or teacher to detect this. In the morning, an audience is far more attentive to a speaker than in the afternoon. During the afternoon, there is a withdrawal of consciousness from the physical realm, resulting in a sluggishness of those within the field. Scientifically, this phenomenon has been referred to as post-cranial dip, and is a predictable neurological event. Regardless of the various biological and psychological explanations, the underpinning of the phenomenon is etheric. In this simple example, we see the drama of lesser cycles occurring during the day as they exist within a greater cycle (the out-breath of daytime wakefulness).

> *There are lesser etheric cycles within the greater ebb and flow. This the creator must surely know.*

Interestingly, within this lesser cycle there are still shorter rhythms operating. For example, during the vital period of the morning, there will still be experienced a lesser oscillation of etheric vitality within that period. Even though the larger energetic movement is toward increased vitality, there are small cycles of highs and lows within this larger cycle. The same is true during the afternoon period, as it tends toward etheric depletion. During that time, there are lesser cycles when there is a rise in etheric vitality for abbreviated periods of time. Sometimes this is a natural secondary undulation, while at other times the magician himself has triggered it through his communicative influence. Again, a good public speaker recognizes this when presenting to an audience. Something said or done can cause a brief surge of vitality, even though the larger trend of the etheric field is moving toward depletion.

After expressing something of importance and demonstrating a measure of elaboration on the idea, it is wise to provide a pause in the presentation, even if for only a few seconds. This permits the environment the time to incubate the ideas thus far given. On a very small cycle, this pause represents the gestation phase and is as much a tool to be used by the magician as is the conception midpoint. Silence is particularly effective when it is strategic. Such is the value of gestation periods, either of the greater or lesser kind.

Silence is an indispensable tool on the downward arc of vitality.

The Ancient Fires

To begin this discussion, we must recall that all of creation is living substance. This is true at whatever level we may be considering, including the mental, emotional and physical realms of experience. Thoughts and emotions are things. They each represent an assemblage of living elemental lives. The assembled configuration of a thought or an emotion *is* the thought or emotion itself. When we have a thought or feeling, we are actually experiencing a construction of substance that, at its core, is animated by godly fire.

When a human being creates a thought, that thought then has a life (fire) of its own, quite apart from the thinker who conceived it. Its life represents the assembled value of livingness inherent in the elemental substance that composes it. In truth, a thought is synergistic. That is to say that the intelligence within a thoughtform is greater than the collective intelligence inherent in the elementals that constitute it. However, the living nature of that thought will remain active and vital only as long as the thinker continues to place attention upon it. In short, the more one thinks about something, the stronger the thoughtform becomes. Conversely, when we think a thought, but only for a short time and never again, that thought will dissipate, for the will of the thinker did not continue to reinforce it by repeated focus upon it. Therefore, thoughts are powerful inasmuch as the thinker remains attentive to them. This represents the physics behind thoughtform longevity.

Because of the importance of remaining focused on one's thoughtform, there is a tendency for the thinker to overly invest himself in it. People can become too attached to their cherished ideas. This also reinforces the thoughtform, though adversely so. When an innovative idea is first conceived, it is usually helpful to that person (or to others) in some way. That is to say, we tend to adopt ideas as paradigms that make sense of our lives, thereby bringing order and meaning to it. These paradigms of thought are useful. However, they eventually become obsolete, for they can only bring a person to a certain level of development. They then must be abandoned in favor of newer thoughtforms that

A living (fiery) thoughtform is fortified through repetitive focus upon it.

will serve as evolutionary paradigms for continued growth.

An occult axiom states that what we value today will defeat us tomorrow. This notion is particularly true with regard to the adoption of thoughts and philosophic ideas that help us to grow and evolve. We discover and accept those truths that move us forward, only to eventually see them as hindrances to further spiritual development. As such, an idea or philosophic truth is only useful within a certain range of growth and development. When the wisdom of a cherished idea has been fully integrated into one's consciousness, it serves no further developmental value, and must be respectfully discarded.

The discarding of a prized idea or belief is usually quite difficult. This is because, as one commits to an idea (or ideal), there is an unconscious tendency to identify with it. It becomes cherished, and we begin to define who we are by what we believe. This is of course an illusion, for the self is transcendent to all thoughts, ideals and beliefs. Yet for every evolving human being, this tendency is operative.

Thoughts are fiery energy manifested as form. And when they have a long history of influencing us (both individually and collectively), their energy is referred to as the *ancient fires*. These ancient fires of thought are strong and are resistant to change, even when change is needed in order for evolution to move forward. Yet, freeing ourselves from these ancient fires is extremely difficult. We only need to look at our lives to see the truth of this notion. All of us have adopted ideas and attitudes in life that have assisted us in our growth and development. As time progresses however, we see that many of these attitudes begin to be less effective and even counter-productive. Even with this realization, we have difficulty letting them go, for the personality is fearful of such relinquishment.

Today's temple shall become tomorrow's prison.

Entrenched thoughtforms have difficulty letting go of us, as we of them.

For example, we may have long cherished the marital vow "till death do us part," only to later realize that such an attitude is no longer supportive of either person's continued growth. People often grow in different directions. What was originally accepted as a sacred and immutable vow (thoughtform) is later recognized as a limitation. Yet, the attachment we have had to the idea has been strong, and letting it go may be quite difficult, even though we deeply realize that we must.

Indeed, it is not simply that we have difficulty letting go of old and cherished attitudes. It is also that they have difficulty letting go of us. Again, a thought is a living thing. When it is old and entrenched, this means that its sacred fiery core has for long been confined within a well-established form. Just as a human being is fearful of letting go of an old habit (form), so too does an archaic thoughtform fear letting go of its entrenched pattern of expression.

Again by analogy, just as one abandons an old habit leading to the development of more useful patterns to live by, so too is this the case for thoughtforms in process of change. In forfeiting their long-held pattern, they reconfigure themselves into new and progressive forms that support the future. This is a form of reincarnation, understood at the level of living thoughtforms. When we face within us the feelings and attitudes that limit our growth, we are actually facing the ancient fires. Our resistance to change is as much a fear experienced by the old ideas themselves as it is our own. Until one is fully enlightened and therefore liberated from the limitations of form, this will be an inescapable challenge that we, and they, must face.

In Search of the Enemy

There is a common notion that when a person is soul-aligned, things will work out as they should. It is thought that one's life becomes effectively coordinated and spiritually fulfilling due to this inner alignment. This is most certainly true. When the soul is guiding, it suggests that the spiritual realm is now participating in the expression of one's outer life of service. With soul participation, opportunities emerge—opportunities that would not occur without the soul's influence. In short, doors open that would never have opened otherwise. Yet, it would be a mistake to therefore assume that difficulties cease to challenge the disciple, even when the soul is involved. Quite the contrary, true discipleship presupposes that one's life is directed toward finding, then doing battle with, the enemy.

At first glance, the idea that there is need for spiritually committed people to search for an enemy may be interpreted adversely. Spirituality typically holds high the mantle of peace and harmony. To understand this principle, we must first define what is meant when using the word "enemy." Our initial tendency is to consider it as a call against various people or organizations that are in opposition to us in some way. However, such is not the true enemy. To the occultist, people and organizations are never the adversary. Instead, the enemy is archaic thought.

Societally considered, the obsolete thoughtforms that condition humanity are the ancient fires that must be dealt with. Instinctively, these fires resist the emerging ideas destined to forge humanity's future. Outworn thought is rooted in the past, and is most certainly the enemy of the future. It has been said that evil represents the good that should have been outlived. This idea has much usefulness in light of what we are

People and institutions are never the enemy of human evolution. Instead, obsolete thought is holder of that title.

considering here. Broadly viewed, evil is any idea that was once progressive to human evolution, but is now entrenched, obstinately resisting change.

To reiterate, all thoughts represent the embodiment of sacred fire. However, the fire found within obsolete thought, though sacred, is encased in a form that is no longer supportive of humanity's evolutionary needs. This is what defines them as obsolete. The core fire is the fire of Divinity itself, but its manifested form is what determines its usefulness or lack there of. The ancient fires simply represent the fire of God clothed in forms (thoughtforms) that have outlived their usefulness. Magic is governed by the understanding that humanity cannot fully progress unless these archaic truths (fires) are transformed into progressive thoughts that support the future of human development.

The ancient fires represent the living energy of God clothed in outworn attire.

In practical terms, let us consider a disciple whose service leads to public speaking of some sort. To such a person, an audience is not just an assemblage of people. More fundamentally, it must be viewed as a sea of thoughtforms. Within this sea is found a mixture of progressive and archaic ideas. Though these thoughtforms are contained within the minds of those in attendance, they are fundamentally living things in their own right. The magician must focus less on the personalities of those holding archaic beliefs, and more on the etheric field containing those beliefs. In other words, the transformation of outworn ideas is facilitated when they are approached impersonally. This is not to say that the human component is unimportant. Quite the contrary, it is very important in that the service rendered is designed to support human betterment. Nonetheless, the magician will be more effective when he directs his attention upon the sea of thoughtforms facing him, rather than the individuals who happen to hold them.

When we examine this in relation to the magical process, there are really three categories of ancient fires to be considered. They correspond to the obsolete thoughtforms, emotional forms and physical forms contained in the consciousness of those within the field. These ancient fires are therefore triple, and are often arrayed against the new vibration being introduced into the field.

When an evolutionary thoughtform is presented, the ancient fires feel threatened by it. In response, they will often rise up in defiance. The white magician must therefore learn to detect these flames lying beneath the surface of the environmental field. They are extremely powerful, and even dangerous. Without keen alertness, the message conveyed by the magician can be mortally attacked by these ancient fires. Beware, for they are often hidden behind smiling faces.

It may well be asked, how does one prepare to counter the effects of the ancient fires? At this juncture, the use of the intuition provides both detection and solution. Intuition gives insight into the energetic undercurrents existing within the field. In addition, it reveals the formula that will disarm the ancient fires should they arise. Normally, these ancient rhythms lie in stealth, and will only emerge into view when they perceive that the fire of the new and progressive thoughtform (sometimes called solar fire) threatens their existence.

To reiterate, these older thoughtforms were at one time considered progressive. In the past, they truly provided light and understanding to those people who adopted them as essential truths to live by. However, when these older ideas have given all of the intelligence they are capable of giving, they then must be forfeited in order that newer truths can carry evolution onward. Yet because they are well-entrenched thoughtforms, often

The ancient fires lie in wait, often veiled by smiling faces.

valued by millions of people for many years (even centuries), they are not willing to yield their authority to the next generation of thoughtforms destined to carry humanity forward. This is particularly true when a person has used these older forms as reference points for self-definition.

At the core of outworn ideas is found the sacred energy of the One Life, abstract and profound.

When an individual expresses a soul-inspired idea, his purpose is to uplift human consciousness to a higher vibration and quality. In short, he seeks to provide others with new ideas that have the power to transform. Such progressive thoughtforms act as catalysts to further the spiritual and personal development of those who are ready to move forward in their evolution. As such, magical work has much to do with helping people to rise above ideas that once were useful paradigms for living, but are now archaic. In time, all thoughtforms become counter-evolutionary. It is a fact built into the physic of evolution itself. When ancient fires are operative in one's life (as is the case for all people at various times), they act as agents of imprisonment, for they arrest one's freedom to grow further. If not modified or forfeited, they will prevent a person (or society) from seeing the next step forward in evolution.

One of the key strategies to overcome the menacing power of the ancient fires is to transform them, rather than combat or suppress them. They are a part of the One Life, and are therefore inherently sacred in their essence. That is to say, every thought is sacred and truthful at its core. Without exception, all thought demonstrates an essential truth if one looks deeply enough into it. Core truth is divinely rooted and is recognized, not as rigid dogma, but as abstract principle. The sacred core within an obsolete thoughtform *is* the ancient fire we have been discussing.

In the context of this topic, it can be rightly stated that fire and divine principle are synonymous. Sacred fire reveals itself as thoughtforms or guiding truths within the human mind. Over time, such truths develop shells of distortion around them. These distorted encasements represent the dogmatized rendition of the divine principles found at their core. Sadly, these perverted shells are eventually accepted as truths, and the divine principles that gave them birth are no longer seen. Yet, truth is a working hypothesis, and is best understood as relative. What is *the* truth at one point in life is later understood as *a* truth. Another occult axiom of monumental import, to be sure.

Admittedly, it is difficult for the human personality to accept the relativity of truth. What is seemingly the all-inclusive truth at one stage of life is later understood as a lesser truth having limited application. Hence the difficulty when the magician is confronted by the ancient fires. These fires, though sacred, are encased within thoughtforms that have long been viewed as truths, yet are now antiquated and regressive. Because these thoughtforms are living, they perceive the magician's newer message (solar fire) as a prescription for their own demise.

Through the utilization of the intuition and the third eye, the magician will begin to discern the formula that will overcome the obstacle that the ancient fires pose. This formula will come when one remembers that it's not the ancient fires that are the problem. Rather, it is the archaic forms enwrapping these fires that need attending. Again, these ancient fires are sacred and eternal. As such, the strategy to transform an obsolete thoughtform is to convey to it the understanding that its essence is sacred and eternal, and will therefore never die.

It is wise for the magician to seek the golden threads of truth within old ideas and attitudes, for they represent the divine principles hidden within archaic forms. It is to

Thoughtforms of ancient fire fear their demise when solar fire emerges. The root of their defiance is here found.

also recognize that older thoughtforms (as well as the personalities that advocate them) feel threatened by the fire of new ideas. Yet at the level of pure essence, these archaic thoughtforms hold sacred principles that are eternally true. Indeed, it is only the distorted shell of dogmatic inflexibility that is temporal, and it is this that must yield to the newer and greater truth.

In many ways, magic is the process of transferring the fiery life at the core of an old idea into a new and progressive form. It is to reconfigure the old so that it supports the magician's expression of solar fire. When such transference has occurred, the power of the newer thoughtform is heightened immensely, for it now has more sacred fire giving animation to it. Such is the reward when one is able to merge the fires of the past (ancient fires) with the fires of the future (solar fire).

An analogy may be helpful at this point. Just as with a thoughtform, a human being can be understood as a shell of substance encasing a spark of sacred fire. This fire is the soul or spirit within, and it is seeking to express itself through its personality vehicle, which is its encasing form. For all of us, there are times in our development when we resist changing our personality tendencies. When someone external to us tries to give us insight into our personality shortcomings, we often respond by taking a defensive stance. In many ways, the practice of psychotherapy is designed to facilitate this personality transformation. When done well, a therapist is able to avoid eliciting the defensive reaction of the client by first navigating to the core of the individual's inherent self-worth. The client will be much more willing to look at his personality problems if he senses that the therapist honors his essential personhood. It is to lift up and acknowledge a person's sacred core (the integrity of essential being) that is a prerequisite to

Through intuition, a formula comes forth within the mind. The golden thread holds the key that blends the fires as one.

helping the client transform his counterproductive personality traits.

This same principle is true when we consider the transformation of archaic thoughtforms. They too represent living fire encased within a shell of substance. Like the human personality, they will resist changing their form unless the eternal flame is recognized within them. When the magician is confronted with an older thoughtform, he must be able to see the sacred truth that its hidden fire conveys, then lift it up in honor. While holding it high, he can then begin to work at reconstructing its form. If done correctly, and with wise and steady patience, the ancient fires eventually yield to the solar fire called forth by the magician.

To illustrate this idea, we shall briefly consider an example. Let us suppose that a person is found to have racist tendencies. By today's standards, such ideas are viewed as archaic and counter-productive to humanity's evolution. At first glance, such bigotry may even be offensive to the magician's personality. Yet, the wise creator knows that at the core of racist views is found a golden thread of truth. That truth is, by definition, a divine principle within creation itself. In this example, the sacred fire at the core of racist ideas is the Principle of Purification. However, racism is a gross distortion of this sacred principle. It has been wrongly applied to considerations of the human body, rather than as it is divinely intended. The intended form through which this principle is to be expressed relates to the purification of the heart and mind, not the separation and belittlement of categories of people according to their genetic endowment.

The Principle of Purification is foundational to the evolution of all units of life within cosmos. As such, it must be honored. Recognizing the distortions of this principle (manifested through racist ideas), the magician

Hold high the core, its sacredness in view. The work of reconstruction then pursue.

must find the formula (of expression) that will liberate this ancient fire from the distorted thoughtforms that imprison it. This is truly an art, and the directive power of the third eye is the tool that the magical artist must use to transform the elementals that are configured as racist thought. When this expression is done correctly, the elementals then willingly reconfigure themselves anew around the sacred fire of purification. A new form is then built. It still resonates to the Principle of Purification, but now in a form that more closely approximates the higher purpose (previously noted) of this sacred fire. Racist thought is then no more.

Magic is occultly understood as the art of triggering environmental kundalini.

Kundalini Magic

When we examine the deeper implications of spiritual creativity, it becomes apparent that magic has intimate connection to the kundalini force. In fact, from a certain vantage point, white magic can be understood as kundalini magic. Why is this so? To see this we must first define what is meant by the word kundalini. Technically speaking, it is a term that speaks of a fiery phenomenon occurring within the etheric body of the disciple when nearing enlightenment and liberation. It is described as the rising of a serpent of fire along the spine of the disciple, arching from the base chakra to the crown within his etheric vehicle. There are also many lesser kundalini experiences that people commonly claim. Though these are far from the kundalini phenomenon just described, they nonetheless suggest that a measure of fire has risen within the etheric body and is experientially unmistakable.

At this point, it would be well to consider the nature of kundalini fire, for in it is found its connection to magic. Kundalini represents the fire within substance as it is being freed from its form-bound condition. Every elemental within the personality contains a fiery core. Because the personality has impurities within it, this fire is locked within imperfect form. As such, kundalini can be thought of as fire that is finally released from its condition of form imprisonment. This is experienced by the initiate as a thrusting up of a flame along the etheric spinal column to join the fire of the spirit/soul waiting at the heights, the crown chakra. When the full kundalini occurs, it indicates that the disciple is purified to such an extent that the old and new fires of spirit can reunite. The impurities of form no longer hinder their union. Indeed, this is a triumphant event for the monad during its long sojourn within the human kingdom. It marks the achievement of relative perfection in its spiritual unfoldment. The fire of the spirit and that of form find each other and fuse as one.

The fires of the past fuse with those of the future, and thus the work is done.

In this light, magic's connection to kundalini can now be seen. White magic is the art of transforming old thoughtforms into newer expressions of truth. Such transformation occurs when the fire inherent within an old idea is released so that it may unite with the solar fire at the core of the magician's thoughtform. In this regard, every act of successful magic is an act of kundalini. Evolution moves forward when the fire invested in the past willingly fuses with the fire that forges the future. In the broadest sense, this is the definition of kundalini, and the art of magic is the means to its end.

This marks the end of the magical process, as performed by the individual disciple. When successful, the outer world of thought, feeling and physical activity is uplifted, and this, in support of the evolution of life. The process began with the emergence of a point of light, the intuitive germ of a thought to be. From this light a thoughtform takes shape, and the warmth of emotion is wisely added. Finally, the outer *garment that uplifts* comes into being, the etheric-physical sheath itself. When skillfully conveyed, its power to transform is certain, and thus the work is done!

Part III

The Larger Agenda

Greater Life Shines Forth
- The Magic of the Logos -

We shall now examine the magical process from a larger perspective, for it entails the creative processes of God. As conveyed in the esoteric teaching, our planet is ensouled by a vast entity whose physical body is the entire globe of Earth. Every expression of life upon this planet is a part of this great and expansive entity. Indeed, all units of consciousness (human or otherwise) are mere fragments of Its consciousness. When we speak of the evolution of a human being, we are actually discussing the development of a single cell within the body of this entity, occultly called the Planetary Logos.

Though God is a relative term, in the context of this discussion we shall refer to our Planetary Logos as God. In truth, any unit of life that has evolved beyond the human stage can be considered a god. Certainly, the entity that ensouls our planet is such a being. However, this being is only a unit within a yet vaster entity, namely the Solar Logos. Solar Logos is the name given to the entity that ensouls our entire solar system, and all planetary gods are lesser expressions of life within it. This is the basis of the so called chain of life and is rooted in the hylozoistic principle. As such, the Solar Logos is a god of higher order than that of our Planetary Lord. The nature of our discussion is related to the magical process demonstrated by God. Though we will be considering God as being the Planetary Logos, it must always be remembered that the same creative principles are applicable to the Solar Logos and beyond.

It has been said that every disciple is destined to become a white magician. But what does this mean? As

Every human being is a cell within the living entity that ensouls our planet.

we have learned, magic is simply the process of translating soul-inspired thoughts into outer tangible effects. We often speak of the soul as being the origin point of the magical process. For pedagogic reasons, this idea is useful. Holding this idea gives us clearer understanding regarding the distinctions between personality and soulful magic. Yet in the larger drama, the soul is not really the origin point of the creative process. Instead, it is merely a conduit for the creative will and intention of the larger life of which it is a part. This is an important idea to ponder. White magic is really founded on the notion of co-creation. That is to say that the goal of disciplic development is to become an agent on behalf of God's creative intention. And, as already stated, in the context of this discussion, we shall consider God to be the ensouling entity of our Earth, the Planetary Logos.

It must be recalled that all entities in manifestation are constitutionally the same. As such, every unit of life (large or small) is enwrapped in layers of substance that compose its vehicles of expression. For example, just as a human being has a mental, emotional and physical body, so too does a cosmic being. Our Planetary Logos is no exception in this regard. However, there is a distinction inasmuch as these vehicles (of the Planetary Logos) are composed of substance of a much higher order than that of a human being. For example, a person's mental, emotional and physical bodies together are simply a part of the physical body of the Planetary Logos. In fact, the seven planes of consciousness, in total, are merely the planes whereon the Planetary Logos finds his etheric-physical body *(see Figure 6, The Human Constitution, page 117)*.

It is easy to lose sight of the enormous difference in the relative scale of life between a human being and the Planetary Logos. Yet to truly understand occultism, the

The human soul is not the place of origin for magical expression, but a conduit for it.

capacity to rightly gauge this difference is essential. Correct proportional thinking is central to esoteric perception, and is foundational to the *Law of Correspondence*. Sometimes called the "as above so below" principle, this sacred law makes it possible to understand the nature of God, though only if right proportion is maintained when reasoning in this way.

Essentially, the creative manifestation process is the same for both a human being and a god. You will recall that the spiritualized mind is the instrument used to begin the creative process. Through the inspiration of the soul, the mind becomes engaged to create thoughtforms. These thoughtforms represent the seeds of the future. If truly inspired by the soul, they will have transformational and uplifting effects upon the outer world. In this way, the disciple becomes a participant in the evolution of life beyond himself. This is essentially the role of spiritual magic. The disciple thinks, and by so doing, creates forms in support of evolutionary change. The same is true for the Logos. Our planetary deity thinks, and by so doing, causes all life on Earth to come into being and gradually evolve. It can therefore be said that life upon our planet is merely the out-picturing of God's consciousness. What we call evolution is really the externalization of God's thought, and it demonstrates itself in the variety of evolving life forms upon our globe.

All forms of life upon our planet represent the out-picturing of God's consciousness.

The Effect of Divine Thought

Every kingdom in nature is in a state of evolutionary development, and it is the consciousness of God that perpetuates such change. For example, within the mineral kingdom, God's thought results in various forces that have tremendous ramifications for our planet. Physical phenomena, such as plate tectonics and the dynamics of world climate, are indicative of this. Both represent forces impulsed by the consciousness of our planetary deity. Mineral development is also an indication of God's thought in action. The application of pressure and heat in the formation of crystalline structures and the development of precious stones over vast periods of time give evidence of God's thought evolving through these categories of mineral form. These forces are aspects of God's consciousness evolving through this kingdom in nature.

It should be noted that all life, as it evolves within the lower kingdoms, is an aspect of the *unconscious* expression of the Planetary Logos. That is to say that the evolution of life within those kingdoms represent the out-picturing of His consciousness at its lowest level of expression. It is below His threshold of awareness and is an aspect of His unconscious nature. Interestingly, it is not until we touch the plane of abstract mind that the *conscious* life of the Planetary Logos is realized. This is the level where the human soul (causal body) is found. Given this fact, we can see that it is only at the level of soul, within a human being, that the conscious life of God can be touched.

> *Within the lower kingdoms, life is an aspect of God's unconscious mind.*

Through its evolutionary processes, the mineral kingdom gradually out-pictures the lowest level of God's consciousness. As earlier discussed, geometric symmetry is a quality that is seeking to evolve through this kingdom in nature. The acme of its development can be witnessed in the geometric precision evident within crystals. This mathematical precision is a divine attribute that is contained within the consciousness of the Planetary Logos, and at its lowest level is evolving through mineral forms.

Within the higher kingdoms, this divine attribute continues to be refined. For example, in the human kingdom, this quality is evident in the intricate organization and symmetry of the human body. It can also be detected in humanity's ability to organize and manifest its many societal structures and institutions. All organizational tendencies within creation are truly divine. It is in the mineral kingdom that such energy expresses itself in the most rudimentary fashion. At the level of mineral, this energy simply indicates the lowest expression of this divine energy manifesting as a result of God's thought.

Within the plant kingdom, this energy manifests as the wide diversity of plant forms evident on Earth, and facilitates their evolution and change over time. The acme of this influence is indicated in the manifestation of fragrance, and the quality of harmony and color as it naturally appears in the plant domain. It is also within the plant kingdom where the consciousness of the Logos is developing the quality of magnetic appeal at its most primitive level. This is the quality of magnetism that plants emit. In the human kingdom, we experience this same divine quality, but at a higher level of realization. We call it love.

In addition, the plant domain is receptive to the energy of aspiration. At its lowest level, this divine energy manifests as a plant's upward yearning toward the light of the sun. Not surprisingly, this quality has higher expressions within the higher kingdoms. For example, in the human kingdom, spiritual aspiration is sensed and developed. As a result, human beings begin to yearn for the soul, which is the inner sun within each of us. As such, our mystical yearnings simply represent a higher participation in the divine energy of aspiration, which at its lowest level manifests in the plant as a striving toward sunlight.

Within the animal kingdom, God's consciousness manifests as animal instinct, and is driving that kingdom toward the production of increasingly perfected forms.

Each kingdom is evolving attributes, which are aspects of the Planetary Logos that He is evolving within Himself.

> *The human kingdom is a single living entity within the life expression of our Planetary Logos.*

The countless species that have emerged, or become extinct, represent the out-picturing of His thought upon this kingdom over aeons of time. Also evident in the animal kingdom is the development of the divine quality of devotion. This is particularly true when we consider domesticated species, for their consciousness is being conditioned by devotion to humanity. Suggested by this is the idea that devotion is an attribute inherent in the consciousness of God, and is developing its lowest anchor of form expression through the animal kingdom. This is rudimentary devotion, and is experienced by domesticated animals as devotion to a human master.

As with all divine qualities, devotion is relative and is evolving through time. Indeed, it is an energy developed at continuously higher levels of existence. At the level of the Masters, it is a much loftier and more refined expression of devotion than is found within animal or human consciousness. An example of this is the devotion the Christ has toward our planetary God.

From this, we can see that all kingdoms in nature are outward manifestations of God's thought, and the human kingdom is no exception. Each of us is a part of the collective consciousness of humanity as a whole. Indeed, from the esoteric perspective, humanity is considered a single entity within the body of our planetary god. As such, the human kingdom is a fragment of the consciousness of God, and our evolution (in consciousness) represents a small aspect of His evolutionary progress.

The demonstration of this is evident in humanity's evolution over time. Our capacity to build thoughts and ideas in support of human betterment is clear indication that God's consciousness is evolving through our species. The evolution of science, philosophy and the arts each give testament to this fact. All social structures and institutions are merely forms attempting to reflect the consciousness of God with increasing precision over time. This is evolution in the truest sense, though it is a bit different than what we have been conditioned to believe by science and the Darwinian model.

The Nature of Change and Evolution

Science has taught us that evolution is a fact in nature, and that it is based upon the survival of the fittest forms. Occultism, on the other hand, suggests that this idea is correct in its premise, though erroneous in its conclusion. Evolution is a foundational notion to all expressions of life. However, ancient occult knowledge strongly asserts that it is the evolution of consciousness, not form, that is the basis of creation.

Consciousness is that which evolves, and does so *through* form. All units of life (whether subhuman, human or superhuman) incarnate for the purpose of evolving. In the process, and over aeons of time, form gradually changes in response to the evolving consciousness expressing through it. Regrettably, science has been preoccupied with the evolution of form, and has assumed that consciousness is simply an emerging by-product. However, it is in the reverse that the greater truth can be found. Consciousness is that which is striving toward a higher and more refined state, while the body is merely adjusting itself (over vast periods of time) to this inner change.

What science is calling human evolution is not evolution at all, but merely the study of its effects. In truth, evolution theory must eventually be recognized for what it truly is—an investigation into the development of consciousness as it evolves through form. This is evolution as understood spiritually. When we consider that humanity is a mere subset of a Greater Life, we must

Evolution is based upon changes in consciousness. The evolution of form is merely an effect.

then conclude that our evolution is simply a response to our planetary god's urge toward betterment.

The Evolution of Societal Systems

In the Esoteric Tradition, it is understood that all human institutions and social structures represent the manifestation of various aspects of God's thought. This is true no matter what social organization we may consider. National government, for example, is the manifestation of divine ideation. That is to say that political philosophy is merely the demonstration of an aspect of God's thought seeking to externalize itself through the fourth kingdom in nature, the human.

The manifestation of government has much relationship to the *will to evolve* aspect of God's consciousness. Through government, this will drives humanity forward as a species. This it does through the application of power in order to facilitate evolutionary change. The many political views existing today are nothing more than attributes of this divine will manifesting through groups of human beings, resulting in political attitudes and biases. As such, when people identify with certain political views, they are really demonstrating sensitivity to a particular current of God's thought. Interestingly, oppositional political perspectives are simply the out-picturing of cognitive dissonance within the mind of the Planetary Logos.

Another example of this can be seen in the educational institutions humanity has created. Though they are conceived by the human mind, such ideas were initially seeded by the thoughts of the Planetary Logos. Essentially, the Logos is expressing an aspect of Himself through the many educational institutions worldwide. These institutions, like all others, are evolving, and the manifestation of this is recognized in

All institutions within society are categories of divine thought evolving through the human domain.

the new and emerging methods now being employed to educate. The purpose of this aspect of God's thought is to condition human consciousness with the knowledge of the Real. Such knowledge is destined to incorporate both spiritual and traditional ideas, and eventually demonstrate the inseparability of the spiritual from the secular aspects of life.

Gradually, humanity is adjusting its view and approach to education in an effort to move in this direction. Particularly in the West, education is slowly adopting teaching strategies that demonstrate the interdependence of academic disciplines. For example, a university class may have two instructors from different disciplines (such as Psychology and History) team-teaching. This trend is clearly moving toward the deeper implications of knowledge as it is revealed through interdisciplinary understanding. Through such efforts, an underlying unity of knowledge will surely emerge.

Fundamentally, evolution is based upon movement toward synthesis. Indeed, interdisciplinary education clearly represents that motion. The point to keep in mind is that education, as a collection of ideological views, represents divine thought being sensed by humanity. It then manifests as various educational institutions and initiatives throughout the world. When in line with the evolutionary intention of the Planetary Logos, education will evolve toward the amalgamation of knowledge. The day will come when this form of synthetic knowledge will be viewed as a prerequisite to wisdom.

As a final example, let us consider the economic structures evident within a given society. These too are manifestations of God's consciousness. An aspect of logoic thought is touched and acted upon by humanity, and the economic structures we live within are the resultant forms. The purpose of this aspect of divine ideation is to slowly condition human consciousness

As time passes, evolution tends toward synthesis. This can now be glimpsed within societal forms.

with the *principle of right distribution*. In other words, the deeper purpose of economics and business, as transmitted by the Logos, is to gradually teach humanity how to rightly distribute resources for the betterment of the entire human family, not simply the prosperous few. Such conditioning will only emerge when humanity begins to see its Oneness. Over the last several decades, indication of this is beginning to emerge. International cooperation, as well as the recognition of economic interdependence among nations, is evidence that humanity is beginning to realize its economic unity. This is the agenda that is driving the Logos to express through society's business and economic structures.

> *Human evolution moves forward through successive approximations.*

It may well be asked, if God is the source of all social institutions, then why are these systems so tainted and corrupt? The answer to this question is so close to us that it is sometimes difficult to see. God's thoughts are perfect (relatively speaking), but they are being transmitted into the consciousness of a category of lesser lives that are comparatively impure, namely, human beings. As such, humanity manifests its social institutions imperfectly. This is not a statement of condemnation. As a category of life, we are manifesting ourselves (and our institutions) to the degree of evolutionary development we have thus far achieved. All life exhibits its form nature in parity with its level of development, and humanity is no exception.

As human consciousness evolves, so too will its capacity to more perfectly create its social institutions. This is what is meant when, in occultism, there is discussion of divine archetypes. These archetypes are God's idealized thought, and represent the pattern of things to be. Indeed, the evolution of human consciousness is based upon our growing ability to approximate these archetypal patterns in the outer world of human living. This is what humanity is trying to do, and has been, since the dawn of our existence. It is a principle grounded in the notion of incremental enlightenment. Spiritual evolution is very gradual, and this whether we consider individual people, societal institutions or humanity as a whole. From the esoteric perspective, the evolution of human consciousness is gauged upon humanity's attempts at successively approximating (in outer form) these divine archetypes. Parenthetically, this principle is also the basis for the acceptance of reincarnation as a fact in nature.

Often, people are deeply disturbed by the misuse of power and the wrongful behaviors that exist within our institutions. We feel anger toward politicians for their seeming misuse of power; we balk at religious institutions for their entrenched dogmatism; we disdain social service organizations that promote welfare policies that inadvertently degrade human dignity. Yet though these criticisms have validity, they often overlook a more important truth. That is that human institutions are imperfect, but they are nonetheless evolving, even if ever so slowly.

No social structure or institution is without flaw, but all are higher expressions than they were hundreds of years ago. One need only examine the history of human civilization to see that our institutions have come a long way. If only an institution's imperfections are seen, then one's natural response toward them will be distrust or disdain. Yet, we must learn to recognize each and every societal system as a demonstration of sacred principles imperfectly expressed. At the same time, comfort can be found in the knowledge that they are gradually evolving toward higher forms of expression.

Over aeons, humanity gradually evolves, and this is detected in the changing nature of the many social systems it has created. At first glance, this would suggest that evolution is a smooth upward tending arch

All social institutions are flawed, yet evolve toward perfection over the vastness of time.

leading toward an eventual state of perfection. While it is true that evolution is moving toward the divine, the journey is far from smooth. Over the course of time, there have been many downturns in humanity's evolutionary journey. At such times, humanity becomes less sensitive to logoic thought (God's ideation), and our social systems become increasingly corrupt and ineffective. The Dark Ages in Western history stand as clear example of this notion.

Other instances of this, though perhaps less severe, are scattered throughout history. Yet if one were to graphically track the rise and fall of human development, a wave pattern would be detected (*see Figure 11, Evolutionary Trend and the Lesser Cycles of Variability, page 297*). Evolution always proceeds in cycles. As such, there are times when society becomes increasingly crystallized and *seemingly* regressive, followed by periods of progressive creativity and renewal. On a large scale, the Renaissance period is a classic example of this upward thrust in humanity's evolution, both from an individual and societal perspective.

The point to remember therefore is that the general trend of evolution is not easily recognized when we are preoccupied with the lesser cycles occurring within that trend. We must examine humanity's evolution within the context of many hundreds of years to really see that the general trend is upward, even though there are isolated periods when a lesser downward tendency may occur. It is well to note that though we have been discussing this idea in the context of humanity as a whole, it is equally applicable to an individual.

Evolution is always occurring within cycles of variability.

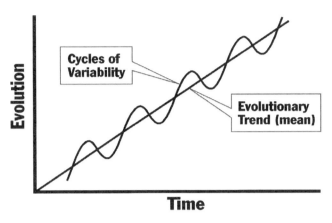

Figure 11

To assess one's place upon the path, the mean of experience is a reliable gauge.

Every human being is growing within the context of rhythms and cycles. Often, disciples will mistakenly evaluate where they stand upon the path by these lesser rhythms, rather than the larger trend of life. All people have times when they are sensing a deep connection to the soul within, followed by periods when contact seems to be despairingly lost. These highs and lows are not useful measures of spiritual status or achievement, for they often lead to erroneous conclusions. A person is never as evolved as his high moments would suggest, and never as undeveloped as his low points seem to indicate.

The correct measure of place and direction is always found at the mean between the extremes of experience. It is simply another example of walking the noble middle path, as was advocated by the Buddha. A preoccupation with our spiritual highs and lows is simply indication that an aspect of the self is overly identified with these experiences. Detachment is the antidote to this problem. It is through one's capacity to remain removed from experience that liberation and spiritual freedom is eventually achieved. This is true whether considering the development of an individual or of humanity viewed as a single evolving entity.

The Magical Nature of Logoic Thought

Returning now to our subject, let us examine the nature of God's thought as it impresses itself upon the consciousness of humanity. In truth, it is a process that is magical. The Planetary Logos thinks, and through the inherent power within such thought, our world, and all life upon it, comes into manifestation. It is an act of white magic on a cosmic scale. Indeed, the principles of magic relevant to a human being are identical to those governing the manifestation of worlds and the kingdoms of life existing upon them. The Law of Correspondence holds true here. As such, it is well for us to review the initial aspects of magic. For in their comprehension comes understanding as to how God shapes the larger patterns of thought within humanity's collective mind.

You will recall that thoughts are things. Every human thought is a form composed of the substance of the mental plane. However, this substance must not be viewed as inorganic. Every element of substance is actually a living entity of minute size and development. As we have learned, a thought is really the assemblage of a myriad of these elemental lives that have come together in cooperative rapport. They do so in response to the vibration emitted by the thinker, be it the soul or the personality.

The will and intention of the thinker, at any given moment, has a quality related to it. When this will is projected (by the thinker) into the mental body, the elementals respond to it as moths to a flame. They then assemble themselves into a geometric configuration that

When the Logos thinks, worlds come into being.

becomes the thoughtform itself. When we have a thought, we are actually experiencing an inner structure composed of millions of minute lives of mental substance.

The quality of any thought is determined by the nature of the vibration that gave it birth. Lofty intention breeds lofty thoughtforms, while degraded intention does the reverse. You may recall that elementals are of different grades. The mental plane is composed of countless elemental lives, ranging from those that are highly developed to those that are much denser and less mature. When the thinker is the soul, it creates thoughts from the reservoir of mental elementals, and this substance will be of a high grade. On the other hand, when the personality gives birth to a thought, the mental substance it attracts will be comparatively less developed. On a planetary level, this is precisely what is happening when the Logos magically projects His thought and intention into the human kingdom.

In the eyes of our Planetary Logos, human beings are elemental lives.

Human Elementals

The correspondence between the magic of the disciple and that of the Planetary Logos is important. To our planetary deity, human beings *are* the elementals used in the manifestation of His thoughtforms. From the perspective of our Logos, humanity is a field of living substance, and each elemental within that field is a human being.

At this point in our discussion, it should *not* be assumed that the collective consciousness of humanity is contained within the mental plane of our Planetary Logos (God). His thoughtforms are created on levels transcendent to all categories of human awareness. Nonetheless, the thoughtforms created by this Entity will eventually descend into humanity's collective mental field and be registered there. This registration is realized as an intuitional idea by those human beings sensitive to Its impress.

Our response is one of construction in that we begin to form societal institutions around these impressions, as well as their philosophic platforms. As such, we respond to God's downward radiation in the same way that the elementals respond to the soul when it constructs a thoughtform. We organize ourselves and call it a social institution, philosophic platform or collectively agreed upon view of life, just as the elementals organize themselves into a thought or innovative idea. With humble spirit, we therefore must accept the notion that to God, we are the elemental lives who collectively give tangible expression to His thought.

A collection of like-minded people, grouped around a new and progressive idea, is a manifestation of divine ideation.

As an example, let us consider the field of science. All progressive ideas that have emerged from the scientific community are related to impressions of logoic thought. When the Logos downwardly asserts His evolutionary intention (which is vibrational thought), vast numbers of people in the world begin to assemble around its note and quality. In time, these people become a community of like-minded individuals, all of whom are committed to a common set of scientific ideas. As a collective body, they *are* the manifestation of a thoughtform impulsed by the Logos. Though these people believe themselves to be independent thinkers, they are all resonating to a larger will being impressed through them. They become the form manifestation of an aspect of God's will. In truth, this group is a collective thoughtform (on the human level) that will have evolutionary influence in the world.

To illustrate this, let us say that a group of scientists resonates to the principles of quantum physics. In such a case, this group is the embodiment of God's thought as it has been stepped down into the domain of human consciousness. The entire field of quantum physics, with all of its essential principles, represents the out-pictured thoughtform created by the Logos. And, though it is far less than a perfect reflection of God's initial thought (archetype), it represents the level of humanity's capacity to receive this divine vibration and build thoughts around it.

Though woefully less than what it is essentially, the collective thoughts of humanity (pertaining to quantum physics) will nonetheless exert an influence upon society as a whole. By so doing, they (those people who are attracted to quantum theory) gradually perpetuate human evolution. They do this by educating humanity on the principles of quantum physics and its implications for human betterment. Collective humanity then benefits from this knowledge, for it gives to us a deeper understanding of the Real. By so doing, humanity's consciousness is nudged toward a more enlightened state of being. In this way, our species more closely approximates the divine archetype that gave birth to quantum theory as that theory was conceived by the human elementals destined to intuit it.

The Logos bathes humanity with the archetypes to be. Progressive ideas then emerge within human thought.

As a reminder, this principle is operative within all departments of human enterprise. It is relevant to political ideologies, religious precepts or newly emerging forms of artistic style. All social structures represent impressions of God's thought working through intelligent people, and this according to their individual mental proclivities. Such is the means by which the Logos facilitates His evolution. The Logos energetically fecundates the collective consciousness of humanity, and creative ideas emerge within groups of human minds in response to this divine fertilization. Through this process, humanity is uplifted into a wiser understanding of life and circumstance.

Strange as it may sound, the primary purpose of the creative work of the Logos is to facilitate His evolution, and humanity's development is merely an incidental effect. Here an analogy may be useful. Let us say that, as a human being, you decide to improve your eating habits, believing that by so doing your life will improve. With conviction, you direct your thoughts to making the needed dietary changes. Every cell within your body is also a living entity, and they too are evolving. As a result, they will be the recipients of the benefits of your dietary change. Even though the reasons for changing your diet were based upon the uplifting benefit it will have to you (as a whole being), the lesser lives within your body (cells) are indirect beneficiaries. By analogy, such is the case when we consider the Logos. It is His consciousness that is evolving upon this planet, and all the cells within His body (including human beings) are incidentally uplifted.

Unlike the personality, the soul is capable of rightly sensing impressions from above.

Grades of Elemental Receptivity

From this understanding, we can more clearly see why the disciple's magical work should be impulsed from the soul, rather than the personality. For it is the soul, not the personal self, that is able to rightly register impressions from the Logos. When the mind of the disciple is aligned with the soul, the process of thoughtform-building will be along the lines intended by the divine impression. When soulfully aligned, the disciple then begins to build a series of thoughtforms in accordance with the subtle intuitive impression inwardly sensed. Here we can see the challenges existing within every social institution. In every organization, there will be more people who are not aligned with the soul than people who are. As such, most people will think thoughts that are impulsed by their personalities, not their souls. These thoughts will tend to have little if any connection with the descending impression coming forth from the Planetary Logos.

The hope of the future rests in the fact that within all institutions are found people who yearn to introduce the new and emerging paradigms. Though comparatively few in number, it is they who are sensitive to the archetypes working through the institutions they serve. We therefore see that in any organization are found those who advocate its positive evolution, while the majority are resistant to such movement. Most often, these two types are antagonistic toward each other, hence the foundation of much strife in society. In many ways, humanity is torn between these two categories of people—those who are sensing a higher truth and seeking to live according to it, and those who are not. People who are not yet sensitive to the soul's impression will tend to be attracted to ideas from the past. They will resist change, and will do so by clinging to tradition and archaic ideas. From the polarization thus created, societal conflict emerges, sometimes violently.

From our earlier discussions you will recall that some elementals are of higher development than others, therefore further evolved. When the human soul seeks to construct spiritually progressive thoughtforms, it does so only when it is able to attract the more refined elementals to construct these ideas. These mental elementals are more intelligent, and demonstrate purity in their nature and motive. Herein is the reason the magician seeks to utilize higher elemental lives. Only through them can a thoughtform be constructed that will properly reflect the formless impulse coming from the soul. Lower elementals are not sensitive to the soul's vibration. As such, they remain uninvolved in the soul's creative work.

Within any organization are found those who advocate the new, while most remain committed to the archaic view.

The evolutionary spectrum of consciousness is wide within the human family, as it is in every kingdom of nature.

With this in mind, let us now reconsider the magical work of the Logos as He seeks to create impression within the collective consciousness of humanity. He too seeks to work with higher grades of elemental lives, and it is advanced humanity who are these elementals. To the Logos, humanity represents a category of elemental substance of varying grades of intelligence and purity. He too seeks to utilize elementals of a higher grade in order that the vibration He sends forth will be rightly registered. They who are the more evolved within the human kingdom provide the Logos with this possibility. Such people are sensitive to their souls, and by extension are sensitive to God's impression.

Over countless incarnations, human evolution has been governed by a slow and persistent expansion of consciousness. Through this process, the soul is eventually discovered within oneself. Yet, this does not mean that human beings are all at the same level of development. Quite the contrary, the range of evolutionary development is wide within the human kingdom, as it is within the animal and plant domains of life. The most evolved among us are those who are fully soul-conscious, and are able to selflessly serve the outer world without personality distortion. At the other end of the human spectrum are the very young souls. They are people who are most recent in their participation in human existence and are far from the time when even a fleeting glimpse of the soul is possible. As such, they are naturally inclined toward comparatively primitive (almost animal-like) behaviors. Needless to say, the majority of people are developmentally found somewhere between these two extremes.

In the eyes of the Logos, this wide spectrum of human development simply represents the differing grades of substance within the human kingdom. From His perspective, the consciousness of a human being is equivalent to a single elemental life. As such, He uses human elementals, in mass, to construct thoughtforms needing to be realized and integrated into humanity's consciousness. Disciples are those within the human family who have a measure of soul alignment and awareness. Because of this, they are the human elementals that the Logos uses when building evolutionary thoughtforms destined to uplift humanity.

Due to their soulful alignment, disciples are able to register the subtle vibrations coming forth from our planetary god. Collectively, they respond to this vibration and organize themselves around it. In short, God's thoughts do not manifest through individuals, but through groups of people. Indeed, in their assemblage, they themselves become God's thoughtform manifested within the consciousness of humanity.

As a reminder, we are discussing a vastly stepped-down thoughtform, for God's thoughts are far removed from the consciousness of even the most advanced groups within the human kingdom. Instead, it is around a reduced reflection of logoic thought that spiritually committed people intuit and build progressive thoughts. Though far from its divine source, it is a vibration that nonetheless has the power to free humanity from some aspect of its existential predicament.

When a collective thoughtform has developed enough structural integrity, it will begin to influence humanity as a whole. Stated differently, when enough people intuitively sense the same progressive idea or principle, they will gradually find each other and organize around their common vision. It is in the nature and effectiveness of their organization that the power of God's thought can influence humanity. This is true whether we consider a group of environmentalists who organize themselves in order to advocate a particular environmental cause, or a group of united economists in

The organization of people around a commonly intuited principle is what is needed for a divine archetype to take form, and thus begin to shape societal opinion.

support of a newly conceived economic theory. All societal organizations are formed around some idea or set of principles.

When governing principles are supportive of God's evolutionary plan, humanity's evolution then moves forward. This is the basis of the progressive arm within any and all social institutions. Interestingly, because logoic thought is collectively registered, revolutionary ideas are (in most cases) conceived simultaneously. An example of this is the theory of evolution advocated by both Charles Darwin and Alfred Wallace in the nineteenth century. In their independent investigations, both men arrived at the conclusion that evolution exists as a cornerstone of life. Though they confined their views to the evolution of form (rather than of consciousness), they both deeply sensed that all life evolved toward higher states of existence. They each presented sound empirical evidence in support of what they intuitively were led to study, and at roughly the same time. On its heels, the scientific community further researched their theories before they became widely adopted by humanity. This is simply an example illustrating that even though individuals are intuitively receptive to logoic thought, its transformational power (to society as a whole) is in its collectivity.

New and progressive ideas are usually intuited by more than one individual.

The Dual Edge of Social Systems

In closing this discussion, it would be well to note that, because all societal structures are evolving, they will manifest a leading and trailing edge, so to speak. By this is meant that social systems have elements within them that are progressive, as well as regressive. Much of this can be accounted for by the reasons already mentioned. That is, some people within a given system are aligned with the soul, while others are not. Because of this, some can sense the higher archetypes seeking to manifest in support of the future, while others are inclined toward ideas that are already established and often obsolete. Considering this, it is best to view an institution (and society as a whole) as a single living entity in movement from the past to the future.

Every organization has both a leading and trailing edge voicing its position and concerns. The voice of the leading edge is always sensitive to those principles and ideas that support human and organizational betterment, and therefore cuts into the future. Conversely, the trailing edge tends to hold onto the past, and therefore resists change. And, though these two edges may seem a dichotomy, they really represent the two extremes of a single spectrum. When perceived as a dichotomy, no resolution of them can be found. They will seem to be irreconcilable forces at constant odds with each other. However, if we begin to see these extremes as elongated expressions of one thing, then perhaps solutions can be found. It is true that the leading edge is where the more progressive ideas are to be found. Yet, this does not negate the fact that the trailing edge of any social system has something important to give.

To highlight this, let us consider the institution of religion. Generally speaking, most world religions have a strong relationship to tradition. As such, religion tends to be less supportive of the emerging paradigms revealing higher spiritual truths. Instead, they repulse the suggestion that spirituality is a dynamic and evolving thing. Even so, within all religions will be found those who do see and yearn for the new. Often, they are not heard, for their ideas seem antithetical to the traditional views dearly held by the majority. The result is that both the traditionalists and the religious visionaries become intolerant of each other.

Within the human condition, every social system is a spectrum in its expression, and has both a leading and trailing edge.

From the occult perspective, the leading and trailing edges of any religion (or organization) are only able to advocate a half truth. For example, those who hold onto the past are often fearful of change, and wrongly believe that humanity's relationship to God is static, rather than dynamic. They must eventually see that all things in creation evolve and change, including their cherished forms of worship and ritual. This will be accepted when they realize that institutions are living things. And, just as they will admit that they themselves are evolving and changing over time, so too must their prized religion do the same.

Conversely, those who yearn for the new paradigm are sensing a higher spiritual truth, yet they often become disrespectful of the traditional views held by the trailing edge. Importantly, the evolution of any system does not mean the complete rejection of its former principles. Instead, the *essence* of the past must be brought forward to unite with the paradigms of the future. It is only its outdated expression (form) that must be abandoned. There are aspects of traditional theology that are true, and eternally so. For example, there is essential wisdom hidden within long-established ritual, such as its reliance on sacred geometry and numerology. These attributes are eternal, and must be carried into the future. It is only the outer form (out-of-date ritual expression) that must be abandoned. Indeed, the wisdom hidden within the older forms must serve as the seed for new and progressive ritual expressions. Spiritual evolution mandates changing forms, while essence ever remains. This is a fact often forgotten by those who loudly proclaim the righteousness of their progressive ideas.

The thoughts we have been considering here are true regardless of the social system. Whether we speak of the arts, sciences, business or the political arena, all are

The leading and trailing edges each express only half the truth. The entire truth is found in their union.

evolving thoughtforms initiated by the Logos. Indeed, every societal institution has a leading and trailing edge functioning within it. The day must eventually come when the sacredness of both edges is seen. For the destiny of the leading edge is to reveal the new and evolving thoughts of God, while the trailing edge ever ensures that the lessons of the past are not forgotten in our yearning to manifest the future.

Final Remarks

In the long drama of human evolution, every human being is destined to become a spiritual magician. The inevitability of this lies in the fact that the creative manifestation process is woven into the fabric of the soul's nature. In truth, the soul's purpose is actually twofold. Fundamentally, its intention is to *shine forth* its essential nature through form, and this without encumberment. Secondly, the soul yearns to make an uplifting contribution to that which is beyond itself. It is this fact that gives foundation to the claim that destiny will eventually lead to magical living. It simply cannot be otherwise. The importance of studying the magical process is therefore undeniable.

White magic is both an art and a science. As such, it doesn't truly emerge into one's life until the heart is filled with love, and the mind can soundly reason while remaining fixed upon higher purpose. Indeed, the heart and mind are equally important to successful creative work. The heart ensures that the magical work is done within a field of loving unity, while the mind gives clarity of thought and directional assistance to the creative process.

In our study, we have learned about the magical process, particularly as it pertains to thoughtform-

When the heart is filled with love, and the mind sound and true, the soul's magic shall then ensue.

building. Much was offered related to the physics of the process, particularly how thoughtforms emerge from the formless intuitions shining forth from the soul. The value of knowing that thoughts are living things cannot be understated. With this understanding, the magician discovers how to cooperate with the livingness of thought in order to facilitate the upliftment of a larger whole. This is white magic in the truest sense.

Magic also demands that the creator understand the role of emotion in the creative process. Emotion gives warmth and magnetism to the ideas we seek to express, but it can also victimize the would-be magician if he is not careful. As we have learned, the science of emotion involves giving the correct amount of feeling to one's creative ideas, while simultaneously remaining detached from them. This is truly the antidote to the dangers inherent in creatively working with emotion.

Finally, white magic is meaningless unless one's soul-inspired thoughtforms find expression in the outer world. When brought forth successfully, the effects are transformational to the people and institutions that the magician seeks to serve. When the magical process is done without flaw, uplifting effects are inevitable. Right timing is crucial in this regard. For if the timing of expression is gauged poorly, the thoughtform will surely die. It then becomes a stillborn child, for it dies at the moment of its birth. Therefore, a profound etheric sensitivity must be developed by the magician. With such faculty, the energetic undercurrents become evident within the outer field of service, and the time for magical opportunity can then be rightly sensed.

When broadly considering white magic, we realize that it is best described as a co-creative process. For when the magician is conscious of his soul, then he is aligned with the Larger Life to which his soul is an integral part. This Larger Life is the Planetary Logos,

> *Always remember that magic is a co-creative process. The human soul is merely a conduit for the expression of something greater.*

the entity that ensouls our entire planet and all life upon it. As human beings, we are mere cells within the vastness of this entity's consciousness. When we create according to the soul's intention, we are participating in a much larger creative drama, one coming forth from our planetary God. If we narrow our focus to the human domain, we see that the out-picturing of this entity's creative intention has led to the rise and fall of countless civilizations throughout history. The many societal systems existing within today's modern civilization are merely the effects of this Larger Life's creative agenda.

Taking the theme of magic to the highest level possible, there is only one creative agency in existence. It is the One Life, the one existence. The universe, with its incomprehensible size and diversity, is the out-pictured consciousness of this Universal Life as it incarnates itself. As human beings, we are minute atoms of intelligent life within its body of manifestation, and we are guided by its incarnational objective. What that objective truly is, we haven't the capacity to know. Nonetheless, it can be said that a small aspect of it pivots on the notion that the One Life is projecting itself into outer form, and the eventual perfection of that expression is its goal. As such, we must do the same. There is simply no other choice, for we are constituent parts of it.

From this we see that all entities within creation are propelled to take form through the force of externalizing life coming from above. In truth, there is only one universal decree, and it is proclaimed from the lips of the One Life. The sound of this decree is breathed forth, and the universe (and all life within it) comes into existence. In this way, all units of life (whether large or small) are driven toward actualizing their Beingness through form. Though language cannot possibly convey this universal fiat, striving humanity still needs words to

The universal decree is that all units of life must one day fully Shine Forth.

grasp the indescribable. Let us simply say therefore that the One Life's magical decree is for all units of life to *Shine Forth!*

Bibliography

Abraham, Kurt. *The Threefold Method for Understanding the Seven Rays*. Cape May, New Jersey: Lapis Press, 1984.

Agni Yoga Society. *Agni Yoga*. New York: Agni Yoga Society, Inc., 1980.

—*Brotherhood*. New York: Agni Yoga Society, Inc., 1982.

—*Fiery World, Volume I*. New York: Agni Yoga Society, Inc., 1948.

—*Hierarchy*. New York: Agni Yoga Society, Inc., 1977.

—*Infinity, Volume I*. New York: Agni Yoga Society, Inc., 1980.

—*Supermundane, The Inner Life, Book I*. New York: Agni Yoga Society, Inc., 1994.

Bailey, Alice A. *A Treatise on Cosmic Fire*. New York: Lucis Trust, 1962.

—*A Treatise on White Magic*. New York: Lucis Trust, 1979.

—*Discipleship in the New Age, Volume I*. New York: Lucis Trust, 1981.

—*Discipleship in the New Age, Volume II*. New York: Lucis Trust, 1986.

—*Esoteric Psychology, Volume I*. New York: Lucis Trust, 1984.

—*Esoteric Psychology, Volume II*. New York: Lucis Trust, 1981.

—*Glamour, A World Problem*. New York: Lucis Trust, 1988.

—*Initiation, Human and Solar*. New York: Lucis Trust, 1980.

—*Telepathy and the Etheric Vehicle*. New York: Lucis Trust, 1986.

—*The Destiny of the Nations*. New York: Lucis Trust, 1949.

—*The Externalization of the Hierarchy*. New York: Lucis Trust, 1989.

—*The Light of the Soul*. New York: Lucis Trust, 1989.

The Rays and The Initiations. New York: Lucis Trust, 1988.

Barborka, Geoffrey. *The Divine Plan*. Adyar, India: The Theosophical Publishing House, 1964.

Barker, A. T., compiler. *The Mahatma Letters to A.P. Sinnett*. Facsimile Edition. Pasadena, California: Theosophical University Press, 1975.

Beckham, Carole. *Cycles of Opportunity*. Mariposa, California: Source Publications, 1998.

Besant, Annie. *A Study in Consciousness*. Los Angeles: Theosophical Publishing House, 1918.

—*Thought Power*. Wheaton, Illinois: The Theosophical Publishing House, 1966.

Blavatsky, Helena, P. *The Secret Doctrine, Volume I*. Pasadena, California: Theosophical University Press, 1988.

—*The Secret Doctrine, Volume II*. Pasadena, California: Theosophical University Press, 1988.

—*Isis Unveiled, Volume I*. Pasadena, California: Theosophical University Press, 1988.

—*Isis Unveiled, Volume II*. Pasadena, California: Theosophical University Press, 1988.

Capra, Fritjof. *The Tao of Physics*. Boulder: Shambhala, 1975.

—*The Turning Point*. New York: Simon & Schuster, 1982.

Cedercrans, Lucille. *The Nature of the Soul*. Whittier, California: Wisdom Impressions, 1993.

Collins, Mabel. *Light on the Path, Through the Gates of Gold*. Pasadena, California: Theosophical University Press, 1976.

Dass, Ram. *Journey to Awakening*. New York: Bantam Books, Inc., 1985.

—*The Only Dance There Is*. New York: Bantam Doubleday Dell Publishing Group, 1973.

DeMotte, Charles. *The Inner Side of History*. Mariposa, California: Source Publications, 1997.

Eastcott, Michal, J. *The Silent Path*. London: Rider & Co. Ltd., 1969.

—*I, the Story of the Self*. Wheaton, Illinois: The Theosophical Publishing House, 1980.

Gibran, Kahlil. *The Prophet*. New York: Alfred A. Knopf, Inc., 1973.

—The *Voice of the Master*. New York: Bantam Books, 1967.

Grof, Stanislav. *Beyond the Brain*. Albany: State University of New York Press, 1985.

Hall, Manly P. *Collected Writings of Manly Hall, Volume III*. Los Angeles: The Philosophical Research Society, Inc., 1962.

—*The Secret Teachings of All Ages*. Los Angeles: The Philosophical Research Society, Inc., 1988.

Hodson, Geoffrey. *The Kingdom of the Gods*. London: The Theosophical Publishing House, 1952.

Holmes, Ernest. *The Science of Mind*. New York: Jeremy P. Tarcher/Putnam Edition, 1997.

Krishnamurti, J. *The Awakening to Intelligence*. San Francisco: Harper & Row Publishers, 1973.

Laurency, Henry, T. *An Introduction to Esoteric Philosophy*. Skovde, Sweden: The Henry T. Laurency Publishing Foundation, 1984.

—*The Knowledge of Reality*. Skovde, Sweden: The Henry T. Laurency Publishing Foundation, 1985.

—*The Philosopher's Stone*. Skovde, Sweden: The Henry T. Laurency Publishing Foundation, 1979.

Leadbeater, W.W. *Man Visible and Invisible*. Wheaton, Illinois: The Theosophical Publishing House, 1980.

Lyon, Bruce. *Standing for the Sacred*. New Zealand: Bruce Lyon, 1997.

Murchie, Guy. *The Seven Mysteries of Life*. USA: Houghton Mifflin Company, 1981.

Prater, Rick. *Bridge to Superconsciousness*. Mariposa, California: Source Publications, 1999.

Richmond, M. Temple. *Sirius*. Mariposa, California: Source Publications, 1997.

Robbins, Michael, D. *Infinitization of Selfhood*. Mariposa, California: The University of the Seven Rays Publishing House, 1997.

—*Tapestry of the Gods, Volume I*. Jersey City Heights, New Jersey: The University of the Seven Rays Publishing House, 1990.

—*Tapestry of the Gods, Volume II*. Jersey City Heights, New Jersey: The University of the Seven Rays Publishing House, 1990.

Satprem. *Sri Aurobindo on The Adventure of Consciousness*. Mt. Vernon, Washington: Institute for Evolutionary Research, 1993.

Suzuki, Shunryu. *Zen Mind, Beginner's Mind*. New York: John Weatherhill, Inc., 1984.

Zukav, Gary. *The Seat of the Soul*. New York: Simon & Schuster, Inc., 1990.

Index

A

Adept 169–170
Ageless Wisdom 240
Agni
    lord of the mental plane 178
Ahamkara 126
    countered by decentralization 143
    desire gives birth to 191
    heart center transcendent to 131
    imbuing idea with I-ness 7
    used to measure motive 219
Air 202
Ajna Center
    (See also chakra, ajna)
    location of personality integration 104
    magical triangle 131–133, 251
    relation to third eye 174
Alignment
    emerging point of light 111
    function of meditation 99
    registration of vibration 305
    soul and personality 94, 98
Alta Major Center 174
Ancient Fires 269–279
Angel
    Guardian 84
    of the Presence 85
    Solar 84–86
Anima 210
Animal
    consciousness, species defined 52
    domestication 50, 68, 290
    foundation of psychic experience 205
    harmony further developed 44
    instinct 49
    instinct, matrix of individualized mind 49
    kingdom 48–51
        horizontal extension 48
        instinct as God consciousness 289
    rays governing 48
    relation to mass consciousness 209
    source of human nourishment 46
    temperament 67
Antahkarana
    as communication medium 101
    at third initiation 163
Aquarian Age 77, 207, 212
Aquarius 212
Archangels 74
Archetype
    geometry underlying thought 181
    God's idealized thought 294
    perfected design or prototype 24
    relation to buddhic plane 120, 130, 166
    relation to third ray 78
    retouched through contemplation 133
    third eye uses as measure 131, 173
Arhat 166, 168
Art
    as evolving thoughtform 308
    related to fourth ray 79
    reveals evolution of consciousness 290
    society the product of 260
    white magic as 7
Aspect
    first 62
    second 62, 226
    third 62, 184, 223, 226
Aspects
    the three 61–64
Aspiration
    gives way at third initiation 164
    relation to plant domain 46, 289
    Sixth Ray of 47
Astral Body
    (See also emotional body)
    adding emotion to thoughtform 128
    difficult to detach from 158
    emotion experienced within 181

filling with lofty emotion 160
long dominated consciousness 243
second initiation, rise above 157
Astral Plane
   (See also emotional plane)
   corresponds to water 186
   danger to magic 216, 217
   magic on 185
Attraction 65, 135
Aura
   of fifth kingdom, entrance 152

B

Baptism
   Jesus in Jordan River 160
   second initiation 157–160
Base Center 133, 135
Beauty
   fourth ray influence 78–79
   fourth ray, resolution of conflict 52
   God's intelligence 31
   magical process as 7
   plant kingdom 43–45
   product of correct geometry 181
   synonymous with truth 79, 181
   unfolded through personality 152
Being
   All and part awareness 57
   archetype of identity 24
   condition of synthesis 63
   destiny as by-product of 227
   experienced by immature monad 34, 39
   expression of pure identity 31
   identification with oneness 164
   memory of unitive state 20
   monad as center of 85
   sensed indirectly 73
   subjective end of pole 127
   vertical axis of 219
Beingness
   actualized through form 311
   nature of the monad 85
   transcendent to consciousness 73
   transcendent to forms that symbolize 72
   transcends thoughts 183

Bible 161
Black Magic 217
Bodhisattva 168
Born-again 149
Boundless All 34, 35, 39
Brahma 62, 78
Brahman 21, 114
Brain 250
   cavity 103–105, 109
   ventricles 106
Breath
   prana from God 250
   soul creates personality through 115
   symbol of etheric vitality cycle 264–266
Buddha 194, 297
Buddhi
   (See also intuition)
   corresponds to air 202
   intuition, formless truth 120
   nebulous impressions 228
Buddhic Plane
   en rapport with heart center 132
   geometric archetypes 181
   raincloud of knowable things 166
   relatively formless content 120
   source of archetypes 130
Buddhic Sheath 165
Burning Ground 171
Business
   as evolving thoughtform 308
   purpose of 294
   seventh ray people attracted to 83
   third ray 78

C

Capricorn 161
Causal body
   connection to the cave 111
   destined unfoldment 52
   destruction at fourth initiation 166
   equipment needed to individualize 51
   formation of 83
   introspection made possible 72
   located on higher mental plane 92
   one's body of causes 84

provides containment for wisdom 71
referred to as the treasury 166
relation to fifth ray 53
represents father and mother 71
substance of the solar angel 85
symbolizer of being 73
synthesized into buddhi sheath 165
Cave 103–107
    harmonic connection to soul 111
    location of third eye 174
    meditation for finding 105, 108–110
    standing steady within 133
Chain-of-life 148
Chakra
    ajna
        magical role 132
        personality integration 104
        third eye relation 174
    base, transference to head 135
    crown, relation to cave within the head 105
    heart
        conscious used in magic 251
        first initiation 152
        magical role 131
        source of magnetic appeal 188
    sacral, transference to throat 135
    solar plexus, transference to heart 135
    throat
        carrier of creative wisdom 252
        magical role 131
Chakras
    environmental sensors 253
    intersection points of nadis 249
    kundalini 280
    repolarization 136
    reversal of polarity 133–135
    triangle of magical endeavor 132
Change
    a function of evolution itself 291
    atomic substance 143
    due to father principle 23
    emergence of pain 23
    feminine (mother) contribution 30
    occult perspective 291
    resistance by ancient fires 271
    resistance of society's trailing edge 307

resistance to 272, 303
right timing 256
self-identity 20
seventh ray disciples 82
transformational power of words 259
vertical axis of being 219
Christ
    also called Bodhisattva 168
    as multilevel term 153
    birth within the heart, first initiation 152
    full grown man in 162
    gestation within the heart 151
    his devotion to the planetary God 290
    officiates first and second initiations 156
    viewed by Christian church 137
Christ Principle 151, 153
Christianity
    archangels and seven rays 74
    axiom of Christ and heaven 137
    creative power of the Word 260
    evangelists 233
    prodigal son 35
    Satan as God, blasphemous 13
    the Word of God 114
    transfiguration story 161
    virgin birth motif 153
Circumstance 253
    as revelatory 142
    energetic undercurrent 253
    governed by causal body and karma 84
    hiding unified field 175
    magical potential within 261
    principles evolving through 75
    recognized as living whole 16
    soul reveals through 225
Climate 288
Co-creation 58, 262, 286
Communication
    antahkarana 101
    attributes conditioning message 260
    relation to meditation 99
    with the master and Christ 168
Compassion
    higher emotion within consciousness 160
    inversion of 200
    Lord of 169

second ray manifestation 76
Conception Midpoint 266
Consciousness
   animal 67, 68
   animal kingdom 48–51
   antahkarana 163
   as continuum of self 106
   as sentiency 67
   atomic matter 143
   based upon hierarchy 147
   beingness 73
   benefit of meditation 100
   causal body 107
   contrasting opposites 14, 16
   degree of defines hierarchy 211
   emergence of 29
   etheric body 250
   evolution of 5, 8, 20, 290–291
   expansion of 234, 247, 304
   field of manas 93
   full-spectrum 107, 127
   God
      cells benefit 302
      evolving through human 6
      evolving through kingdoms 288–290
      out-pictured 287
      units as fragments of 285
   governed by law of periodicity 257
   group 94
   group versus mass 208
   higher 247
   human being as element 304
   human kingdom 51–57
   individualized 27, 69, 72
   initiate 95
   initiation 144
   instinctual 205
   interaction of Father and Mother 22, 26, 255
   mass, based on herd tendency 209
   mass, inversion of group 208
   Masters of Wisdom 213
   measure of polarization 142
   menacing vacuum 125–127
   mineral kingdom 35–41
   monadic 33, 163
   personality 58, 98, 188
   physical body 153
   plant kingdom 41–47
   relation to
      Being 164
      beingness 85
      causal body 68
      circumstance 5
      duality 15
      etheric body 106
      hylozoism 138
      Identity 126
      initiation 141
      sentiency 69
      substance 26, 113, 177, 180
   requires form 72, 85, 181
   resting 166
   sleep 268
   societal structures 291
   solar angel 85
   soul 61, 137, 152, 166
   successive approximations 295
Constitution of Human Being 117
Contemplation 130
Conviction 186
Cosmic Father 23–25
   division of the One Life 21, 255
Cosmic Mother 25–27
   division of the One Life 21, 255
Creation
   developmental distinction 211
   expression of One Life 21
   God's manifested knowingness 26
   great geometrician 181
   magical work of co-creation 262, 286
   master's magnum opus 170
   oneness manifested in diversity 17
   principle of hierarchy and equality 146
   seven rays 74
   thoughtforms 114, 122
   trinity of 61
   ultimate purpose of 18
Creativity
   art of impregnation 254
   cycles of variability 296
   inner point of synthesis 247
   magic of the soul 6

relation to kundalini 280
sound as governing force 123
Creator 58
Crisis
    as burning ground 171
    related to
        all initiations 144–145
        fourth initiation 168
        lunar initiations 171
        probationary path 150
        second initiation 158
Crown Center 84, 119, 174
Crucifixion 167
Crystal(s) 37, 39, 288
Cycles
    etheric 259
    incarnational, and lesser rhythms 257
    seasons, day and night 43
    societal 296

D

Dark Ages 296
Darwin, Charles 306
Death
    associated with first ray 75
    companion to resurrection 144
    rooted in law of periodicity 257
    triumph over at fourth initiation 168
    veiled resurrection in waiting 233
Decentralization 143
Desire
    ancient emergence 134
    antithetical to spiritual development 185
    astral plane attuned to 113
    blessing hidden within 193
    dilemma and mystery surrounds it 190
    distinction from will 191
    enlightenment through renunciation of 81
    inversion of love 204
    misapplication of vertical energy 191
    obstacle to enlightenment 185
    overcoming 195
    problem of 187–198
    relation to karma 193
    rise above, baptismal demand 160

root of ahamkara 191
self-satisfaction motive 129
self-validating force 195
solar plexus, principle of attraction 135
Destiny
    dominion over lower etheric triangle 137
    express innate divinity 52
    glamour of 226, 240
    loving use of cave 108
    monad in human kingdom 53
    of leading edge of humanity 309
    rise above misidentification 209
    soul versus personality perspective 242
    to be spiritual magician 5
Detachment
    antidote to highs and lows 297
    between thinker and thoughtform 182
    from
        emotion, defines effective use 245
        emotional experience 158
        previously desired forms 192
        sexual longings, first initiation 155
Deva 182–184
    aid in creative aim of soul 180
    give intelligence to manifest purpose 119
    intelligence itself 178
Deva Lord
    elementals loyalty toward 203
    loyalty of elementals toward 178
    seeming battle with thinker 179
Devotion
    animal 50, 290
    ray of 47, 48, 81
    to guru or spiritual leader 159
Diminishment Factor 120–122
Disciple
    ability to sense underlying quality 227
    application of rod of initiation 156
    aspires toward soulful expression 164
    believes soul is eternal 166
    chakra repolarization 136
    challenge of desire 187
    Christ to Sanat Kumara 156
    committed to serving humanity 155
    danger of obsession 124
    danger of sex magic 155

decentralized introspection 173
destined to be white magician 285
diminishment of selfishness 156
freedom from slavery of ideas 159
inconsistent soul experience 94
measure of soul infusion 87
meditative distinctions 100
need to rise above sentiment 158
relation to larger life 55
relation with deva substance 182–184
sense of inner group 160
shining forth of Christ-like love 153
sounds emitted by vehicles 123
thinks in support of evolution 287
transcending emotional body 188
translator of intuitive impression 87
use of eye of vision 101
use of right timing 256
use of third eye 131
used to facilitate evolution 87
wielding of destructive power 179
Discipleship
battle with enemy 273
etheric registration 253
etheric repolarization 133
reversal of creative tendency 252
Discipline
inculcated on probationary path 151
meditation to discover cave 105
to distinquish truth and falsity 80
Discrimination 234–235
between soul and imposter 220, 231
inverted into criticism 214
monad develops 34
needed to overcome desire 196
Distribution 261
Divine
essence of God 82
force that enlivens 42
light at core of substance 101
sun as source 250
Divinity
beauty proclaims it 79
buddhic plane 166
causal body reveals 52
fire within forms 274

forms represent 175
its vision revealed 81
magnetic power of love 204
manifest through tangible effects 82
revealed through correct knowledge 80
revelation of its purpose 75
soul acting on behalf of 58
soul as quality of 73
Duality
astral, the middle path 246–247
being shines forth into field of 18
cosmic level 21
cosmic prototype 60
emerging mother and father 21–23
experienced by probationer 150
holds key to transformation 173
inherently paradoxical 15
internal, human kingdom 52–53
resolution at transfiguration 161
resolution leads to synthesis 15
sexuality, soul and personality 155
soul versus imposter consideration 225

E

Earth 138, 285, 287
Economics 226, 293, 306
Education
second ray governs 76
seventh ray people attracted to 83
Educational institutions 292–293
Elementals
atoms of intelligence 26
cellular intelligence of devas 178
consciousness of vaster deva 203
found upon any plane 113
grades of 143
humans as 299
law of economy 184
need for right relationship with deva 183
passive lives 115
racism, purification 280
respond to will 298
supplicate to soul, third eye 164
synergy created through assembly of 118
synergy of thought 118–119, 270

Index

Emotion
    attributes 185–187
    distorting direction 218
    dualistic force 195
    giver of warmth and magnetism 310
    impulse toward activity 216
    measured application 243
    mist emerges when fire added 215
    problem of desire 187
    problem of inversion 198
    relation to instinct 205
    relation to intuition 204
    self is transcendent to 247
    surrender to soul's agenda 197
    tends to invert intuition 202
Emotional
    relation to law of love 188
Emotional Body 185–188, 195–198
    (See also astral body)
    adds feeling to thoughtform 125
    becomes tranquilized 102
    composed of intelligence substance 30
    dangers related to 128–130
    diminishment of thoughtform 121
    impulse to act 216
    incompatible with fiery thought 214
    lack of stability, soul challenged 91
    mastery, then trusted 217
    psychism, negation of mind 206
    reflects intuition 204
    soul makes contact through 59
    subtle influence on personality 157
    tends to magnify ideas 244
    water as symbol 160
Emotional Plane
    (See also astral plane)
    duality particularly potent 246
    incompatible element with fire 214
    most prone to inversion 202
    teeming with elementals 203
Emotions
    assemblage of substance 180
    danger of repressing 197
    distorting force 8
    effective when tranquilized 102
    lack of stability challenges 91

    learning to observe 196
    nationalism 209
    nurturing of higher 160
    over-stimulation 129
    purification of 140
    related to likes and dislikes 158
    subtle guiding mind 157
    transfiguration 136
    when attached to thoughtform 129
Empathy 200–201
Enemies, near 200
Enemy
    archaic thought 273
    as desire 198
    in search of 273–280
    one's own personality 7
Energy
    as anima mundi 64
    circulatory, soul and personality 111
    converted into force 250
    distorted by elementals 203
    etheric body transmits 252
    etheric vitalization cycle 263–269
    father principle, dynamic will 23
    father, purpose and identity 28
    follows thought and the eye directs 176
    inherent in plants, softening 42
    intersecting nadis 249
    Law of Attraction 65
    moving between crown and ajna 174
    of
        ahamkara 126
        aspiration, plant domain 289
        desire, personal longing 158
        enthusiasm, creates veil 215
        God, blended energy 31
        personality, vertically redirected 101
        prana 45, 250
        sexual magic 155
    Seven Rays 73–83
    solar plexus to heart transfer 132
    soul accumulates surplus 96
    taking form as circumstance 253
    that drives things to manifest 189
    thoughts as fiery manifestations of 271
    transfer between chakras 133

transmitted by Sanat Kumara 156
Enlightenment
    causal body radiates, no distortion 52
    desire as obstacle to 185
    incremental in nature 140, 173, 295
    renunciation of desire 81
    resolution of duality 22
    soul radiation without distortion 38
Enthusiasm
    causes distortion of thought 127
    due to excessive emotion 8
    essential to manifestation 186
    must be measured 244
    veils next step 215
Entification 69, 139, 189
Equality
    father and mother principles 23
    most fundamental truth 212
    relation to hierarchy 145–147
Etheric
    eye of vision 173
    health of the physical body 250
    magical triangle 131, 251
    relation to cave in head 103
    relation to dense physical 249
    reversal of polarity 133
Etheric Body
    as intermediary 250
    conduit for prana 250
    kundalini arousal 280
    millions of threads (nadis) 249
    must withstand initiation rod 165
    needed for brain registration 106
    use in magical process 251
Etheric Field
    distribution of vibration 261
    ebb and flow 257
    penetration of vibration 262
    question of timing 256
Etheric Web
    magically applied 251
    midway point 263
    reading its condition 257
Evil
    good that has outlived usefulness 273
    not conceivable without good 15

    part of the One Life 13
    secret revealed, initiation 142
Evolution
    ancient fires 275, 281
    based upon gradual awakening 152
    cosmic father gives impulse for 24
    cosmic mother provides intelligence for 26
    cycles of 296
    deva 119
    first ray force 76
    goal, right relation with substance 182
    gradual process of detachment 189
    harmonization of extremes 263
    Higher Way of 170
    human 5–10, 19, 21, 52, 53, 57, 64, 208
    imposter 235
    inverse to desire 189
    law of economy 184
    logos 285, 287, 300, 301
    memory of Original Condition 29
    monadic life within mineral forms 37
    prehuman 46, 49, 288, 289
    principle of hierarchy 146
    principle of oneness needed 14
    psychological inversions 202
    purification 279
    rediscover inherent oneness 63
    societal systems 292, 308
    soul experiences, as all things do 140
    vehicles 133, 143
Eye of Vision
    (See also third eye)
    control of building process 164
    directs magical process 101
    discern hidden purpose 142
    etheric organ of perception 173
    witness soul in all things 175

F

Faith
    assurance of immortality 9
    confidence in God's existence 137
    superseded by experience 149
Fanaticism 124, 150, 159
Fear

based on perception of lack 192
governed by mass consciousness 209
harmful to manifestation 129
non-existent at fourth initiation 168
of change 308
of mortality, imposter 232
repression and mistrust of emotion 197
thoughtforms, experience of 272, 277

Feelings
   ancient fires 272
   category of substance 180
   crisis at second initiation 172
   directing trend of thought 157
   dualistic swings 246
   experience of motherly substance 25
   pleasurable and painful, equal 247
   soul confused itself with 96
   untangle from thought 158
   used to build self-construct 126

Feminine 28, 29–32

Feng Shui 259

Fifth Kingdom
   entrance into 152
   masters are members of 86
   relation to fifth ray 235
   rite of entrance 55
   soul already potential member 152

Fire
   ancient 274, 276, 278
   hidden behind all forms, third eye 175
   human spirit, encased in substance 278
   kundalini 280–281
   of
      mind, producer of thought 214
      new thoughtform threatens 275
      purification 280
   solar 102
   synonymous with divine principle 276

Form
   as effect 122
   causal body 72
   evolution of soul through 8
   God's perfected expression 18
   human 70
   identity transcendent to 192
   initiation as measure of mastery 170
   inseparable from life 36
   kundalini, fire inherent within 280
   liberation from 272
   magical externalization of 105
   mind gives to intuition 120
   misidentification with 192
   monad evolving through 32
   nature of personality 123
   objective end of polarity 127
   parity to level of development 294
   personality defined by 188
   personality identified with 98
   purification of 156
   relation to ancient fires 271
   relation to desire 190
   relation to number four 102
   representation of intuition 177
   root of uniformity 210
   soul manifesting through 57
   subtler than physical 113
   thoughtform 119

Forms
   etheric, environmental web 258
   in-breath devitalizing 267
   intelligent organization of substance 69
   mineral 37
   physical, need of etheric 250
   plant 43
   product of disciplic thought 287
   thoughts and feelings are 72
   unity underlying 17, 21

Freedom 199
   detachment leads to 298
   experience of the masters 169
   masters struggle to achieve 193
   opposite of predetermined life 15

G

Garment 96, 99, 282

Geometric Symmetry 38

Gestation
   causal body's role 72
   Christ within the heart 151
   contemplative withdrawal 267
   etheric field 254

presentational pause 269
    principle of 26
Gestation Midpoint 267
Glamour
    caused by desire 190
    easily creeps into self-perception 220
    misperceptions, ungoverned passion 199
    of destiny, imposter prone to 226
God
    (See planetary god)
    (See planetary logos)
    (See solar logos)
    as cosmic father 23
    as cosmic mother 25
    creative processes of 285
    definition 13, 14, 21, 23, 32, 65
    earth as His out-pictured thought 287
    faith in, versus experience of 137
    great Geometrician 181
    human soul as quality of 73–83
    laws of nature 123
    masculine pronoun description 31
    mind of 162
    nature of His thought 298
    out-pictured as kingdoms 287–291
    personal relationship with 139
    planetary, Sanat Kumara 156
    prana, breath of 250
    relativity of 51, 138–139
    seven rays as emanations of 47
    soul as 139
    the Word 260
Goodness 143
Government 76, 292
Gravity 66
Group
    contemplative rapport 94
    inner 208
    no relation to physical location 208
    orientation of soul 94
    relation to intuition and purpose 207
    relation to mass consciousness 208
Group Awareness 56, 160
Group Consciousness
    inversion 207–209
    service 207

Groups
    as collective thoughtform 300
    freedom from conformity 210

H

Hall of Wisdom 141
Happiness 14, 79, 194, 246
Harmonic Relation 43
Harmony
    dependent on beauty 44
    higher refinements 44
    plant kingdom 289
    ray of 78–79
    within etheric field 254
Healing 76, 250
Heart
    birth of Christ, first initiation 152
    equal to mind 309
    gestation of Christ, probationary path 151
    intuition is felt by 206
    recipient of solar plexus transference 188
    sacrifice and initiation 144
    transcends self-reference 133
Heart Center
    access to buddhic plane 132
    magical triangle 131–133, 251
    recipient of solar plexus transfer 135
Heart Chakra
    conscious use in magic 251
Heresy of separation 194
Hermetic 19
Hierarchy
    ashramic 169
    foundation of initiation 145
    inversion of 210–214
    principle of 141, 145–148, 210
    resistance to 212
Hierarchy of Masters
    entering into the aura of 152
    initiate aware of 162
    soul as agent of 86
    vast field of radiation 94
Hierophant 169
Higher Way of Evolution 170
Hitler 147

Holy Spirit 78
Horizontal Extension 48, 50
Human
    affiliation with ashram 169
    as god 138
    constitution 117
Human Being(s)
    causal body emerges 51
    cell within planetary logos 285
    consequences of thought 116
    destined to be magician 5
    distinction from animal 67
    elementals to logos 299
    emit vibrations unceasingly 123
    must eventually face desire 189
    rise above instinct, individualized 9
Human Kingdom
    desire as nemesis 190
    development of spiritual aspiration 289
    formation of causal body, legend 83
    governing rays 52
    great heritage 9
    hallmark, individualized mind 53
    hierarchical development 212
    I-ness emerges (individualization) 71
    internal duality realized 53
    introspection emerges 68
    inward extension realized 54
    manifestation of God's thought 290
    monad's, entrance into 51–57
    relation to deva kingdom 119
Humanity
    Aquarius, influence upon 212
    as single entity 63
    conditioned by great illusion 199
    destined to promote amalgamations 207
    emotionally driven consciousness 157
    gives opportunity to elementals 119
    governed by collective opinion 208
    gradual evolution 295
    limited understanding of life 180
    misuse of hierarchical structures 146
    problem of obsolete thoughtforms 273
    relation to religion 149
    two categories of people 303
Humility 172

Hylozoism 285
    cell within vaster being 138
    definition 36

I

Identification 163, 164
Identity
    desire foundational to search of 190
    disassociation from thought 182–183
    imposter 232
    moving target 19
    principle of 24, 27, 31
    renunciation of previous views of 167
    represented by self-construct 126
    self-construct represents 31
    soul as individualized 71–73
    soul as, personality reflection of 8
    soul versus imposter, experience of 242
    transcendent to form 192
    transformation via cave 105
Illusion
    arrests spiritual development 190
    evolution necessitates it 192
    finite existence, fourth initiation 168
    heresy of separateness 194
    misapprehensions of the mind 199
    needed to test discrimination 235
    of no personal gain, imposter 225
    rooted in identification with feeling 247
Imagination 108
Imposter of the Soul 219–242
    characteristics of 223–228
    comparison with soul (table) 242
    definition 220
    emerges through soul-infusion 222
    part of the personality 222
    positive aspect of 234
    source of inflated status 171
    surreptitious nature 229
    types, strategic and innocent 231
Incrementalism
    enlightenment based upon 140
    evolution of consciousness 16, 57
    governs individual and society 295
    monad through kingdoms 41

spiritual path is based upon 173
Individualization
    earlier kingdoms set stage for 51
    middle of Lemurian epoch 83
    monad enters human kingdom 41
    similarity to first initiation 152
Initiation
    common features of each 141–145
    death to something cherished 173
    fifth 168–170
        revelation of higher way 170
        title of master bestowed 168
    first 151–157
        as important as individualization 151
        begin entrance into fifth kingdom 151
        Christ force becomes radiatory 152
        Christ officiates 156
        confused for the third 171
        dangers of sex magic 155
        triumph over fleshly appetites 153
        yearning to serve 155
    fourth 165–168
        abstraction of wisdom 165
        destruction of causal body 166
        percentage of atomic substance 143
        release from personal karma 168
        renunciation and crucifixion 167
    hierarchical nature of 145
    location of event, causal body 156
    milestones of development 55
    second 157–160
        detachment from cherished ideas 159
        group means more than self 160
        involves emotional crisis 158
        measure of emotional detachment 158
    third 160–165
        antahkarana fully built 163
        aspiration no longer used 164
        dominion of soul over personality 160
        duality fused into singularity 161
        intimacy with master felt 169
        law of sacrifice dominates 162
        light of monad touched 56
        personality is transfigured 161
        Sanat Kumara officiates 165
        soul fully expressed 56

        soul gazes in three directions 95
        timing of 157
Initiations
    lunar 171
    solar 171
Initiations on the Threshold 165
Initiator
    first and second initiation 156
    Sanat Kumara 156
    third initiation 165
Instinct
    animal kingdom 49
    basis of psychic experience 205
    foundation of reason 49
    humans to rise above 68
    life in animal kingdom 9
    relation to base center 134
    relation to mind, third ray 48
    toward defining oneself, masculine 24
Intellect 141, 208
Intellectualism 53
Intelligence
    animal 49
    as third aspect 62
    assembly as thoughtform 177
    causal body (solar angel) 85
    custody of cosmic mother 26
    devas are 178
    devas provide in support of purpose 119
    elementals, building blocks of 118
    found within substance 30
    higher order in causal body 84
    revealed as attributes 70
    soul organizes according to purpose 69
    strata of substance 113
    synergy of 270
    third ray 48, 77
    within mineral domain 36
    within old ideas 275
Introspection
    decentralized 172
    monad first experiences 54
    not possible in animals 68
    second initiation 158
Intuition
    (See also buddhi)

art of magic requires use of 7
discerning the formula 277
distinction from psychism (table) 206
evolutionary goal of human life 49
experience of motherly substance 25
formless realization 204
formless truth 120
higher rendition of instinct 49
inversion of 204–207
related to element of air 202
sense of larger whole via its stillness 216
third serves as agent of 257
thought gives representation to 177
used to counter ancient fires 275
Intuitive germ 112
Inversion
    cause of great illusion 199
    of
        empathy 200
        group consciousness 207
        hierarchy 210
        intuition 204
        love 203
        unanimity 210
    problem of 198
Involution 190
Inward Extension 54
Isolated Location 39, 41

J

Jesus
    baptism, second initiation 160
    contrasted to Hitler 147
    crucifixion, fourth initiation 167
    transfigured on the mount 161
Jewel in lotus 71
Joy
    experienced by ignorant monad 34
    momentary seeing soul 149

K

Karma
    aftermath of personalty response 97
    freed from at fourth initiation 168
    related to third ray 78
    relation to causal body 84
    relation to desire 193
Knowledge
    accumulation after third initiation 165
    death, as self-imposed 168
    evolution of consciousness, not form 291
    fifth ray of 52, 53, 80
    measure of imposter's authority 227
    of
        monad 33
        reality 35
        solar logos 18
    revealed through logoic thought 293
    transcendent to elemental intelligence 119
    wisdom supersedes 141
Kundalini 280–282

L

Language
    magical potency of 82
    manas, broad and abstract 93
    society exists because of 259
    words of power 260
Law
    of
        Attraction 65, 66
        Correspondence 287, 298
        Economy 184
        Love 186
        Periodicity 257
        Sacrifice 162
Laws of Nature 122
Leadership 76
Left handedness 216
Left-hand Path 216
Lemuria 83
Life 62
    all substance imbued with 113
    beauty, gate to its mystery 79
    characterized with sentiency 66
    correlation to first aspect 62
    deva lord gives 203
    doctrine of hylozoism 36
    evolution of 27
    fire within created thought 270

identification with 164
Larger
    co-creativity 58
    components interacting 16
    establishing rapport 55
    planetary logos 310
    serving its intention 155
    soul communing with 94
    soul is servant to 6
monadic 56
prana as breath of 250
principle of equality 146
resolution of paradox 15
seeks to evolve through form 74
units of, all have soul 64
units of, definition 32
Light
    bridge of 101
    initiation 148, 171
    mind 128, 130
    monad 56, 167
    monad, blocked at fourth initiation 167
    nature of 73
    personality 101
    point of 32, 111, 112, 121
    seven ray expression 74
    soul 46, 100, 102, 140, 161
    yearning for 45, 46
Lord
    Agni 178, 179
    deva 179, 203
    of
        Compassion 169
        Mars 211
        World 165
    Planetary 285
    Rishi 74
Love
    buddhic plane 132
    Christ radiation 152
    companion to mind 198
    contains magnetic appeal 65
    desire as inversion of 203
    emerges from law of attraction 65
    enlivens vision of oneness 42
    essence of all things 14
    heart chakra 251
    law of 186, 188
    memory of original condition 65
    relation to desire 188
    rooted in plant kingdom 289
    rose as symbol 42
    second ray of 47, 76
    soul as center of 93
    soul as representative principle 64–66
    transcendent to ahamkara 131

M

Magic
    as kundalini force 280
    as sexual intercourse 254
    astral plane 185
    attraction of elementals 115
    black 128, 217
    co-creative effort 58
    emerging point of light 111
    etheric-physical plane 249
    mental plane 91
    of logos 285
    power of words 259, 262
    rhythmic nature 94
    science of thoughtform-building 6
    seventh ray of 82
    sex 154
    spiritual
        partnership of four 102
        sound creates effect 122
        top-down process 92
    use of the cave within the head 103–108
    white
        art and science 7
        bringing wisdom into form 105
        consciousness and circumstance 5
        definition 6
        science of thoughtform-building 83
        soul's creative urge 58
        soul's downward gaze 94
Magical
    process
        antidote to dangers 130, 133
        astral vitality 186
        building an etheric sheath 251

correct measure of emotion 243
dangers of
    astral neglect 128
    hidden motive 219
    imposter 219–233
    left-hand path 216
    obsession 124
    unbridled thought 127
    urge to act 219
    vacuum 125
diminishment of idea 121
distribution, etheric 261
etheric timing 254
externalizing master's ideas 87
field as womb 254
magical triangle 251
magnetic appeal 186
objective view 247
penetration, etheric 262
problem of desire 187
right relations with devas 182–184
soul gathers itself 97
transforms archaic thought 273–280
use of etheric midway points 263–269
use of third eye 173–182

Magical Triangle 131, 251
Magician
    cave, as standing place 103
    cooperates with livingness of thought 310
    destiny of every human being 5
    detachment from thoughtform 126
    directional uncertainty 215
    gray 218
    importance of disciplined meditation 99
    seeks to use higher elementals 303
    sensing readiness of etheric field 252
    use of the third eye 164
    words chosen define effect 123

Magnetic Appeal
    attribute of emotion 186
    begins in plant kingdom 42
    heart and solar plexus 188
    Logos developing 289
    relation to love 65
    role of emotion in magic 244

Magnetism
    added to soul-inspired thought 243
    added to thoughtform via emotion 186
    magical role of emotion 310
    personality yearning converted 188
    plants, higher level in humans 289

Mahapralaya 29
Manas 84, 93
Manipulation 77
Mantram 51, 151
Mars 211
Masculine 23, 24, 28
Masculine Pronoun 29–32
Master
    fifth degree initiate 169
    greatest of white magicians 170
    must demonstrate his masterpiece 170

Masters of Wisdom
    acme of evolution 213
    differ from Lord of Compassion 169
    disciple enters aura of 152
    freedom from desire. 193
    soul as agent of 87
    source of the Plan 224
    vaster field of life 94

Matter
    atomic 143
    intelligent substance 70
    more subtle than usually considered 25
    organic versus inorganic 180
    perfect relation with spirit 18
    teaches monad 35

Maya 199
Meditation
    construction of antahkarana 101
    contemplative form as antidote 130
    role and benefits 99–103
    technique for finding cave 108
    utilization of cave 103

Memory 20, 28, 61
Mental
    discrimination 234
    elementals 115
        attracted to vibration 116
        build around point of light 121
        cells within Lord Agni 178
        disciple takes control of 182

    join together, create a thought 114
    passive lives 115
forms
    symbolizing identity 72
Mental Body
    composed of intelligent substance 30
    soul in partnership with 102
Mental Plane
    (higher) soul is found 92
    composed of elemental substance 177
    fifth ray animates 53
    intuition takes form upon 112
    nature of its substance 113
Middle Principle
    corresponds to second aspect 62
    principle of relationship 61
    soul represents 65, 93
Middle Way 246
Midpoint(s)
    conception 266
    gestation 267
    within etheric cycles 265
Milky Way 138, 146
Mind
    abstract, registration of intuition 205
    abstract, soul resides upon 59, 93
    antidote to problem of astrality 158, 198
    building aggregates of elementals 114
    danger of ahamkara 7
    dangers of thought construction 123
    devas implanting spark of 84
    disciple John as symbol 161
    discriminative nature 197
    distinction between truth and falsity 80
    emerging point of light 111
    first etching, domesticated animals 51
    gives gives directional assistance 309
    God's cognitive dissonance 292
    group 207
    hall of wisdom through transcendence 141
    hallmark of human evolution 53
    held steady in the light 130
    higher 205
    higher, soul engages 93
    illusion 199
    importance of meditation 102
    individualized in human kingdom 54
    instinctual 48
    instrument of diminishment 120
    introspective 71
    mastery, transfiguration 136, 162
    perceives dualistically 79
    picturing making faculty 108
    receiver of intuition 206
    relation to fifth ray 53
    relation to fire 214
    son of 93, 162
    soul projects into 96
    steady in the light 112
    subtle guidance by emotions 157
    tendency to stray 178
    third ray, mind of God 77
    tool in magical process 5
    translator of intuition 120
    used to assess astral body 128
Mineral Kingdom
    bottom of arc 35
    God's consciousness 288
    governing rays 39
    isolated location 39
    levels of development 37
    monad's entrance into 35–41
    plate tectonics 287
    rudimentary monadic life 36
    traits developed by monad 37
Minerals
    advanced categories 39
Misidentification 192, 209
Monad
    as beingness 85
    as highest self 32
    attributes gained in animal kingdom 48
    attributes gained in human kingdom 53–54
    comes home at sixth initiation 56
    consciously touched at third initiation 56
    individual and universal 33
    origin lost 33
    paradoxical existence 56
    purpose of its human experience 70
    qualities developed in plant kingdom 42
    relation to antahkarana 163
    represents father principle 168
    spark of God's flame 32
    synonymous with spirit 33

traits acquired in mineral kingdom 37
transcendent soul 86
ultimate being 32
unit of life 32
uses causal body to focus itself 72
Monadic
   consciousness 33
   sojourn 32
Money 78, 167, 226
Moon 146
Motive, hidden 218
Mulaprakriti 21, 60
Musical scale 74

N

Nadis 249
Nationalism 209
Near-Enemies 200
Necessity, Sons of 189
Nervous System 250
New Age Movement 216

O

Obsession 124, 159
Occultism 36
OM 110
One Life 14
   as God or Brahman 21
   breaths itself into manifestation 115
   cosmic father, purpose 24
   cosmic mother, intelligence 26
   doctrine of hylozoism 138
   emergence of relationship 61
   evolving toward perfection 29
   forcing all lesser units of life 35
   manifests as quality 73
   mother and father interact 22
   mystery of its manifestation 60
   original condition 20
   primary principle 13–15
   process of manifestation 21
   purpose expressed through diversity 17
   trinity expression 61
   universal fiat 17–19
   urge to manifest 191

Oneness 13–15
   humanity, as fact in nature 63
   inescapability of 36
   love and unitive field 43
   simultaneous to diversity 17
   soul as representative of 61
   underlying multiplicity, soul see 224
Opposites 16
Original Condition
   bring parts into right relation 63
   cosmic synthesis 20
   love reestablishes 204
   memory of 28, 61

P

Pain
   due to heresy of separateness 194
   equal to pleasure 247
   facilitates evolution itself 23
   misaligned elements of circumstance 16
   personality feels through sacrifice 144
   relinquish form, spiritual identity 172
Paradox
   desire and fear, relation to soul 192
   diminishment of idea 120
   lighten darkened areas 140
   monad exists in 56
   nature of desire 190
   obscured vision and impulsivity 215
   resolution of 15–17
   take eyes off oneself 172
   voice of the silence 100
Penetration 262
Periodic Table 74
Periodicity
   law of 257
Personality
   alignment with soul 98
   as extension of soul 96, 233
   at transfiguration 95
   atomic matter of vehicles 143
   attenuated in substance 96
   communication with soul 97
   defense mechanism 124
   defiant toward soul 145
   definition of 58, 188

enthusiasm validating 129
essential in magical work 58
fears relinquishment 271
identified with organized form 98
integrated, definition 20
integration, ajna chakra 104
karmic aftermath 97
magic 218
magic, self-serving 6
meditative practices of 99
needed in magical work 92
one's greatest enemy 7
prone to ahamkara 219
reflection of soul 8, 45
relation to desire 187
relation to initiation 141, 145
relation to love 204
relation to sacrifice 144
represents third aspect 62
root of distorted ideas 7
soul gazing toward 94, 95
source of imposter 222
traits in animals 67
transfiguration 161
triple nature 57
with soul-infusion 57
Phenomena 85, 159, 247
Photosynthesis 45
Physical
   circumstance 253
   form
      animal identified with 209
      etheric body underlies 249
      evolves as reflex 37
   forms
      have etheric underlying 250
   plane
      composed of living substance 180
      divided into two categories 249
      magic upon the 249
      out-breath phase 267
   sensation
      animated by soul 96
      identification with 96
      identity transcendent to 126
Physical appetites
   tamed 102
Physical Body
   appetites transcended 154
   disciple Peter, correspondence 161
   etheric sheath underlies 106
   health and well-being 250
   intelligent organization of substance 70
   intelligent substance 30
   mastery, first initiation 153
   maya, distortions of 199
   of planetary logos 285
   purification of 151
   related to base center 135
   relation to sleep 265
   soul's outer activity 59
   transmitter of soul's message 91
Piscean Age 77
Plan
   of evolution 165, 224
   of God 169
Planes
   as substance of varying grades 25
   of consciousness
      elementals compose 177
      intuition hovers lower 202
      law of periodicity 257
      seven subplanes 115
      strata of substance 113, 180
      total as physical, logos 286
Planetary God
   devotion of Christ toward 290
   evolution, urge to betterment 292
   rode of initiation used by 156
   vibration coming from 305
Planetary Logos 285–287
   compared to human 211
   human beings, elementals to 299
   institutions seeded by 292
   larger life that ensouls planet 310
   thinks and world manifests 298
   unconscious aspect of 288
Plate Tectonics 287
Point of light
   emerges within mind 111
   intuitive germ 281
   soul's creative idea 114

Polarization
    etheric 133–136
    level of development 219
    within society 303
Politics
    animated by first ray 76
    as evolving thoughtform 308
    seventh ray people attracted to 83
Power
    essence, monad 38
    first ray of 39, 75
    gathered by soul 97
    of
        destruction 179
        God 305
        human reason 49
        imposter 226, 229, 231
        love 64, 203
        magnetic appeal 186
        magnetic radiation 42
        manipulation 77
        propaganda 208
        radioactivity 38
        relationship 63
        sex magic 155
        speech 122
        third eye 164
        words 32, 82, 122, 254, 259
Prana 45, 250
Presence
    angel of 85
Primary Principle 13–15, 16
Principle
    of
        attraction 135
        equality 146
        expansive life 138
        gestation 26, 27
        hierarchy 146, 210
        identity 24, 27, 31
        love 59, 64
        mind 93
        purification 279
        radiatory life 38
        relationship 61–62, 66
        right distribution 294

        unanimity 210
Probationary Path
    gestation of Christ-like love 152
    monad, recaptures universality 55
    path of purification 148–151
    relation to orthodoxy 150
    repolarization begins 136
    spiritual touch 149
Prodigal Son 35
Projection
    cave origin for 107
    personality defense mechanism 124
    soul towards higher pole 107
Psychism 204–207
    distinction from intuition (table) 206
    rooted in instinct 49
Psychoanalysis 198
Purification
    change in atomic matter 143
    incremental enlightenment 140
    path of 148–151
    prepares for rod of initiation 156
    principle of 279
Purpose
    as expressed through outer forms 175
    between first and second initiation 159
    creative work of the logos 302
    manifestation of first ray 76
    manifesting through circumstance 240
    of
        cosmic father 23
        creation 18
        creative work of the logos 293
        economics and business 294
        evil 142
        form 82
        human evolution 5
        personality 58
        soul 69, 140, 198, 276, 309
        spiritual groups 209
        spiritual magic 121
        universal life 19
    relation to
        cave within the head 108
        cosmic mother 28
        desire 190, 192

head centers 252
jewel in the lotus 71
spiritual group 208, 210
revealed through eye of vision 101, 142
Purusha 21, 60

Q

Quality
    gives birth to form 242
    soul as 73
Quantity 227
Quantum Physics 300

R

Racism 279
Radioactivity 38
Raincloud of Knowable Things 166
Ray
    fifth 53, 80, 235
    first 39, 75
    fourth 47, 52, 78
    second 47, 76
    seventh 39, 82
    sixth 47, 50, 81
    third 48, 77, 80
Rays 75–83
Reason
    bridge, mass and group consciousness 208
    built upon instinct 49
    causal body capacity 71
    law of correspondence 287
Rebirth 75, 257
Reflection
    instinct is to intuition 205
    of
        air on water 202
        the One Life 60
        the soul, personality 45
        unanimity 210
    personality is to soul 8
    sexuality, soul and personality 155
Reincarnation
    no longer mandated 168
    reconfigured thoughtforms 272

successive approximations 295
Relationship
    between thinker and devic life 182
    inter-elemental 183
    principle of 61, 63
Religion
    animated by sixth ray 82
    resists emerging paradigms 307
    unconscious force led to 149
Renaissance 296
Renunciation
    fourth initiation 165–168
    of desire, enlightenment 81
Repolarization
    chakras 134–136
    etheric sheath 133
    shift due to initiation 142
Repression 197
Repulsion 195
Resistance
    experienced by old ideas 272
    leads to pain 23
    to principle of hierarchy 212
    wanes over time 98
Resurrection 144, 233
Revelation
    fifth initiation 168–170
    gradual, nebulous, difficult to recall 242
    offered by imposter 228
    speed of reception 240
Rhythm
    human growth occurs in context of 297
    law of periodicity 257
    lesser within greater 269
    sensed within circumstance 177
    sensing magical opportunity 94
Ritual
    seventh ray people attracted to 83
    wisdom hidden within it 308
Rod of Initiation 156

S

Sacral Center 133, 135
    relation to first initiation 154
Sacrifice 144, 167

law of 162
Sanat Kumara 156, 165
Satan 13
Science
 as evolving thoughtform 308
 manifestation of fifth ray 80
 preoccupied with evolution of form 291
 rooted in vibration of logos 300
 white magic as 7
Self
 as a construct 24, 126
 as continuum 106
 before third initiation 182
 defined by 19
 lower, as personality 57, 96
 masculine side of nature 31
 motion in search of 195
 over identified with experiences 297
 placed within cave 103
 pulled into vacuum 126
 vertical axis of being 219
Selfish Magic 128, 216
Self-Realization
 happiness as barometer of 194
 oneself as possessor of form 192
 relation to identification 164
 Son of Mind emerges 162
 working hypothesis 20
Sentiency 66, 67, 69
Sentiment 158, 207
Separateness 56, 214
 heresy of 162
Service
 aquarian age 207
 defined by soul ray 155
 definition of 176
 first degree initiates 155
 heightened vibration translates into 170
 related to group mind 207
 relation to cave 108
 relation to throat center 135
 role of emotion 197
 second degree initiate 160
 sixth ray, sacrificial 81
 soul in service to monad 86
 third degree initiate 162

Seven Rays 74–83
Sex
 drive 135, 154
 magic 154
 symbol of spiritual creativity 254
Sexual
 lower expression of larger principle 155
 turmoil 154
 yearnings 154
Shiva 62, 78
Silence 269
 voice of 100
Social Systems
 becoming corrupt 296
 dual edge of 306
 reveals humanity's evolution 295
Solar Angel
 (See also angel, solar)
Solar Fire 102
Solar Logos
 confined by desire 193
 definition 18
 entity with grander cosmic being 138
 relation to planetary gods 285
 second ray entity 77
Solar Plexus
 energy transfer to heart 132, 135, 188
 relation to psychism 206
Son
 of mind 93, 162
 of necessity 189
 prodigal 35
Soul
 acts as co-creative conduit 286
 alignment through cave 104
 always in state of meditation 97
 as
  anima mundi 64
  consciousness of causal body 167
  higher-self 32
  identity 8, 20
  individualized identity 71
  inner sun 46
  middle principle 93
  organizing principle 69
  personal god 139

    principle of love 64
    quality of divinity 73
    sentiency and consciousness 66
    universal matrix 59
  asserts creative intention in mind 114
  attenuated as personality 96
  beginning point of magic 92
  challenge to convey wisdom 91
  conduit for buddhic impression 120
  detection of its note 115
  direction of communication 93
  dominion over personality 160
  enemies of 192
  experiential proof of existence 9
  expression of a ray energy 74
  expression of loving mind 93
  extracts itself during sleep 265
  faith in, superseded 149
  imposter of 219–242
  infusion 145, 148, 203, 218
  initiation and polarization 142
  kingdom of 152
  magic of the 6
  meditation, always in state of 97
  middle principle 61
  misidentified with desired substance 190
  nature of 57–83
  ray defines service 155
  relation to third eye 173
  resides on abstract mental plane 93
  second aspect expression 62
  seeks mastery over personality 55
  spectrum of its evolution 304
  third initiation 56
  use of etheric triangle 131
  wins loyalty of elementals 184
  words of power 260
Soul-Infusion
  indication of disciple 87
  nature of 220
  personality substance abdicates 203
  readiness for magical work 57
  recognition of inauthentic self 229
  relation to imposter 222
  relation to initiation 145, 148
Sound
  as creator of effects 122
  attracts mental elementals 115
  becomes another tone 121
  creative power, mythology 260
  emerges through movement 123
  governs all in existence 123
  manifesting force in creation 114
  soul emits 114
  vehicles of personality, emit 123
Spirit
  conscious of beingness 56
  correlates to father aspect 23
  kundalini, fires reunite 281
  relation to universal fiat 18
  resolution of opposites 16
  synonymous with monad 33
  transcendent to soul 86
  uses language to express itself 82
  utilizes soul to assert its intention 69
Subplanes 115, 249
Substance
  as intelligence 71
  as livingness of forms 25
  causal body is vehicle of 51
  deflecting power of 201
  deva kingdom represents 180
  devoted to devic superior 203
  elementals, grades of 143
  etheric, cave 103
  etheric, nadis 249
  etheric, third eye location 174
  feelings, category of 180
  field as womb of 254
  grade defines nature of thought 181
  humanity as field of 299
  manipulation of, fifth degree initiate 169
  mental elementals 118
  One Life incarnates into and as 18
  personality composed of 98
  planes of consciousness, strata of 113
  provides intelligence 69
  represents cosmic mother 25
  sentient, impressionable 66
  soul loses itself in 192
  thought, category of 180
  vessel for incubation 26

Sympathy 200
Synergy 118
Synthesis
    cosmic, original condition 20
    duality and oneness 15
    evolution is movement toward 293
    harmonization as prerequisite 16
    intuition tending toward 206
    of being 63
    of intelligence as a thought 183
    white magic, governed by 247

T

Taoism 27
The Human Constitution Graphic 117
Thinker 100
Third Eye 173–182
    (See also eye of vision)
    agent of intuition 257
    discerning formula 277
    eye of the soul 17
    fully open to initiate 164
    meditation facilitates opening 101
    relation to ajna center 132
    relation to cave 107
    relation to initiation 142
Thought(s)
    antidote to human misfortune 76
    archaic, enemy 273
    built upon instinct 49
    category of substance 180
    fiery manifestations of energy 271
    fifth ray, precision 80
    God's
        as societal systems 292
        effect on kingdoms 287
        life upon planet 287
        working through groups 305
    imprecision of 128
    logoic, magical nature 298
    nature and composition 112–118
    opposite exists as potential 14
    personality defines itself by 58
    representation of formless intuition 120
    soul confuses itself with 96
    soul's ability to influence 9
    synergy of 118–119
    third ray animates 77
    used to build self-construct 126
Thoughtform(s)
    adding etheric sheath 251
    as fearful entity 272
    astral vitality added 186
    attractive, magnetic appeal 186
    building
        efficient design 83
        science of 6
    dies at birth 256
    dissipation of 270
    effect on etheric field 260
    geometric patterning 181
    sacred truth at core 276
    seeds of the future 287
    symbols of identity 72
Three Aspects 61–64
Throat Center
    magical triangle 131–133
    transfer of sacral energy 135, 154
Throat Chakra 252
Time 224, 238
Timing 256
Transfiguration 160–165
    awakened ajna center 174
    imposter nearly eliminated 231
    Jesus on the mount 161
    law of sacrifice 162
    mastery of the mind 162
    personality infused by soul 95
    relationship to repolarization 136
    Sanat Kumara as initiator 165
    wielding destructive power 179
Transformation
    resolution of duality holds key to 173
Trinity 61
Truth
    core, abstract principle 276
    discern from pseudo-truth 234
    fifth ray, distinguish from fiction 80
    golden thread 277
    inversion of 202
    paradoxical 15

rearrangement of ideas 77
synonymous with beauty 79, 181
thoughts essentially demonstrate 276
working hypothesis, relative 277

U

Unanimity 210
Unicorn 161
Uniformity 210
United Nations 79
Unity
    empathy as reflection of 200
    establishment of right relationship 63
    field of love 309
    gate leading to oneness 63
    interaction between the poles 66
    inversion of 207–208
    of inner group 56
    radiation in plant kingdom 42
    realized through consciousness 21
    relation to unanimity 210
    revealed through second ray 76
    simultaneous with diversity 17
    third eye perceives 101
    transcendent to duality 15
    undetected by five senses 175
Universal Fiat 18

V

Vacuum 125
Vegetarianism 45
Vehicle(s)
    etheric 106
    of personality 57
    of the soul, causal body 27
Ventricles 106
Venus 211
Vertical Extension 46
Vibration
    experience recorded in causal body 166
    first etched in etheric vehicle 106
    humans emit through three bodies 123
    lofty, innate within thoughtform 261
    of soul, no longer threatening 98

of soul-inspired thoughtform, effect 260
relation to etheric body 252–253
relationship, commonness of 62
responded to by elementals 298
Virgo 153
Vishnu 62, 78
Vision
    eye of 101, 142, 164
    of divinity, sixth ray 81
    relation to ajna center 132
    synthetic, first ray 75
    unitive 225
Visualization 107
Vital Body 251
    (See also etheric body)
Vitality
    astral 186
    condition of etheric body 259
    greater and lesser cycles 268
    middle point of 263
    soul's idea 102
    within etheric field 256

W

Wallace, Alfred 306
War 79, 82, 209
Water
    condenses upon a thoughtform 186
    second initiation, immersed and detached 160
    symbol of emotion 128
Waters
    condition of 128
White Magician
    comparatively few 57
    destiny of every disciple 285
    master as greatest 170
    proven mastery of emotion 217
Will
    creative, the three aspect 102
    destructive aspect of God 14
    distinction from desire 191
    first ray of 75
    leaves wake behind it 23
    of
        God, co-creation 112

God, master has intimacy 169
　　　monad, incarnate into form 70
　　　One Life 35
　　　soul, control elementals 179
　　　soul, devas seeks to serve 184
　　　soul, personality surrender 144
　　　spirit, utilizes soul 69
　　　thinker, motivation 116
　　　thinker, projected into mind 298
　　　thinker, reinforce thoughtform 270
　　　thinker, thoughtform building 70
　　　thinker, thoughtform emerges 114
　　planetary god transmits 156
　　related to first aspect 62
　　relation to base and head centers 135
　　relation to government 292
　　to evolve, cosmic father 23
Wisdom
　　coming from causal body 85
　　demonstrates as understanding 76
　　emerges upon intellect 141
　　externalized by soul 91
　　form of love 76
　　from intuitional plane into denseness 105
　　gained through experience 71
　　Hall of 141
　　hidden within ritual 308
　　second ray of 76
Words of Power 259–262
　　nearing conception point 266
　　spoken at midway point 264
World disciple 162

Y

Yin-Yang 27

Z

Zodiac
　　Capricorn 161
　　Virgo 153

About the Author

William Meader is an international teacher and lecturer currently working in the United States, Canada, New Zealand, Australia, as well as several countries in Europe. With more than twenty years experience in his field, he offers both ongoing study opportunities and public presentations on a variety of subjects found within the Esoteric Spiritual Tradition. For more information regarding his work, or to contact him, please see www.meader.org.